PROBLEMS OF THE MODERN ECONOMY

The Battle Against Unemployment

PROBLEMS OF THE MODERN ECONOMY

General Editor: EDMUND S. PHELPS, *Columbia University*

Each volume in this series presents
prominent positions in the debate of
an important issue of economic policy

THE BATTLE AGAINST UNEMPLOYMENT

CHANGING PATTERNS IN FOREIGN TRADE
AND PAYMENTS

THE GOAL OF ECONOMIC GROWTH

MONOPOLY POWER AND ECONOMIC PERFORMANCE

PRIVATE WANTS AND PUBLIC NEEDS

THE UNITED STATES AND THE DEVELOPING ECONOMIES

LABOR AND THE NATIONAL ECONOMY

INEQUALITY AND POVERTY

DEFENSE, SCIENCE, AND PUBLIC POLICY

AGRICULTURAL POLICY IN AN AFFLUENT SOCIETY

THE CRISIS OF THE REGULATORY COMMISSIONS

The Battle
Against
Unemployment

Edited with an introduction by

ARTHUR M. OKUN

THE BROOKINGS INSTITUTION

REVISED

NEW YORK
W·W·NORTON & COMPANY·INC·

The Human Costs of Unemployment, by Elliott Liebow, originally entitled "No Man Can Live with the Terrible Knowledge that He Is Not Needed," © 1970 by The New York Times Company. Reprinted by permission.

The Costs of Inflation, by Arthur M. Okun. Reprinted by permission of New York University Press from *Inflation: The Problems It Creates and Policies It Requires* by Arthur M. Okun, Henry H. Fowler, and Milton Gilbert, copyright © 1970 by New York University.

Unemployment, Inflation, and Economic Stability, by Herbert Stein, from *Agenda for the Nation*, Kermit Gordon (ed.), © 1968 by The Brookings Institution, 1775 Massachusetts Avenue, N.W., Washington, D. C.

The Case for High-pressure Economics, by Alvin H. Hansen. From *The American Economy*, by Alvin H. Hansen. Copyright 1957. McGraw-Hill Book Company. Used by permission.

The Case against High-pressure Economics, by Henry C. Wallich, from *United States Monetary Policy*, by Henry C. Wallich. Reprinted by permission of Frederick A. Praeger, Inc.

The Cruel Dilemma, by James Tobin, from *Prices: Issues in Theory, Practice and Public Policy* by Phillips and Williamson, © 1967 by The University of Pennsylvania Press. Reprinted by permission of The University of Pennsylvania Press and James Tobin.

Weak Links in the Multiplier Chain, by Milton Friedman, from *Capitalism and Freedom*. Copyright © 1962 by The University of Chicago Press. Reprinted by permission.

The Need for Balanced Federal Budgets, by Maurice H. Stans, from *The Annals of the American Academy of Political and Social Science*, Vol. 326, November 1959. Reprinted by permission of the Academy and Maurice H. Stans.

Toward a Flexible Tax Policy: Automatic and Discretionary Stabilizers. The Report of the Commission on Money and Credit, *Money and Credit: Their Influences on Jobs, Prices, and Growth*, © 1961. Reprinted by permission of Prentice-Hall, Inc., Englewood Cliffs, New Jersey.

Organization for Monetary Policy, by G. L. Bach, from *Making Monetary and Fiscal Policy* by G. L. Bach, © 1971 by The Brookings Institution, 1775 Massachusetts Avenue, N.W., Washington, D. C.

What Monetary Policy Can Do, by Milton Friedman, originally "The Role of Monetary Policy," *American Economic Review*, March 1966. Copyright © 1966 by the American Economic Association. Reprinted by permission of the American Economic Association and Milton Friedman.

Doubts about Monetarism, by Walter W. Heller, from *Monetary vs Fiscal Policy*, by Milton Friedman and Walter W. Heller, W. W. Norton & Company, Inc., 1969. Copyright © 1969 by The Graduate School of Business Administration, New York University.

A Rule for Monetary Policy? by Henry C. Wallich, from *Deutsche Bank Studies*, 1969. Reprinted by permission of the author and The Deutsche Bank.

The Fiscal Route to Full Employment, by Walter W. Heller. Reprinted by permission of the publishers from Walter W. Heller, *New Dimensions of Political Economy*, Cambridge, Mass.: Harvard University Press. Copyright, 1966, by the President and Fellows of Harvard College.

The Fiscal Fiasco of the Vietnam Period, by Arthur M. Okun, from *The Political Economy of Prosperity*, by Arthur M. Okun, W. W. Norton & Company, Inc., 1970. Copyright © 1970 by The Brookings Institution.

A Monetarist Critique of the New Economics, by Beryl Sprinkel, from a speech to the Illinois Chamber of Commerce on October 27, 1967.

Economic Policy and the Lessons of Experience, by Paul W. McCracken, from *Republican Papers* edited by Melvin R. Laird. Copyright © 1968 by Melvin R. Laird. Reprinted by permission of Doubleday & Company, Inc.

Wage-Price and Other Structural Policies, by Committee for Economic Development, *Further Weapons Against Inflation*, A Statement on National Policy, November 1970, pp. 37–47, 52–60.

What Price Guideposts? by Milton Friedman, from *Guidelines, Informal Controls and the Market Place*. Copyright © 1966 by The University of Chicago Press. Reprinted by permission.

Unreasonable Price Stability—The Pyrrhic Victory Over Inflation, by Edmund S. Phelps. Used by permission of the author.

The Basis for Lasting Prosperity, by Arthur F. Burns, from a lecture delivered at Pepperdine College on December 7, 1970. Reprinted by permission of the author.

The Costs of Wage-Price Controls, by William Poole, from *Brookings Papers on Economic Activity*, No. 2, 1971, © 1971 by The Brookings Institution, 1775 Massachusetts Avenue, N.W., Washington, D. C.

After the Freeze, by George L. Perry, from *Brookings Papers on Economic Activity*, No. 2, 1971, © 1971 by The Brookings Institution, 1775 Massachusetts Avenue, N.W., Washington, D. C.

Library of Congress Cataloging in Publication Data

Okun, Arthur M ed.
    The battle against unemployment.

    Bibliography: p.
    1. Unemployed—U. S.—Addresses, essays, lectures.
    2. Labor economics—Addresses, essays, lectures.
    3. U. S.—Economic policy—1961-   —Addresses,
essays, lectures.   I. Title.
HD5724.O35 1972   339.5'0973   79–38987
ISBN 0–393–05446–2
ISBN 0–393–09846–X (pbk.)

                    4 5 6 7 8 9 0

Contents

v

Introduction

PROSPERITY IS RIVALED only by peace as the key political issue in the United States. Unemployment and recession hit people hard in their pockets and pocketbooks and threaten their security and freedom of action. In presidential and congressional election campaigns, the record of economic performance by the "ins" and the promises of the "outs" represent one of the central issues. Our entire political process is conditioned by the mandate of the Employment Act of 1946, which declared: "It is the continuing policy and responsibility of the Federal Government . . . to promote maximum employment, production, and purchasing power."

The Employment Act's conclusion that social action to curb unemployment is necessary and desirable was neither trite nor self-evident. Until the 1930s, most economists believed that the private enterprise system, functioning competitively, had an automatic tendency to balance supply and demand in the aggregate at the right level. Wide fluctuations in economic activity and excessive unemployment were generally interpreted as either inevitable features of a growing economy or the results of misguided government interferences in economic life. Such views pointed toward a hands-off policy of neutrality for the government.

The Great Depression had a permanent impact on attitudes toward public policy against unemployment. At the depths of the depression, one-fourth of the nation's labor force was unemployed; and the unemployment rate did not fall below 14 percent throughout the 1930s. No individual escaped the impact of this great collapse and no individual could combat it on his own. With the sole exception of the Civil War, no episode in our nation's history has so strained the fabric of American society. The public refused to accept this deep and persistent depression as inevitable, nor could it be convinced that the depression was attributable to the errors of the government. The call for social

action was insistent and persuasive; it was answered by the innovations of the New Deal. Meanwhile, at a theoretical level, the
great British economist John Maynard Keynes dealt a mortal
blow to Say's Law, the doctrine that supply creates its own demand, and thereby destroyed the logical foundation for faith in
the basic stability of the private economy. Thus, the battle of
public policy against unemployment took shape in the 1930s.

The Employment Act gave recognition to the overwhelming
economic and social significance of adequate job opportunities.
This volume opens with Elliot Liebow's discussion of some of the
broader social aspects of joblessness. He stresses that unemployment can mean spiritual as well as material deprivation. Work is
an "admission ticket to society" and the absence of work is the
denial of that ticket: it tells a man that he has no productive
contribution to make to society. Moreover, Liebow emphasizes,
"unemployment strikes from underneath, particularly at those at
the bottom of our society." Thus it becomes divisive and destructive of social stability.

The nation's efforts to curb unemployment have had a reasonable degree of success since the Second World War. In the first
postwar decade, unemployment rates of 4 percent or lower—
generally accepted as essentially full employment—were the rule,
broken only during and immediately after two brief recessions.
Subsequently, although unemployment averaged nearly 6 percent from late 1957 through 1964, the full employment zone was
regained by late 1965 and maintained through 1969.

THE UNEMPLOYMENT-INFLATION DILEMMA

The record shows, however, that periods during which the unemployment performance can be regarded as satisfactory have
been periods in which price performance has been unsatisfactory.
The nation has not been able to combine an unemployment rate
as low as 4 percent with rates of price increase that remained less
than 4 percent. Indeed, the need to curb the inflation of the late
sixties led to the restrictive fiscal and monetary policies that
brought on the fifth postwar recession at the end of 1969 and
created our most recent bout of excessive unemployment. The
battle against unemployment can be understood only in light of

the "trade-off" between full employment and price stability.

While the initial article below by Liebow discusses the costs of unemployment, the second selection, by the editor of this volume, looks at the other side of the trade-off by appraising the costs of inflation. The factual evidence may be surprising when compared with many widely held beliefs about the evils of inflation: rising prices do not normally squeeze the real income of the poor or the average worker. Nonetheless, inflation does impose significant costs on society. It does adversely affect the real incomes of the aged, and it does introduce an undesirable lottery element into the distribution of real incomes. It has even more important effects on the wealth and the ability to save of many groups. In particular, it may deprive small savers of the opportunity for holding a reliable store of value and thus may turn them into "suckers" while sophisticated "sharpies" reap gains on rising prices. There are excellent reasons why the American people will not accept inflation as a way of life and why we must strive for a socially tolerable compromise on full employment and price stability.

In the third selection, Herbert Stein argues "as a minimum, the desirability of reducing the rate of inflation from 4 percent to the 2 percent we have averaged earlier." He argues that the process of reducing inflation is surely less painful in the long run than in the short run and, indeed, may involve little or no extra unemployment beyond a transition period. Stein stresses that, during the transition, manpower policies and income supplement systems can contribute a great deal to alleviate the burdens on those most vulnerable to unemployment. Moreover, he argues that if the disinflationary process to a 2 percent rate is executed satisfactorily, it may be feasible and appropriate for the government to set its sights on a zero rate of inflation as a long-run economic goal.

In sharp contrast, Alvin H. Hansen urges us to create a high pressure economy, accepting the risks of inflation rather than the danger of stagnation. He argues that the evils of inflation have often been exaggerated and that an attempt to ensure absolute price stability would gravely weaken our long-term economic performance. While recognizing that no formula for balancing the risks can rest on a firm analytical foundation, Hansen offers his own preferred rule: tolerate price increases "so long as percentage increases of aggregate output exceed the percentage increases in the price level." That rule does not satisfy Henry C. Wallich. He points to the risks of hyperinflation, economic collapse, and price controls that may stem from tolerance of "creeping inflation." He concedes the appeal of more output and more employment in the short run but warns that the "chickens may come home to roost."

In the concluding essay of the first section, James Tobin sets forth the simple analytics of the unemployment-inflation dilemma. He discusses the well-known and frequently used Phillips curve approach which "forces us to confront squarely the fact that our goals for prices and employment are not wholly reconcilable." One option is to try to shift the Phillips curve down—so that less inflation is associated with low unemployment. Such an effort relies on techniques to improve the labor market, mobility, competition, and the rate of growth of producitivity; or on the use of government moral suasion and controls. An alternative strategy is to mitigate the social costs of either unemployment, inflation, or both. For example, the social costs of unemployment may be reduced by strengthening unemployment compensation and increasing the placement and training of the hard-core unemployed. The social costs of inflation might be reduced by offering "cost of living" bonds to small savers. But Tobin offers no assurance that such measures can provide a reliable escape from the dilemma.

FISCAL POLICY

Fiscal and monetary policies are the principal weapons in the battle against unemployment. The selections of Part Two are devoted to fiscal policy. The mechanics of an expansionary fiscal action are explained in the 1963 Council of Economic Advisers' discussion of the multiplier. Budgetary policies can raise the take-home pay of the American public—through tax reduction, increased transfer payments, or higher government purchases of goods and services. Since households generally gear their outlays to their disposable incomes, they will tend to increase their expenditures for consumer goods and for services, thus generating more incomes for others and further increases in demand. Furthermore, the gains in sales, profits, and retained business earnings will encourage investment. In this way an initial fiscal stimulus can generate a multiplied increase in overall income. Similarly, a restraining fiscal measure can have a multiplied effect in curbing the growth of national product. The state of the economy determines whether we should want expansionary, neutral, or restrictive fiscal measures. If demand is weak in relation to the supply capabilities of the economy and idle resources abound, fiscal measures that add to demand will improve the overall supply-demand balance. On the other hand, if demand is so high as to strain the productive capabilities of the economy, a restrictive fiscal policy can help to curb excess demand inflation. When there are idle resources, increases in total spending are likely to be translated into more employment and production. When resources are fully employed, however, added demand will primarily raise prices, rather than real GNP. The Keynesian analysis of the multiplier process is at the heart of the belief that budgetary policies have important effects on the economy, and that these effects can be constructive if fiscal policy is appropriately geared to the state of overall demand.

Milton Friedman contests the central tenet of fiscal economics, questioning the potency of budgetary measures. According to Friedman, many links in the multiplier chain are weak. In some instances, he argues, government spending may displace rather than reinforce private spending. In particular, when the government finances its expenditure increases or tax reductions by borrowing funds from the public, Friedman doubts the stimulative character of these actions. Because of these weak links, in Friedman's view, fiscal policy is not a reliable and effective technique of stabilization, nor does it pose a great threat of destabilization.

In contrast, Maurice Stans does not doubt the power of the federal budget but rather emphasizes the likelihood that it may be used to produce harmful results. Stans fears that, once the rule of budget balancing is ignored, deficits become much more likely than surpluses for political reasons. Ignoring the rule thus creates a bias toward inflation. Stans is also concerned that discarding the balanced budget rule removes the guide to decisions

on the level of government expenditures and may thus encourage an irreversible growth of the public sector. The Stans
article was written in 1959; it is hard to find a serious expression
of this point of view in the 1960s or 1970s, and yet it does have a
continuing pervasive influence within the political process in
federal policy-making. Many congressmen and some members of
the executive branch are uncomfortable about budget deficits;
while they do not display the religious devotion to budget
balancing that once marked political rhetoric, neither will they
embrace the deliberate use of fiscal policy to influence the nation's economy. They want some guide or rule of discipline in
fiscal policy and long for the old beacon of the budget-balancing
rule.

The 1971 Council of Economic Advisers' discussion of the full
employment budget offers an alternative guide. The Council argues that "the actual deficit or surplus . . . can be grossly misleading" as a measure of the impact of fiscal policy. For the actual surplus or deficit is the compound result of (a) fiscal policy
decisions on public spending and tax rates and (b) the automatic process by which the strength of the economy influences
tax revenues. When the economy is rising sharply, tax revenues
jump, reflecting gains in private incomes, and thereby tending to
move the budget into surplus. But such a surplus does not necessarily imply that the fiscal dials are set in a restrictive pattern;
it is like the furnace shutting off because the outside temperature has risen rather than because the thermostat has been reset.

The confusion can be avoided by use of a measure that dis-
tinguishes the effects of tax and expenditure decisions from the
effects of the strength of economic activity on the budget. The
measure proposed by the Council calculates the budget surplus
(or deficit) on the assumption that the economy followed a full
employment path and thus generated the tax revenues stemming
from full employment incomes. The full employment surplus is
influenced by decisions to change public expenditures and tax
rates, but it is not affected by changes in economic activity that
influence actual tax revenues. The full employment surplus thus
describes the setting of the budgetary thermostat and abstracts
from the temperature of economic activity.

In addition to its use as an indicator of what fiscal policy *is* doing, the full employment budget is taken by some economists as a guide to what fiscal policy *should* be doing. In a period of weak economic activity, the Nixon Administration's fiscal policy called for a bare balance in the full employment budget (on the "unified" budget measure) but opposed a full employment deficit on principle. The old and naive rule of balancing the budget was thus supplanted by a new rule of balancing the full employment budget. Nonetheless, as critics pointed out, a full employment deficit could be a desirable stimulative strategy to pull the economy out of recession or stagnation. The principle of balancing the full employment budget is designed to reduce the magnitude of swings in fiscal policy. Advocates of steadier fiscal policy point out the large and inappropriate stimulative swing in the federal budget during the Vietnam war buildup. Others read that economic lesson differently as demonstrating the need for greater flexibility in tax rates, rather than for more stability in fiscal policy.

The need for greater flexibility in varying tax rates was emphasized by the Commission on Money and Credit in its 1961 report. The Commission recognized the contribution of built-in stabilizers to the performance of our economy. Because federal tax receipts share significantly in any economic decline or expansion, a dollar drop in GNP means substantially lower government receipts and hence much less than a dollar reduction in private after-tax income. As a result of this cushioning, the multiplier is reduced in size and the economy is made more stable. Unemployment compensation also acts as a shock absorber for disposable income during recessions. But while these built-in stabilizers can limit the magnitude of the decline, they cannot in general reverse the direction of economic trends. For such a task, discretionary changes in tax rates may be required. When such changes were proposed for stabilization purposes by President Kennedy in 1963 and by President Johnson in 1967, a prolonged debate and apparent stalemate ensued in the Congress; roughly a year elapsed in each case before a tax measure was enacted. The Commission on Money and Credit foresaw this danger at the beginning of the 1960s and proposed congressional action to vest the President with conditional powers to raise or lower personal income taxes, subject to congressional veto. The proposal was designed to guarantee swift action that would make tax policy a more effective device for promoting economic stability. In part, the stress on tax reduction as a stimulative measure reflected the experience that increases in most types of federal expenditures are slow to implement and very difficult to reverse, once undertaken. If the legislative delay could be overcome, variability in taxes could be the generally preferred technique of altering fiscal policy. Nonetheless, while the Commission's proposal has been debated and discussed and even supported in modified form by both Presidents Kennedy and Johnson, it has had very little appeal to the Congress, which jealously guards its prerogatives over changes in tax rates.

MONETARY POLICY

Monetary policy is the partner of fiscal policy in stimulating or restraining overall demand. But it is a legally divided partnership. While the President and the Congress determine fiscal policy, the authority over monetary policy rests with the Federal Reserve System. In the first selection of Part Three, G. L. Bach discusses the organization for monetary policy-making and the significance and appropriateness of Federal Reserve independence. Bach argues that, as an important branch of macroeconomic policy, monetary policy cannot realistically be made independently. In particular, no Congress or Administration would acquiesce in policies of the central bank that overrode the legislative and executive conception of the basic strategy for achieving the nation's economic goals. And yet Bach sees a strong case for Federal Reserve independence as it is now established and practiced. First, he favors the dispersion of power accomplished by Federal Reserve independence. Second, and most important, he argues that "the entire American democratic political process has an inflationary bias," and that Federal Reserve independence allows the System to act as a buffer against inflation within that process.

Milton Friedman is much less sanguine than Bach about the role the Federal Reserve has in fact played as a buffer against instability. Nonetheless, he accepts the present organization, but argues for a change in the targets and techniques of Federal Reserve policy. Friedman emphasizes that the first and most important task of monetary policy is to "prevent money itself from being a major source of economic disturbance." He believes that drastic and erratic changes in the growth of the money supply have been a major source of economic instability in the past. He relates these errors to the Federal Reserve's "propensity to over-react" by slamming on the brakes or the accelerator in light of current economic conditions while ignoring the necessary delays between policy actions and the subsequent effects on the economy. According to Friedman's prescription, the monetary authority should adopt publicly the strategy of achieving a steady rate of growth of the money stock. As Friedman sees it, monetary policy would thus make a major contribution to economic stability and to the avoidance of either inflation or deflation.

Walter Heller doubts the wisdom of Friedman's monetary rule. Basically, Heller stresses that a steady growth of the money supply offers no assurance of steady growth in national product. He points out the variety of other factors besides the quantity of money that seem to influence national income: the price of money —that is, interest rates; the quantity of other forms of liquidity; the posture of fiscal policy; and variations in private desires to save and invest. To Heller, these other factors produce "twists and turns in the road" that argue strongly against the Friedman proposal to lock the steering gear into place.

The 1969 Council of Economic Advisers' piece on monetary policy is in the same spirit as the Heller selection. It develops a Keynesian view of the way that monetary policy influences output, employment, and prices. The cost and availability of credit are emphasized as the key financial factors affecting the willingness of consumers and businessmen to spend. The supply of money is important in this view insofar as it influences the cost and availability of credit, but the Council stresses that new money "is not something given to the public for nothing as if it fell from heaven." The Federal Reserve has often in the past geared monetary policy to targets for interest rates and credit conditions rather than to growth of the money supply. Accordingly, when the economy expanded and credit demands rose strongly, the Fed accommodated the increased demands for money with a growing supply. Historically, such a strategy produces a close relationship between income and money—without necessarily showing that changes in money *caused* the changes in income. The Council emphasizes the possibility of a misinterpretation of the evidence if the "reverse causation" from income to money is ignored.

Henry Wallich sees defects in both a policy such as Friedman's rule, which is oriented purely toward control of the money supply, and in an orientation directed solely toward interest rates. He stresses that, particularly in boom periods, when interest rates may be swelled by expectations of inflation, high interest rates may not be valid indicators of monetary restraint. However, he fears that a rule of fixed monetary growth would increase the instability of interest rates, thereby impairing the strength of the corporate and government bond markets and compromising balance-of-payments objectives. For these reasons, Wallich doubts that the Federal Reserve ever will adopt a rigid monetary rule. In its policy deliberations and decisions in 1970 and 1971 the Federal Reserve did give much more emphasis to the money supply than in previous years, but, in line with Wallich's prediction made in 1969, it did not set a fixed and unvarying target for the growth of the money stock.

RECORD OF THE "NEW ECONOMICS"

The selections of Part Four illuminate the principles and practices of stabilization policy in terms of the record of the 1960s. Walter Heller documents the success story of the early sixties during which the nation's longest and strongest peacetime expansion was achieved. Inheriting a weak economy which was recovering from its second recession in three years, the Kennedy economists set their sights on catching up and keeping up with the nation's full-employment potential. As Heller indicates, the "new economics" shifted focus from the maintenance of economic expansion (that is, avoidance of recession) to the more ambitious pursuit of a moving full-employment target. In pursuing this target, fiscal strategy became more activist and bolder. Its biggest single innovative measure was the 1964 tax cut, which was unprecedented in many respects: it was a major fiscal stimulus applied while the economy was in an expansion rather than a recession, while the budget was in deficit, and while federal expenditures were still actually increasing. As Heller emphasizes, the expansionary fiscal strategy was supported by an accommodative monetary policy and by wage-price guideposts and other efforts to ensure price-cost stability during a period of strong economic advance. By mid-1965, the economy was finally approaching the zone of full employment and was still displaying a remarkable record of price stability.

At that point, Vietnam intruded upon the economic scene and subsequently dominated that scene for the remainder of the Johnson Administration. In the view of the editor of this volume, the ensuing "fiscal fiasco" reflected not a failure of the new economics, but rather its defeat by the old politics. When Vietnam expenditures were piled on a budget that was appropriately expansionary, fiscal policy became an over-expansionary engine of inflation. A sufficiently prompt and large increase in taxes could have neutralized the budgetary stimulus of Vietnam outlays, but the political process was paralyzed—partly because of the unpopularity of the war. A major curtailment of federal civilian outlays might also have done the stabilization job, but only at enormous social costs to poor, aged, black, and urban citizens. A heavy burden hence fell on the monetary authorities to curb the inflationary boom, and they rose to the occasion in 1966. But the distorting "side effects" of tight money on interest rates, the stability of financial markets, and the balance among sectors (especially homebuilding) were acute. By the time the budget was restored to an appropriately restraining position in 1968, inflation had developed enormous momentum and proved extremely resistant to the slowdown in economic activity.

In contrast, Beryl Sprinkel puts the blame for the economy's going off track in 1966 directly on the new economics rather than the problems of war finance. He contends that the basic position of the new economists gave inadequate attention to monetary growth, and that the activist fiscal strategy presumed an ability to implement rapid changes in taxes and public spending whenever necessary. As he sees it, the war was basically the acid test that the new economists could not pass. It refuted their unreasonable expectations that the economy could be effectively managed by an active and alert fiscal policy.

Paul McCracken's evaluation of the 1961–68 record of economic policy and performance gives substantial credit to the new economics for the results of the early sixties. Yet his enthusiasm is distinctly more restrained than is Heller's. For one thing, McCracken sees much more continuity with the past and less innovation in the policies of the new economics. Secondly, he stresses that the climate of the early sixties—after years of disinflation—made an expansionary strategy particularly appropriate and successful. In his view, fiscal and monetary policies both became overly stimulative in 1965, before the major Vietnam buildup; and erratic policy management contributed to economic problems throughout the Vietnam buildup. To McCracken, one lesson is that the need for fiscal-monetary flexibility has been overstated in the past. Instead, he stresses the desirability of a "steadier and more even-handed management of economic policy."

THE COST-PUSH PROBLEM

McCracken got the opportunity to apply his principles when he became Chairman of the Council of Economic Advisers under President Nixon in 1969. The Nixon Administration inherited an economy plagued by inflation but blessed with low unemployment. Because aggregate demand was still straining productive capacity in 1969, fiscal and monetary restraints were applied in an effort to halt the boom and thereby to curb inflation. Aggregate demand did slacken fairly promptly, but the price performance worsened rather than improving during 1969. The wage-price spiral turned out to have tremendous momentum; cost-pressures continued to push up the price level even after demand stopped pulling up prices and wages. In the first selection of Part Five, the Nixon Council of Economic Advisers explains its strategy of dealing with the inflationary situation, showing how a process of gradual restraint on aggregate demand could produce market pressures for employers to resist wage increases and to temper their price increases. The Council also explains the Administration's initial decision not to revive wage-price guideposts or otherwise to invoke anti-inflationary moral suasion.

The Committee for Economic Development, on the other hand,

concludes that the fundamental monetary and fiscal stabilization policies are not adequate to deal with the economy's inflationary tendencies. It offers a wide variety of proposals for supplementary policies to increase the efficiency of labor and product markets. It also reviews the record of wage-price policies and the need for them, reaching the conclusion that "on balance of considerations . . . the United States should include voluntary wage-price policies among its policy tools for reconciling price stability and high employment." To implement such policies, the Committee recommends the creation of a three-man Board on Prices and Incomes which would promote full consultation among government, business, and labor leaders, and would develop ground rules to define wage-price behavior consistent with the public interest.

In the next selection, Milton Friedman registers his strong opposition to such wage-price guideposts. He argues that cost-push inflation is often an optical illusion, merely the lagged or indirect effects of demand pressures stemming from previously excessive growth of the money supply. Moreover, he insists that, whatever the source of inflation, a system of voluntary controls confuses the big issue of determining overall monetary policy, distorts the allocation of resources, involves the dangerous use of extra-legal powers of government, and compromises the proper role of businessmen and labor leaders.

While the first three selections in Part Five accept the curtailment of inflation as a desirable social goal, Edmund Phelps strikes at "the myth of price stability." In Phelps' view, it would be advantageous for the nation's rate of price increase to be predictable and planned so that people are not surprised and fooled. But he sees no superiority of a zero percent rate of inflation over a steady rate of 4 percent or even higher. Consequently, he argues that the policies of 1969–71 have made important sacrifices of output and employment to achieve the unimportant target of price stability.

In contrast, Federal Reserve Chairman Arthur Burns concludes that the disinflationary process of 1969–70, while imposing important costs on output and employment, made considerable positive achievements. It restored more prudent and efficient financial and business practices and corrected unreasonable expectations. But he notes that the economy continues to be plagued by "pressures and costs arising from excessive wage increases." For this purpose, he considers the adoption of a comprehensive "incomes policy," including many measures to improve the functioning of markets as well as the establishment of a high-level price and wage review board.

After thirty-one months of firmly resisting recommendations like those of the Committee on Economic Development and Arthur Burns for a wage-price restraint program, the Nixon Administration reversed itself dramatically on August 15, 1971 and imposed a comprehensive program of legal controls on wages, prices, and rents. The final two selections in this volume offer contrasting views on the potential success of a restraint program. William Poole contends that a mild, selective, or largely voluntary wage-price policy would be useless, while the benefits of strict comprehensive controls would be swamped by enormous costs, including a loss of individual freedom, distortions of the allocation of resources, and enforcement problems that lead either to widespread evasion or to a huge bureaucracy.

George Perry, on the other hand, argues that a "middle-of-the-road incomes policy" that focuses selectively on the most visible and most critical wage and price decisions could reduce inflation without the enormous burdens that Poole foresees. Perry suspects that the existence of high "habitual wage standards" has been responsible for maintaining an inflationary treadmill in the face of pervasive excess supplies of goods and labor. Particularly because the wage-price control program was launched at a time of excess supply rather than of excess demand, Perry is optimistic that it could offer business and labor an opportunity to get off the inflationary treadmill.

Along with stubborn and continuing inflation, the early 1970s brought a new wave of high unemployment. The year 1971 registered the third highest unemployment rate since the Second World War—below only 1958 and 1961. But the new economic policy of August 1971 was accompanied by tax reductions, expenditure increases, and a stimulative monetary policy, which were soon reflected in a strong rebound of economic activity and a downward movement in unemployment. The closing months of 1971 and the year 1972 also witnessed a significant deceleration of inflation. While economists disagree about the magnitude of the contribution of wage-price controls to that deceleration, most observers credit them with some favorable impact.

By the end of 1972, the economic recovery had developed a strong head of steam, and the Administration began to fashion a less expansionary fiscal and monetary strategy. At the same time, the wage-price control program was reshaped into a more narrowly focused, self-administering system. The big unanswered questions of stabilization policy are highlighted in a strong but incomplete recovery: How much can unemployment be reduced below 5 percent and toward 4 percent through strong overall economic expansion without unleashing the forces of demand inflation? To what extent can a continuing federal program of price and wage restraints offer insurance against a new outbreak of cost-push inflation?

American experience under the Employment Act has provided incontrovertible evidence of the potency of fiscal and monetary actions to stimulate and to restrain economic activity. Clearly the policy-makers can administer effective medicines, and they know a fair amount about how to vary the dosage. But they have not yet learned, or at least not yet demonstrated, the ability to find a tolerable compromise between high levels of employment and economic activity, on the one hand, and a reasonable degree of price stability on the other. That remains the chief challenge to overall economic policy.

PROBLEMS OF THE MODERN ECONOMY

The Battle Against Unemployment

PART ONE

The Unemployment-Inflation
Dilemma

The Human Costs of Unemployment

ELLIOTT LIEBOW

This selection appeared in the New York Times Magazine *of April 5, 1970, and was originally entitled "No Man Can Live With the Terrible Knowledge That He Is Not Needed." Elliot Liebow is an anthropologist at the Mental Health Study Center, National Institute of Mental Health.*

NOW THAT WE HAVE, in effect, seized upon unemployment as a weapon of choice in the battle against inflation, we face the prospect of an unemployment rate of 5 percent (4 million persons) or more. And as the unemployment rate goes up, economists and public policy makers debate the question: How much unemployment can the country stand?

Strictly speaking, it is not "the country" that is being asked to "stand unemployment." Unemployment does not, like air pollution or God's gentle rain, fall uniformly upon everyone, nor does it strike randomly at our labor force of 80 million. Unemployment is directional and selective; it strikes from underneath, and it strikes particularly at those at the bottom of our society. Managers, professional people, scientists, technicians, and others with special skills and training are generally secure in their jobs whatever the unemployment rate. Indeed, even with a 5 percent unemployment rate, there would continue to be a labor shortage at many of these occupational levels. When we talk about unemployment, then, we are talking mainly about those at the bottom of society: the day worker, the unskilled and semiskilled laborer, the Job Corps and the on-the-job trainee, those with little or no seniority in the labor unions and those making their first try at breaking into the labor force.

Since there is little unemployment at the upper and middle occupational level, a 5 percent *average* rate means unemployment rates of 10 percent and 20 percent in our ghettos and other hard-core areas. And among certain groups, such as black and other minority-group youths and women, it means an unemployment rate as high as 25 or 30 percent. Increased unemployment, then, means not only more people out of work, it means mainly more black people, more young people, and more poor people out of work. The question is not simply how much more unemployment we can stand, but whether we can stand, through deepening unemployment, a deepening of the race and class divisions that are already threatening to tear our society apart.

We could, of course, deal with the newcomers to the ranks of the unemployed and the poor in the same way that we deal with those who are already there, but this would be to make believe that we don't know the destructive and self-defeating consequences of our public-welfare programs, whose positive effects are largely limited to the simple maintenance of life at bare subsistence levels.

One difficulty in generating alternative solutions comes from our looking at unemployment too narrowly. We tend to see unemployment as a kind of inevitable exhaust of our economic engine. We fail to see that it is also a social process powered by the values we hold and the choices we make.

It might be useful, for example, to look closely at work and unemployment without regard to poverty. There are, after all, many people who work very hard and yet live in poverty, and there are others who do not work at all and are very rich. For the moment, then, let us ignore poverty and look only at work, in the ordinary, day-to-day meaning of the word as having to do with a job, with earning a living.

From the very beginning of human history, it has been through work that man has provided himself with the necessities of life. So closely is work tied in with the social and psychological development of man that it is almost impossible to think of what it means to be human without thinking of work. Indeed, the connection is so strong, so close, and so obvious that attempts to talk about the importance of work often sound banal. "Work is the fundamental condition of human existence," said Karl Marx; "work is man's strongest tie to reality," said Freud.

It is also through work, as a producer of socially useful goods or services, that the individual—especially the adult male—carries out those social roles (husband, father, family head) that define him as a full and valued member of his society. That work becomes, in effect, a kind of admission ticket to society is not something invented by white middle-class Americans, although many of us often act as if it is. There is nothing especially white or middle-class about wanting to earn a living and support one's family. That is what the working-class man wants, and the Eskimo hunter and the Chinese peasant and the African herdsman —all of them want it, too. "In every known human society," Margaret Mead tells us, "everywhere in the world, the young male learns that when he grows up one of the things he must do in order to be a full member of society is to provide food for some female and her young."

The centrality of work, then, is not new to human experience, and it did not arrive only with the appearance of capitalism and the Protestant ethic, although each of these did add its own embellishments to the meaning and importance of work. What does seem to be relatively new, however, is the appearance of widespread, systematic nonwork—unemployment—as an integral part or by-product of the ordinary functioning of society, an appearance which seems to date from the introduction of market economies and wage labor typically associated with the rise of capitalism.

In subsistence economies, the entire population has to work to produce the goods and services necessary to survival, and there is always work to be done. In such societies, people are not recognizable as being in or out of the work force—the work force is synonymous with the total population.

In industrial societies, unemployment strikes deep at the man, as well as at the way he fits into his family, his community, and the larger society. It can put a man "out of it," and can turn him into a caricature of himself, giving him the appearance of being stupid and lazy with no concern for the future. Some of this can be seen in Marie Jahoda's description of what happened to the workers in the Austrian village of Marienthal when its only factory was shut down in the 1930s:

The unemployed men lost their sense of time. When asked at the end of a day what they had done during it, they were unable to describe their activities. "Real" time . . . was vague and nebulous. Activities such as fetching wood from the shed, which could not have consumed more than 10 minutes, were recorded as if they had filled a morning. . . . The men's waking day was shortened to 12 or 13 hours. Rational budget planning . . . was abandoned in favor of expenditure on trinkets, while essentials could not be paid for.

Edward Wight Bakke's study of white Americans thrown out of work in those same depression years makes it equally clear that there is more going on here than a simple lack of money to live on. He found that public assistance for the unemployed was initially effective. After a few months, however, public assistance, by itself, could no longer hold back the destructive consequences of not working; and the man's relationships with his family, friends, and neighbors, indeed, with the whole community, degenerated dramatically. Once this degenerative process established itself, only work could halt it, and only through work could the man gain again his position as a valued member of society.

Bakke also found that the man cannot wait forever for a job. Being unemployed quickly reaches a point of no return. The man learns to live with his failure by lowering his life goals and by other rationalizing measures which effectively remove him from ordinary society. No longer a producer, a contributor to the commonweal, and no longer the breadwinning husband and father, he is also, in his own eyes and in the eyes of society, no longer a man. Faced with nothing to do, he has no place to go. He hangs around. He is superfluous, and he knows it.

Moreover, if we now widen our view of work and unemployment to include money and poverty, we see that unemployment is only the tip of the iceberg. The unemployed man is just a special case of the man who cannot support himself and his family. For every man who is looking for a job, there are dozens more who have jobs and are still unable to support themselves and their dependents. The effects are, perhaps, no less disastrous for the man who works than for the man who does not, nor are they any less disastrous for their families, their communities, or the whole society.

We can see the general problem most clearly by narrowing our focus to black people and other racial minorities in our society, for they are the principal victims. Black people suffer more from unemployment not only because more of them, proportionately, are unemployed, but because they are more likely than their white counterparts to have been unemployed in the past and to remain unemployed or underemployed in the future. This circumstance of life—a major thread in the collective history and present experience of black people as a group—shapes the way the black man sees himself and is seen by others as fitting into the larger community. It also gives meaning to the assertion that we are a racist society, a racism that is intimately bound up with work and productivity and individual worth.

Let me give an example. The six-year-old son of a woman on welfare was struck and killed by an automobile as he tried to run across the street. The insurance company's initial offer of $800 to settle out of court was rejected. In consultation with her lawyer, the mother accepted the second and final offer of $2,000. When I learned of the settlement, I called the lawyer to protest, arguing that the sum was far less than what I assumed to be the usual settlement in such cases, even if the child was mainly at fault. "You've got to face the facts," he said. "Insurance companies and juries just don't pay as much for a Negro child." Especially, he might have added, a Negro child on welfare.

If the relative worth of human life must be measured in dollars and cents, why should the cash surrender value of a black child's life be less than that for a white child's life? The answer clearly has nothing to do with private prejudice and discrimination. Insurance companies and our legal system take an actuarial perspective. Damage awards are based primarily on the projected lifetime earnings of the individual; they are statements about his probable productivity, not about his skin color. But this child, this Anthony Davis, was only six years old. On what basis do they make lowered projections of earnings for a six-year-old child, before he has acquired or rejected an education, before he has demonstrated any talents or lack of them, before he has selected an occupation, or, indeed, before he has made a single life choice of his own?

There can be only one answer. The answer is, simply, on the basis of skin color and social class. And what is most important for us to know and admit is this: the insurance company was *absolutely right*. Anthony was more likely than his white, middle-class counterpart to go to an inferior school, to get an inferior education, to be sick, to get an inferior job, to be last hired and first fired, to be passed over for promotion, and to live a shorter life. In all probability, then, Anthony *would* be less productive over his lifetime than his white middle-class counterpart. And we are a racist society because we know this to be true before the fact, when Anthony is only six years old.

Typically, we admit the problem, but we place the cause in the Negro (Puerto Rican, Mexican-American, American Indian, Appalachian white) himself. We say that because of their history, or their subculture, or their family structure, these minorities are lazy, irresponsible, and don't want to work. Then, in the midst of an affluence never before achieved by any society, we offer them the most menial, the dullest, the poorest paid jobs in our society, and, sure enough, some of them don't want to work.

But the one most important fact is often overlooked. Most Negroes (Puerto Ricans, etc.), like everyone else in our society, do want to work. Indeed, most of them have been working all along. In Washington, for example, the garbage does get picked up, the streets get swept, hotel beds are made, school and office-building floors and halls get mopped and polished, cars and restaurant dishes get washed, ditches get dug, deliveries are made, orderlies attend the aged, the sick, the mentally ill, and so on. And most of the people whose job it is to do those things are black.

But if most Negroes do have jobs, what is the problem? It is mainly that most of those jobs pay from $50 to $80 or $90 a week. In 1966, for example, 25 percent of all non-white, *full-time, year-round* male workers earned less than $3,000, and this in a year when the Bureau of Labor Statistics said that it required $9,200 to maintain a modest standard of living for a family of four in an urban area. The man with a wife and one or two children who takes such a job can be certain he will live in poverty as long as he keeps it. The longer he works, the longer he cannot live on what he makes.

This situation makes for a curious paradox: the man who works hard may be little or no better off than the man who does not look for a job at all. In a sense, he may even be worse off. The man who works hard but cannot earn a living has put himself on the scales and been found wanting. He says to society, "I have done what needed doing. Now, what am I worth?" and society answers, "Not much, not even enough to support yourself and your dependents." But the man who does not seek out or accept such a job may, for a while at least, fool himself or his fellows into thinking that he has not climbed onto the scales at all.

By itself, then, work does not guarantee full and valued participation in society. Participation requires not only an opportunity to contribute to the day-to-day life of that society, but it requires, reciprocally, an acknowledgment by society that the contribution is of value. That acknowledgment, typically in the form of wages, lets the man know that he is somebody, that he is important, useful, and even necessary. But the man who cannot find a job, or the man who finds one but is still unable to support himself and his family, is being told in clear and simple language, and loud enough for his wife and children and friends and neighbors and everyone else to hear, that he is not needed, that there is no place for him.

No man can live with this terrible self-knowledge for long. Both the youth who has never worked but who sees this situation as his probable future, and the man who has experienced it retreat to the street corner where others like themselves, in self-defense, have constructed a world which gives them that minimum sense of belonging and being useful without which human life is perhaps impossible and which the larger society gives up so very grudgingly or not at all. And after we tell a man that he cannot earn enough to support himself and his family, that he is not a full and valued member of society, what claims have we on his loyalty and goodwill? I strongly suspect that we have none. From his point of view, if we deny his claim on us, he does not owe us a thing, not loyalty, not goodwill, not "responsible" protest.

From this perspective, the problem is how can we change our society so that all who belong to it can become full and valued participants in it?

For a beginning, we must make the poor less poor. We must get money into their hands. We must choose one or a combination of the many income-supplement programs that have been proposed and put them into practice. Another beginning step might be to focus our concerns on the low-paying, menial jobs that have to be done in every society. Since these jobs have to be done by someone, it makes little sense to keep insisting that we must always and only upgrade the person. At some point we are going to have to upgrade the job.

For systematically upgrading jobs such as these, we might use the airline stewardess as a model. Casual observation suggests that, for the most part, her job is that of a waitress. But the airlines, through adroit public relations, through the use of smartly designed uniforms, by setting performance standards, and by paying a decent salary, have upgraded the job of the airborne waitress to a much higher level of respectability and desirability than that enjoyed by her ground-based counterpart.

Not all menial jobs can be upgraded so easily and so far. Many menial jobs are dirty jobs, and there is not a lot we can do at this time to make them less dirty. But that is not the only reason they are despised and among the lowest status jobs in our society. They are also among the lowest paying jobs. They are the kind of jobs a man can work at full time, year round, and still earn less than $3,000, and both the job and the man are despised for this reason, too.

It is very easy to overestimate the extent to which such jobs are despised because they are dirty or hard and to underestimate the extent to which they are despised because they pay so little money. There is little that is intrinsically bad about being a janitor or trash collector. What is so bad about them is that in such jobs you cannot earn a living. Where the pay for garbage and trash collectors approaches a living wage, as in New York City, there is intense competition for the work that is elsewhere shunned and accepted only as a last resort.

That these jobs tend also to be dead-end jobs is probably true, but perhaps we make too much of this also. The job of the lathe operator, the assembly-line worker, the truck driver, the secretary, these tend to be dead-end jobs too, but they are not bad jobs because of it. Not everyone in our society is career-oriented.

We have a large and relatively stable working-class population which does not aspire to moving up a career ladder. The working man who earns a living and supports his family by doing work that everyone agrees is socially useful does not necessarily want to become a foreman, or plant manager, or office executive. If he is dissatisfied, it is probably because he wants more of what he has and wants to be more certain of keeping what he has, not because he wants something different. So would it be, perhaps, with jobs that are presently considered menial, dead-end jobs. If a man could earn a living at these jobs, they would not be dead-end. They would be much like other jobs—a job.

I do not mean to suggest that all unemployed and underemployed men and youths want nothing more than jobs that pay a living wage. Many do want careers and an opportunity to use their brains and their strengths to take them as high and as far as they can go, and they must have these opportunities. The point here is that not everyone wants to scratch his way to the top of something. Most people, black and white, want the creature comforts and the psychic rewards that come with having jobs that enable them and their families to live like most other people in our society.

This brings us to my final proposal. It has been suggested many times by many people, but because it has been labeled unrealistic or too expensive or destructive of free enterprise, it does not seem to be getting the serious attention I think it deserves. . . . If having a job and earning a living is, as I believe it is, the linchpin of full and valued participation in our society, then every able-bodied man must have a right—a legal, statutory right—to a job doing socially useful work which pays a decent wage. To do this would probably require that government—federal, state and local—already the largest employer, become also the employer of last resort. At the federal level, there are many different employment models to choose from: Civil Service, the Tennessee Valley Authority, the Public Health Service, contract, grant and draft mechanisms, the old WPA, and CCC, etc.

The crucial thing here is not the mechanism but the avoidance of contemptible make-work by matching a wide range of job skills and aspirations to tasks that are clearly of a high order of social usefulness, such as construction of public and low-cost housing, restoration of cities, expansion and improvement of mail service, and host of other programs and projects directed at the unmet public need in the areas of health education, child care, urban mass transit, conservation, pollution, and so on. Where appropriate the federal government could subcontract such projects, or parts of them, to state and local governments through a revenue-sharing system, thereby insuring that national programs and policies were matched to local needs.

We have already seen that, by themselves, neither money nor a job is sufficient to guarantee full and valued participation. The two must be linked together. A man must have the right to a job that pays a decent wage. Thus, though income-assistance plans are needed for the immediate future, and indeed always will be needed for those persons—the aged, the sick, the handicapped, and women with dependent children—who cannot or should not work, such plans should be viewed for the working poor as stop-gap emergency measures rather than long-range solutions.

In general, income-assistance plans for the man who works but does not earn a living wage are focused on the wrong end of the employer-employee relationship. We are probably all agreed that, given a wage-labor system, a man who does an honest day's work, whether it be sweeping the floor or simply guarding a gate, is entitled to an honest day's pay. An honest day's pay must mean, at the minimum, enough for the man to support himself and an average number of dependents. If it means anything less, it means nothing at all.

If a business or industry cannot afford to pay the worker enough to live on, the failure lies with the company, not the employee, and it is the employer who needs welfare, not the worker. Enterprises which through inefficiency or other reasons cannot afford to pay their workers enough to live on must leave the field or, if they are deemed socially useful and necessary, must be subsidized by the government—let's call it cost-sharing—so they can pay their workers a living wage. In this way, the stigma, the badge of dependency that goes with being a recipient of public assistance, is removed from the worker (where it did not really belong in the first place) and placed on the employer (where it does belong). . . .

Acknowledgment of every citizen's uncompromised right to earn a living is not proposed as a solution to all of our social problems. It would, however, be an important first step toward dealing with many of them: behind much of what presents itself to us as family instability, dependent women and children, violence, crime, and retreatist life styles, stand men and women, black and white, who cannot support themselves and their families. In addition, raising the social and economic status of its members is the surest and safest way for a society to reduce its rate of population growth. Most immediately and directly, however, the right to a job at a decent wage would go a long way toward removing simple, brutal poverty from our national life. And unlike variations on the welfare theme, it would do this in a way that would help reorder the relationship between citizen and society so that everyone could enjoy that minimum sense of security and self-respect without which talk of freedom, equality, and opportunity does not mean very much.

The Costs of Inflation

ARTHUR M. OKUN

This article is an adapted and updated version of a portion of a lecture presented at New York University in November 1969 and originally published in Inflation: The Problems It Creates and the Policies It Requires *by Arthur M. Okun, Henry H. Fowler, and Milton Gilbert.*

WHEN THE UNITED STATES experiences an economic slump in an effort to curb inflation, the costs are enormous. At the beginning of 1971, the actual annual rate of output of goods and services was running $60 billion below the potential output of this nation. At a time when we are straining to finance state and local programs that meet urgent public needs, to rebuild our cities, to provide for our poor, and to clean up our environment, the loss of $60 billion a year of output is an extravagance of cosmic proportions.

Along with that shortfall of output goes an equal shortfall in real incomes. Roughly $20 billion of the missing $60 billion would be in corporate profits, which are the private incomes most vulnerable to an economic slump. Owners of small businesses, farmers, and self-employed professionals absorb some of the costs, perhaps as much as $5 billion. Our wage and salary payrolls are some $30 billion below what they would be in a full-employment economy. Taxes on these profit and wage incomes would put extra receipts of more than $20 billion in federal, state, and local treasuries.

When the unemployment rate is 6 percent rather than the 4 percent widely regarded as full employment, an extra 1.7 million Americans are jobless. But the slump affects far more than 1.7 million households. Fortunately, few people stay jobless all year long, even in a slumping economy; but the converse of that proposition is that an extra 1 percentage point of unemployment means as much as 5 percent of the labor force feels some stretch of extra unemployment during the course of a year. And millions more lose pay for overtime work that has become a vital margin to supply the amenities of life to many American families. Others find their full-time jobs converted into part-time employment. Statistical evidence from past periods of economic fluctuations suggests that an extra 1 percentage point of unemployment blocked as many as 1 million people from crossing the line of poverty income. In an opinion survey taken in August 1970, 21 percent of all American families reported that they had felt some impact of the curtailment of job opportunities during the preceding year. Their subjective response looks reasonably consistent with the facts.

It is vital to recognize the cost of a slump. But it is not difficult to assess this side of the ledger. It is much more difficult to evaluate the other side: If as a result of the slump we should achieve price stability, what will we get and what is it worth?

One obvious dividend comes in our balance-of-payments position. Even though we have been inflating slightly more rapidly than our major trading partners, the United States surplus on trade account has suffered enormously from the rapid growth and accelerating prices of recent years. Our trade surplus was $5 billion in 1965; it was under $1 billion in 1968 and 1969. That major deterioration in our trade position has not hurt the world role of the dollar. But that result has depended on a series of strokes of good luck—like the shift of the big surplus from gold-hungry de Gaulle to dollar-happy West Germany—and a series of ingenious United States policy actions—including unhappy stop-gaps of controls and forward-looking innovations like Special Drawing Rights.

Still, the balance of payments has only limited political appeal as a rationale for price stability in the United States. To be sure, in early 1968, after the devaluation of sterling, the threat of a world financial crisis was a handy argument in favor of a program of fiscal restraint that the country needed desperately for its own good. The specter of an international financial crisis frightened Congress; even to people who didn't know what "the downfall of the dollar" meant, it sounded far more serious than a few additional points on interest rates or price indices. But this episode was certainly the exception. In 1951 and 1956–57, the United States was fighting inflation because it was unacceptable at home, even though our inflation would have helped to restore world equilibrium and alleviate the dollar shortage. The gut issues about inflation are those of household finance, not world finance.

The costs on the home front are elusive. Because economists do not have good, solid ways to evaluate the costs, they are tempted either to get moralistic about price stability or else, on the other extreme, to dismiss the problem of inflation as an optical illusion. I don't have good answers either, but I pledge utmost effort neither to moralize nor to dismiss the problem. Instead, let me do some arithmetic on the domestic costs of our recent inflation, in terms of the distribution of real incomes and the impact on balance sheets. Prices at the beginning of 1971 were about 11 percent higher than they would have been had we followed a path of 2 percent annual increases since mid-1965. Let us use that as a rough measure of our recent inflation. And let us be sure to focus on the costs of the inflation, as distinguished from the costs of the economic slump.

INCOME EFFECTS

It is remarkably difficult to determine who gained and who got hurt by inflation in terms of real income. The retired aged are the only major specific demographic group of Americans that I can confidently identify as income losers. Since 1964, benefits under the Federal Civil Service Retirement System have had a cost-of-living escalator providing full adjustment. But this is a rare exception. Only a few private pension plans have any escalator provision, although benefits to retirees in some industries have been scaled up as the outcome of explicit collective bargaining agreements.

Social security retirement benefits were increased through new legislation by 13 percent in 1968, and by 10 percent more in 1971. While these legislative actions have undoubtedly been influenced by the rate of increase of consumer prices, it is doubtful that the benefit increases and price movements have been closely correlated. The nation wished to share the benefits of growth with the retired aged, and it probably would have provided nearly as large money gains (and hence larger real increases) if the price level had been more stable.

All in all, retired Americans must have lost at least 6 percent of their real pension incomes as a result of the 11-percent inflation. Greater job opportunities for the aged have cushioned the blow to a degree; for example, the fraction of men over sixty-five still working rose in 1967 and 1968 for the first time in more than a decade. But the extra labor income cannot be any more than 1 or 2 percent of the total real incomes of the aged.

For those earning incomes from the productive process, an arithmetic identity assures that for every extra dollar that a buyer must pay as a result of price increases, an extra dollar's worth of income is generated for some seller. Thus, price increases *per se* cannot create an aggregate net gain or net loss of before-tax incomes for sellers of productive services.

For after-tax incomes, a slight qualification is in order. Price increases add more than proportionately to federal income tax bills because of the graduated character of the tax. The income-elasticity of the federal personal income tax is nearly 1.3—liabilities go up 1.3 percent for each 1 percent rise in money income. For a typical middle-income American household, federal income taxes are about one-eighth of before-tax income. Thus, if the before-tax income of a family just keeps pace with prices, its after-tax income will lag a bit behind—it can be shown that the elasticity of after-tax income would amount to .96. An inflation totaling 11 percent thus puts a small dent of nearly one-half of 1 percent in the real after-tax income of such a family.

Because it stepped up employment and tightened labor markets, inflationary excess demand clearly added to the aggregate real income of wage-and-salary earners between 1965 and 1969. Their share of personal income expanded: total wages and salaries, net of social insurance contributions, rose 44 percent from the second quarter of 1965 to the third quarter of 1969, while the remainder of personal income rose 40 percent. Disposable (i.e., after-tax) personal income per capita in real terms—our best measure of the purchasing power of the average household —advanced by an unusually strong 15 percent over the period, and real disposable wage-and-salary income per capita must have scored a slightly larger gain—perhaps 17 percent.

The most important groups of beneficiaries were those who could gain from the availability of more jobs and steadier jobs. The shortfalls in annual incomes due to unemployment diminished. Many families got an extra paycheck from wives or teenagers who went to work.

Substantial gains were also made by the many people who were upgraded—for example, by shifting from farm to nonfarm employment or from lower paying jobs in services to higher paying jobs in manufacturing. The tightening of the labor market also tended to narrow percentage wage-differentials between unskilled and skilled workers. In general, the reduced unemployment, greater upgrading, and narrowed differentials all tended to be especially favorable to the working poor. Those who had formerly been at the back of the hiring line generally benefited as a result of inflationary excess demand.

Many middle- and upper-level wage groups also fared particularly well. Building tradesmen were one group of skilled workers with outstanding gains. Many families, however, could not benefit from the new developments in the labor market. Men who had steady jobs in 1965 and are still holding those same jobs (and whose wives have not entered the labor force) have generally been squeezed. In particular, for the average factory worker, real spendable take-home pay stagnated on a plateau after 1965 in contrast to its steady rise during the early sixties.

In the light of such dispersions, it is easy to understand the militancy of veteran union members who have been at the same job for years. It is easy to understand the causes of discontent in many quarters, even before the economy slumped late in 1969. The large advances of the aggregates did not tell the whole story. Higher prices raised money incomes in a haphazard, seemingly arbitrary way. Such a reshuffling of real incomes is, in the view of most Americans, unjust. Moreover, it does not even seem to create desirable incentives to shift production or to move resources.

Furthermore, the effects of inflation in raising money incomes may be less visible than the higher prices. Everybody knows that higher prices in our supermarkets and department stores are the result of inflation. When money incomes go up, however, the cause is not so obvious. When the man of the house brings home an 8-percent wage increase, he and his wife are confident that he earned and deserved that raise. If prices subsequently go up by 4 percent, the family is not happy with the 4-percent gain in real income; rather it feels cheated that the wage gain was cut in half by inflation. In point of fact, of course, the husband's 8-percent wage increase may have occurred only because of inflation. Nonetheless, nearly everybody feels that inflation leaves him with the short end of the stick. It is thus divisive and disruptive; and these social consequences are in themselves important.

At the same time, one must be careful about interpreting the public's expression of concern about inflation. We all gripe about our financial positions and our difficulties in stretching incomes to meet aspirations. When the income side of the balance is rising, complaints about difficulties of making ends meet get focused on the outgo side—on high prices. My barber was busily defending his latest price increase, noting all the higher prices he had to pay. In that list, he reported that his electric bill at home had doubled over the past year. When I commented that public utility rates hadn't increased, he replied: "You're right, but I installed central air conditioning."

Let me cite one interesting barometer of public attitudes. The University of Michigan's Survey Research Center asks people at the start of each year to evaluate their current financial situation compared to a year earlier. Recession years stick out like sore thumbs in the post-Korean record, with a peak of 31 percent of the respondents feeling worse off both in 1954 and 1958. But inflation leaves no visible scars. The most favorable appraisals in the 1950s (23 percent felt worse off) came in 1956 and 1957, years of high employment and rising prices. Every January–February survey between 1965 and 1969 yielded more favorable appraisals ("worse off" no higher than 20 percent) than any year prior to 1965. In the survey of February 1970, "worse off" jumped to 28 percent. Apparently it is the cooling off and not the heating up that creates discomfort. Despite the nagging problems of income redistribution, the American public apparently does not consider itself pressed to the financial wall so long as rising prices are accompanied by rapidly rising incomes.

BALANCE-SHEET EFFECTS

In my judgment, the impact of inflation on balance sheets is considerably more serious than that on income statements. In the first place, inflation deprives people of the opportunity to save in a form that gives them a predictable command over future consumption goods. In a noninflationary environment, people can acquire various liquid assets, earn a reasonable return on them, and count on them as the means to acquire a basket of consumer goods in the event of especially large needs or declines in income. To be sure, they can never get a guarantee of future tuition costs, or the prospective price tag on their retirement home, or charges for large medical needs. But these risks are much less serious than those associated with general inflation.

When over-all prices are rising rapidly, their exact course is bound to be unpredictable. If we all knew that 4 percent a year inflation would last through the next decade, nominal interest rates would probably become adjusted to levels offering a reasonable real return, and people would know how much of a consumer market basket their savings accounts could command in 1980. But there simply can't be great confidence that the price level will rise *steadily* at any substantial rate, such as 4 percent. Only if the government is committed to limit the rise to a creep not much above 2 percent can there be reasonable predictability.

The opportunity for safe saving is lost in a period of sizable and unpredictable price increases. Some assets offer a degree of protection against inflation in the sense that their values are likely to move up as consumer prices rise. But no asset shows a good year-by-year correlation with prices; even corporate equities and real estate are not good anti-inflationary hedges by this test. They may actually tend to outpace the price level on the average in the long run, but only with wide swings and great uncertainty.

Our financial system ought to serve both investors who want to earn maximum returns (and are willing to take substantial risks) and holders of reasonably safe assets who view their saving largely as deferred consumption. The latter are not accommodated during inflation; we thereby lose "savers' surplus." Excess-demand inflation creates in this way an unhappy division of savers into

"sharpies" and "suckers," if I may borrow some nontechnical ter-
minology. The former make sophisticated choices and often reap
gains on inflation which do not seem to reflect any real contribution to economic growth. On the other hand, the unsophisti-
cated saver who is merely preparing for the proverbial rainy day
becomes a sucker.

The loss of the opportunity to hold a reliable store of value may
be costly even for a person who has never suffered a real capital
loss on a bond or deposit. But people did suffer substantial real
losses in the inflationary prosperity of 1965–69 and these must be
taken into account. Some were compensated, at least in part, by
higher nominal interest yields. Furthermore, most claims of
Americans have their counterparts as debts of other Americans,
and the changing real value is a transfer from lender to borrower.
However, in the case of the $300 billion net debt of the federal
government, the lender is made worse off with no corresponding
gain on the part of the borrower, since presumably Uncle Sam
doesn't really feel relieved by the reduced real value of the public debt. Our 11 percent of inflation has lowered the real value of
that debt by about $33 billion. In September 1970, the average
interest rate on federal marketable debt was about 3 percentage
points higher than in mid-1965. Over the whole period, the
compensatory rise in interest rates may have neutralized as much
as half of the decline in real value, but the net loss is still a tidy
sum.

Even when the losses of lenders are matched by real gains of
borrowers, these do not necessarily cancel out from a social point
of view. For good reasons, many borrowers do not feel much
better off when the real value of their debt shrinks. Few mayors
or governors have had cause to celebrate the $11 billion decline
of real value on their $100 billion of outstanding debt. Many
homeowners feel no exhilaration about the benefits from the declining real value of their mortgages until and unless they are
selling their homes. Finally, the transfers between sharpies and
suckers is a matter of concern to society. The most significant
real losses are probably incurred by the sizable group of families
in middle and upper-middle income brackets whose liquid assets
are substantial and often not offset by large mortgages. The aged
seem especially vulnerable on capital account, just as they are on

income account. Except for the aged, few low-income families have large holdings of liquid assets; hence the poor are not particularly vulnerable to the loss of real value.

Inflationary distortions of balance sheets have important implications for the entire financial system. The efficiency of investment in physical capital is enhanced by a system which allows investors to borrow and thus to acquire real capital beyond their net worth. But opportunities to borrow depend upon incentives to lend, and these in turn are jeopardized when the predictability of the real value of claims disappears. Our financial system shows remarkable ingenuity in a time of inflation; witness the veritable revolution of 1968–69 in the financing of apartment houses through "equity kickers," special features of mortgages that make them resemble convertible bonds. But there is no complete escape from the important negative impact of an inflationary environment on debt markets.

The costs of inflation as well as the costs of curbing it are significant and serious. We learn to hate that trade-off and wish it would go away. The tally sheet reveals excellent reasons why the American public will not accept inflation as a way of life. Implicitly or explicitly, the government is obliged to set some ceiling on the tolerable rate of price increase, and it will be guided by public attitudes. As a nation, we must experiment with a variety of policy tools, observe how the trade-off operates, and see how public attitudes respond. By testing the terrain, we can hope to come out with a socially tolerable compromise on rates of unemployment and rates of price increase.

Unemployment, Inflation, and Economic Stability

HERBERT STEIN

Herbert Stein was a Senior Fellow at the Brookings Institution before becoming a member of President Nixon's Council of Economic Advisers in 1969 and subsequently its Chairman in 1972. This selection is the first portion of his essay on stabilization policy for Agenda for the Nation (1968), *edited by Kermit Gordon.*

COMPARED WITH PAST PERFORMANCE, the stability of the American economy in the last twenty years has been remarkable. Fluctuations in the rate of unemployment and in the rate of price increase have been smaller than in any earlier period of equal length. Still, it would be premature to file economic stability away in the small drawer labeled "Solved Problems."

There is no assurance that from here on fluctuations will always be as mild as those of the past twenty years. Optimistic statements made in 1929 about the new era of economic stability warn us against overconfidence. The chance of a depression similar to that of the 1930s is as remote as anything in the sphere of human events can be. But there remains the possibility of recessions or inflationary booms more serious than those of the postwar period unless continuous attention is paid to preventing them. . . .

The main reason for present concern with the problem of "economic stabilization," however, is different. While fluctuations of the unemployment rate and of the inflation rate around their averages have been remarkably small, the averages themselves have not been. Unemployment averaged 4.3 percent of the labor force from 1948 to 1957 and 5.3 percent from 1958 through 1967. During the entire twenty-year period the average annual rate of inflation, as measured by the consumer price index, was 1.7 percent. There have been fairly long periods in American history when we did better than this in both respects, and many indus-

21

trialized countries have had lower rates of unemployment than we in the postwar period. In any case, without regard to such comparisons, we want to do better, especially since we have become more keenly aware of the injury unemployment and inflation inflict on those parts of the population on whom their burden falls most heavily. Moreover, the more rapid price increases of the past two years may signal a long period of inflation more serious than that of 1948–66, or at least a troubled course back to a more moderate rate of inflation. Achievement of a lower rate of unemployment and a slower rate of inflation on the average over an extended period is the main problem of economic stabilization today.

UNEMPLOYMENT AND INFLATION

In the middle of 1968 the rate of unemployment was running between 3.5 percent and 4 percent, while the rate of inflation was about 4 percent a year. . . .

We now have to make decisions which will affect the future rate of inflation in the United States, not only for the year or for the presidential administration in which they are made, but for a longer period as well. One way of putting the choice is to ask whether our objective should be to maintain the present 4 percent rate of inflation, to return to the postwar average of approximately 2 percent, or to reduce the rate to zero. There are, of course, other possibilities, but these are the three for which the most reasonable cases can be made.

There is no doubt that the government can, if it is determined to do so, achieve any of these inflation rates, including zero, on the average over a period of years. The means are at hand in monetary and fiscal measures to regulate the rate of growth of total money spending, which in turn controls the prices at which output can be sold and the wages at which labor can be employed. They cannot be employed with such precision as to sustain the rate of inflation at its target level year by year. But they can achieve the desired average over a period of years, which implies compensating for temporary departures in one direction by temporary departures in the other.

The primary question is what the consequences of these

choices would be for the rate of unemployment. While there is much doubt and controversy about this subject, a few important points seem well established. There will be an interval during which unemployment will be higher if we reduce the inflation rate to 2 percent rather than permitting it to continue at 4 percent, and the unemployment rate will be still higher if we reduce the inflation rate to zero. The difference between 4 percent and 2 percent inflation, in terms of unemployment during this interval, will be smaller than the difference between 2 percent inflation and zero. Also, the difference in the unemployment rates will be smaller the more gradually the lower rate of inflation is approached. With the passage of time the differences in unemployment rates associated with differences in inflation rates will diminish.

After several years of rapid inflation, such as we have just had, there is a strong built-in tendency for prices and wages to continue rising rapidly. Some wages and prices are still catching up with price and cost increases that occurred earlier and some are being raised in the expectation of more inflation to come. If the rate at which total spending grows is held down to stem inflation, pressures from businesses and workers will continue to push up prices and wages and this will curtail sales, reduce output, and increase unemployment. However, these developments will in time moderate business and labor pressures, so that prices and wages rise less rapidly, thus further discouraging compensatory price and wage demands. If total spending continues to grow steadily at its new lower rate, the rate of unemployment will diminish. . . .

As price and wage demands and expectations become better adjusted to the actual rate of inflation, that rate will come to make less difference for unemployment. A credible case can be made for the proposition that in time the difference in unemployment rates will disappear, and the average unemployment rate will be the same for various rates of inflation and deflation, including zero, if all the rates are equally steady. On both theoretical and empirical grounds, this proposition has been disputed; but the argument need not detain us, since even if the proposition is valid it does not deny that the period required may be lengthy. We simply do not know how much or how long the rate of inflation influences unemployment. The influence is probably smaller over a period of, say, ten years than would be suggested by observations of the relationship from one year to the next; but it is probably not completely absent even over so long a period.

If unemployment were everything, the problem would be simple. We should then try to hold inflation to its present 4 percent rate, and thus assure a gain of employment for some significant period, if not forever. But unemployment is not everything. Inflation has its costs, or at least most people think it does, and these need to enter into the decision. These costs are mainly inequities resulting from the uneven pace at which different incomes and prices rise during inflation, with the consequence that some people receive less real income than they had expected and bargained for while others reap windfalls. There are some who consider these costs negligible relative to the costs of unemployment, at least short of the runaway inflation of which the United States has no need to be apprehensive. Unemployment imposes real costs involving the loss of real output, whereas the cost of inflation is a redistribution of output that benefits some while it injures others. The redistribution may be unfair, although it is difficult to define that objectively, but—so the argument runs —life is full of unfairness, and the injection of more may not worsen the net result. Therefore, it is concluded, we should give more weight to the tangible fact of loss of output than to the subjective and intangible claim of inequity.

This conclusion, however, almost certainly does not reflect common opinion in the United States. Unemployment is regarded as an evil primarily because of its distributional effects rather than because of its effects on total output. We would not worry nearly so much about 1 or 2 percent additional unemployment if the effects were evenly distributed over the whole population. But the fact that its burdens are concentrated on relatively few, especially if the additional unemployment is prolonged, is the main reason for concern about it. . . .

In addition to inequities, there are other effects which need to be taken into account in considering future policy about the rate of inflation. Rapid inflation here is undoubtedly harmful to our balance of trade, and although this may be offset in part by incentives to invest in the United States, the net effect on the balance of payments is probably negative. Policies such as adjustment of the exchange rate of the dollar might avoid these balance-of-payments consequences at little cost. But we have not adopted them up to this time, in part because their value is much disputed; while the policies we do follow in the attempt to correct our deficits plainly impede efficiency and curtail freedom. In these conditions the effects of rapid inflation on our balance-of-payments deficit, already ten years old, deserve heavy weight. Moreover, we cannot ignore the fact that rapid and continuing inflation is a temptation to direct government control of prices and wages. Most people who have had any experience with extensive wage and price controls would probably agree that continuation of the present rate of inflation is preferable to resorting to them. Nevertheless, controls seem such a simple and direct solution that we cannot be sure of avoiding them if inflation continues at a rate considered to be a serious problem.

This listing of the kinds of effects that should be considered provides no unique goal for the behavior of the price level. It does, however, suggest as a minimum the desirability of reducing the rate of inflation from the current 4 percent to the 2 percent we have averaged earlier. The 4 percent rate has not been in force so long that the country has become adjusted to it. For that reason, its continuation would impose serious and prolonged injustice on many whose incomes have been determined by an earlier and lower rate of inflation, while reduction would cause a smaller and briefer rise of unemployment than otherwise would occur. Moreover, this rate is above the rate of price increase experienced by most of our chief competitors in foreign trade, and its continuation is an obstacle to the restoration of balance-of-payments equilibrium. Finally, we cannot afford to validate the idea that every spurt of inflation will be built into the target for future policy. Doing so would make the task of preserving any steady rate of inflation impossibly difficult. To avoid such a development is ample reason not to accept the recently intensified rate of inflation as the standard for the future.

Whether we should go further and try to reduce our long-term average rate of inflation from 2 percent to zero is a harder question. Even in face of the large numbers who are dependent on assets and incomes the value of which was determined long ago in the expectation that prices would be stable, the case on equity grounds for attempting to halt inflation altogether is weaker. By now many individuals and businesses have made commitments, such as borrowing money at high interest rates, on the basis of expectations of inflation which public policy, if not official statements, encouraged them to hold. They might reasonably consider themselves unfairly treated by a policy-induced cessation of inflation. Furthermore, the cost in unemployment of trying to bring the inflation rate down to zero after all these years would undoubtedly be larger than that we would face if we were now to settle for 2 percent.

One may ask whether it is necessary, or even possible, to decide the difficult question of the rate of inflation at which policy should aim. In view of all the uncertainties about the consequences of different inflation rates, is it not more sensible to feel our way day by day, as we now do, in making monetary and fiscal decisions, continuously balancing unemployment, price level and other objectives in the conditions of the time? The trouble with this apparently reasonable approach is that it inevitably gives much more weight to the short-run consequences of inflation than to its long-run implications. An inflationary bias is thus built into the decisions, because the effect of a little more inflation in reducing unemployment is greater in the short run than in the long run. But decisions made on the basis of short-run consequences affect the choices that will be available later. Inflation resulting from day-by-day decisions is incorporated into expectations and commitments and cannot be counteracted without more unemployment than would have been involved in resisting the inflation initially. The purpose of a long-run goal for the price level is to give the future adequate weight in decisions. . . .

Before considering further the difficult choice of a price level goal, we should look at possible ways to reduce the costs of retarding the rate of inflation.

Wage-Price Policy · The most obvious possible means to brake inflation without unemployment is wage-price policy, perhaps better identified in the United States as "guidepost" policy. It is obvious because it has been discussed so much and tried so often, here and abroad, not because it has been demonstrated to be a solution to the problem. In fact, the main issue is whether wage-price policy is a reality or merely an incantation.

What is meant by wage-price policy is the effort by government to restrain the increases of wages and prices that, in the absence of such an effort, would occur in given conditions of demand, costs, output, and employment. The policy may be implemented or "enforced" by a variety of means, but these are usually understood to stop short of price and wage controls of the type invoked in the Second World War. It has been suggested here that if, after a period in which total spending and the price level have been rising rapidly, we now restrain both, wages and prices will tend to continue to rise for a time as if rapid inflation were still going on. The stronger this tendency and the longer it continues, the more unemployment there will be in the transition to a lower rate of inflation. If wage-price policy can help to shorten the time required for business and labor to adapt to the new lower rate of inflation, it will help to reduce the transitional unemployment. It can thus be regarded as a substitute for the brute fact of unemployment in teaching people that times have changed. An admission that decisions are based on imperfect foresight makes room for such an educational process.

The most recent round of wage-price policy in the United States opened with appeals by President Eisenhower, later made more specific and forceful by President Kennedy, for voluntary restraint by business and labor in making wage and price decisions. The initial basis of the appeal was the moral and patriotic responsibility of citizens, especially of powerful citizens, to act in a way that promoted the best interest of the nation. Participants in the economic process were asked to act as if there were no inflation, in the expectation that if they did so there would actually be none. Beginning in 1962, the policy enjoyed a rapid ascent, only to suffer an even more rapid fall by the end of 1966. The guidepost standards suggested by the administration were simplified and made more precise in an effort to mobilize public opinion behind them; in the process they also became more arbitrary. Instances of threats and coercion increased, and although never widespread, were conspicuous and provoked resentment.

Finally, as the rate of inflation accelerated, the position that labor and business should act as if there were no inflation became untenable; the policy was abandoned or "suspended."

The guidepost policy may have contributed to restraint of inflation during the early 1960s, although the evidence is subject to other interpretations. Moreover, there remain the questions of whether the policy could have survived much longer even without the spurt of inflation after mid-1965 and whether we would have had so inflationary a fiscal-monetary policy if reliance had not been placed on guideposts. The experience of other countries suggests that the life span of wage-price policies is short.

This has not been the only effort in American history to manage the economy by appealing for responsible behavior on the part of labor and business. Herbert Hoover tried to stop the depression in this way, Leon Henderson for a time tried to check inflation at the beginning of the Second World War with it, and the government recently tried it to reduce investment abroad, among other examples. The general lesson is that such efforts either wither or give way to mandatory controls. This does not suggest a cynical view of the moral or patriotic behavior of business and labor. It means only that the 3.2 percent wage increase guidepost, for one example, is not the stuff of which moral law is readily made. . . .

Reducing Unemployment and Its Costs · The problem which confronts us is how, using noninflationary means, we are to reduce the average rate of unemployment and its concentration, or at least mitigate its evil consequences. . . .

The chief noninflationary ways to reduce unemployment and its costs are:

1. Improving the productivity of those job seekers whose productivity is lowest, so that they become more readily employable at effective minimum wages. These minimums are set not only by law but also, and more importantly, by relief standards and by the prevailing expectations of workers and even to some extent of employers, all of which reflect the average earnings of American workers. Persons whose productivity does not match the minimum cannot be employed. In the short run the most promising means of making such people employable is training, in-

cluding repair of educational deficiencies left by the schools; orientation and counseling; and provision of job skills. In the longer run, reducing initial disparities in educational opportunity is essential.

2. Breaking the links that bind the minimum income people receive, the minimum wage at which they can or will work, and the minimum productivity needed for employment at the minimum wage. At present, society's desire to assure at least a basic income, expressed in relief programs and minimum wage laws, inhibits employment of people whose productivity is below the minimum. But this inhibition is not the necessary consequence of providing a minimum income. If the welfare system allowed recipients to retain, net, a substantial fraction of wage earnings, and if the minimum wage were abolished, people would have both more incentive to work at wages commensurate with their productivity and the legal right to do so. Alternatively, a subsidy could be provided for private employment so that work would be available at the minimum income even for those whose productivity is below it. A third approach, much the same as the second, calls for government to provide employment at the minimum wage for those whose productivity is below it.

3. Improvement of information about job availability. Not only unskilled workers but also many skilled and experienced people find that the most economical way to discover what jobs are available and therefore to make a reasonable decision about them is to remain unemployed and canvass the market. This helps to account for the long periods of unemployment often endured by well-qualified people. It is not that they cannot find some job quickly, but rather that they quite sensibly want a good view of the alternatives before making a long-term commitment. In the present state of the labor markets this takes a long time to achieve. Modernization of the employment service through methods, already available, of storing and transmitting information, could contribute significantly to reducing the average duration and total amount of unemployment.

4. Improvement of income-supplement systems, so that persons who have low earned incomes, for whatever reason, would be assured of some minimum level of income reflecting the society's consensus on the value of preventing poverty. This would

reduce the concentration of the costs of unemployment on the unemployed.

Improving training, labor market information, and income supplementation systems can go a long way to reduce unemployment and its costs. Even if inflation were an effective and acceptable way to accomplish this aim, these measures would be required, because inflation will do nothing to improve the condition of the many poor people who cannot be employed or who would be employed only at low wages because of their low productivity.

Full development of programs for manpower training, improvement of labor markets, and income supplementation would still leave unsettled the trade-off between unemployment and inflation, at least as a transitional matter. However, development of these programs would alter the terms of the choice between inflation and unemployment. It would reduce the social costs of unemployment by relieving the concentration of unemployment on a relatively few people, a disproportionate number of whom have low incomes even when they are employed; and it would cushion the impact of unemployment by more adequate income supplements for the poor, including those who are poor because of unemployment. The effect of inflation on the poor is complex. Inflation may encourage employment of the unskilled if, because the minimum wage lags the price rise, it reduces the real cost of the effective minimum wage. But in these circumstances, those who are employed at the minimum, or who receive relief and other benefits at prevailing standards, will suffer from the lag. The more the poor are employed, the more they are covered by programs to supplement income, the more they will have to lose, and the less to gain, from inflation.

The Price Stability Goal · By the methods just discussed we should be able to make the world safer for anti-inflation policy. As we do so, we should be able to push further to slow the average rate of inflation. In any case, as suggested above, we should retreat from the recent 4 percent rate of inflation to the 2 percent which is our postwar average. That having been done, a decision to proceed further to stop inflation entirely would depend on the answers to two questions. First, has the transition from the 4 percent rate of inflation been accomplished without any substantial and persistent increase of unemployment? It is argued here that it can be, but the proposition remains to be tested. Second, are we vigorously and effectively developing programs for manpower training, labor market improvement, and stronger income supplementation systems, in order to reduce unemployment and relieve its consequences for those upon whom its effects are most concentrated? If both of these questions can be answered affirmatively, we can then gradually push on to eliminate inflation.

The government cannot avoid aiming at some price level; zero inflation would be the most satisfactory goal. Even after thirty years of rising prices, it is doubtful whether any goal for inflation other than zero would be credible. Acceptance of a goal such as 2 percent inflation would arouse suspicion that it was only a step toward acceptance of still higher rates. It would signal an increase from the only price level goal the government has ever espoused. Moreover, it would represent an increase from a goal that is intuitively if irrationally accepted as the natural meaning of stability to a goal that seems arbitrary and not obviously superior to many others. Private expectations are more likely to cluster around a target of no inflation, and private efforts will be more easily marshaled to achieve it, than any other goal the government might set. Furthermore, even if the government announces and achieves some goal other than stable prices, a great many people will for a long time act as if they expected prices to remain unchanged, simply because to act in any other way is difficult and expensive and requires more information and sophistication than most people have.

The Case for High-pressure Economics

ALVIN H. HANSEN

Alvin H. Hansen is Lucius N. Littauer Professor (Emeritus) of Political Economy at Harvard University and is generally regarded as the dean of American Keynesian economists. This selection is taken from his book The American Economy, *published in 1957.*

THE AMERICAN ECONOMY has undergone a considerable remodeling during the last quarter-century. I begin with what I regard as by far the most important single factor. It is a new factor, never before experienced in American history. And it is this. We have not had a major depression since 1938. Nearly two decades without a serious downturn. We had, indeed, a minor dip in 1949 and again in 1954—light jolts but no serious depression. And we have had virtually continuous full employment since 1941. Now this is something distinctly new, and we would do well to take a good look at this strange and quite novel experience.

I repeat, we have had virtually full employment and booming prosperity for sixteen years. Past experience has been quite different. Throughout our history every eight or nine years we have experienced serious depression and widespread unemployment. Indeed our economy was for a hundred years the most violently fluctuating economy in the world. And in the 1930s we had prolonged depression and seemingly endless stagnation.

THE MISSING LINK: ADEQUATE DEMAND

What is the essence of the American economic revolution of the last fifteen years? The miracle of production? The economy already had that *potential* back in the thirties, though the steam was unfortunately lacking. Now, however, we have seen what the economy can do under the pressure of *adequate aggregate demand*. We now have acquired at least some confidence in the government's responsibility for the maintenance of prosperity

32

and full employment. When the British Conservative Government, under Churchill, announced its assumption of continuing responsibility for high employment in 1944, that Act was regarded as a new venture of government, and so indeed it was. The Employment Act of 1946 set much the same goal for the United States. But it was not until President Eisenhower's statement with respect to the firm determination of his Administration to use the full powers of the government to prevent depression that general bipartisan acceptance of this program was achieved. It is indeed a revolution in men's thinking. And this revolution is in no small part the result of the vigorous economic controversies which have filled the pages of economic journals, and from there spilled out into the public forums, during the last two decades.

Now someone will say that the miracle of production which we have witnessed during the upsurge of the last fifteen years could never have occurred without the resourcefulness of private enterprise, the technical know-how, the technological innovations, and the capital formation necessary to implement the new technique. This is indeed unquestionably true, and it is a fact that should be stressed again and again. Yet even with respect to these factors it is important to note that the cause-and-effect relations are closely intertwined. The government has made a major contribution to ensure adequate aggregate demand. The upsurge related thereto has stimulated population growth, which in turn has contributed to the upsurge. The war and the postwar upsurge have served to stimulate new techniques, and these in turn reinforce the upsurge. And finally, investment in new capital (together with corporate and individual savings to finance it) is a consequence, no less than a cause, of a high and growing national income.

Thus the American economic revolution of the last quarter-century constitutes a laboratory experiment in which the flow of events has tested on a broad front the Keynesian diagnosis and the Keynesian policies.

The problems of a highly developed economy are different, as we have seen, from those of an economy in the earlier stages of industrial development. The advanced industrial society, having attained a high level of technology together with entrepreneurial know-how and worker skills, has equipped itself with a vast accumulation of fixed capital. The underdeveloped economy is capital-poor; the advanced country is capital-rich.

No one will deny that the developed economies of Western Europe and North America have reached, after 150 years of technological progress and capital accumulation, a high level of productive capacity. These countries have, moreover, within them the seeds of continued growth. Yet the output of the United Kingdom fell far below her potential throughout the two interwar decades, and in the United States the economy performed disastrously below her capacity for more than a decade before Pearl Harbor. How long must an economy fail notoriously to perform before it is generally admitted that something is seriously lacking?

Now it was Keynes' central thesis that the element that was woefully lacking was *adequate aggregate demand*. The classicals had argued that all that was needed was technology and capital, that the economy itself would automatically generate adequate demand. The interwar experience in the United Kingdom and the deep depression in the United States demonstrated, as conclusively as facts can, that the classical thesis, whatever may have been true of the early days of capitalism, was no longer valid.

But facts convinced no one. Facts alone can never destroy a theory. As James B. Conant has aptly put it, men strive desperately "to modify an old idea to make it accord with new experiments." An outworn theory will not be abandoned until it has been superseded by a better one. "It takes," says Conant, "a new conceptual scheme to cause the abandonment of an old one." [1]

In his *General Theory of Employment, Interest and Money,* Keynes challenged the view that the modern economic system can be *depended* upon to make automatically the adjustments needed to ensure full use of productive resources. The thing that private enterprise can certainly do efficiently and well is to *produce*. The thing that it cannot be *depended* upon to do well is to ensure adequate aggregate demand.

Just as the decade before the Second World War deepened the conviction that the classicals were wrong, so the last fifteen

1. James B. Conant, *On Understanding Science,* Yale University Press, 1947, pp. 89, 90.

years have strengthened the conviction that Keynes was right with respect to his positive program. Governments throughout Western Europe, and in the United States, have on an unprecedented scale augmented aggregate demand beyond that generated by private enterprise. And all over the free world, but especially in the United States, we have witnessed what the economy can do when it is put under pressure. Government expenditures, government borrowing, government guarantees and lending operations, government policies in the area of social security, agriculture, public power, rural electrification, securities regulation, deposit insurance, and monetary, banking, and fiscal policies have provided much of the *fuel* needed for the full use of the productive capacity created by technology and capital accumulation.

THE PROBLEM OF INFLATION

Operating under pressure the American economy has performed a miracle. The output response to adequate aggregate demand has surprised everyone, and, what is to many still more surprising, it has not led to any such destructive inflation as was feared. Clearly we are not out of the woods in this matter, but the experience of recent years is reassuring. One thing at least is certain. Our economy is equipped with three powerful safeguards against peacetime inflation: (1) our prodigious capacity to increase production when under pressure; (2) our capacity, both corporate and individual, to save at high-income levels; (3) our demonstrated capacity at responsible fiscal and monetary management. There remains the problem of wages and collective bargaining. This requires, there can be no doubt, statesmanlike action. At all events, I think it is fair to say that experience thus far indicates that the alarmists may well have beaten the drums a little too loudly, and I am happy to note recently a little softer note in the discussion of this very important problem.

A high degree of stability in the value of money must be an important consideration of public policy. Yet we are, I fear, in considerable danger of making a fetish of rigid price stability. This fetish could easily become a serious obstacle to optimum growth and expansion. If we are going to be frightened away by every slight increase in prices, we are likely to fall far below the growth of which we are potentially capable.

We use the term "inflation" far too loosely. The word "inflation" is used to describe the astronomical price increases experienced by Germany after the First World War, and the same word is applied to the comparatively moderate increases in prices in American history. The phrase "inflationary pressures" has often become, I suggest, virtually synonymous with "expansionary forces." Brakes are thereby applied, and output is sacrificed to rigid price stability.

I should like to propose a new definition—one, I hope, which might have some operational value for monetary policy. I suggest that we need a new concept which I propose to call "pure inflation," and I propose to set this concept over against the concept of "price adjustments to output changes." "Pure inflation" (and I emphasize the word "pure"), I should say, is a condition in which prices rise without any appreciable increase in output.

Countries which have suffered in the past from the evils of inflation have typically experienced large price increases with no substantial increase in output. Indeed, in cases of hyperinflation, output has often actually decreased.

There are, to be sure, degrees of pure inflation. And I should like to suggest, to help clarify our thinking, the following general observation. I suggest that at no time in our history, nor indeed in that of any other country, can it be shown that price increases have injured the economy and the general welfare if in the period in question the increase in aggregate output has exceeded percentagewise the increase in prices.

Frederick Mills, of the National Bureau of Economic Research, surveying eighty years of cyclical movements in our history, has shown that, in periods of expansion, for every 1 percent increase in output we have had $\frac{8}{10}$ percent increase in prices—a 5 to 4 ratio. Professor Mills' short-run ratios of output increases to price increases might, of course, develop against the background either of a long-run downtrend in prices or a long-run uptrend.

I repeat, one does not encounter the condition of inflation in any meaningful sense so long as percentage increases in aggregate output exceed by some margin the percentage increases in the price level.

I should be prepared, in special circumstances, however, to go a bit farther. There are times when a tremendous forward push is urgently needed, when a choice has to be made between permitting a price increase substantially greater than my rule suggests or else foregoing the needed increase in aggregate output.

Consider, for example, the situation in 1946 after the removal of price and wage controls and the cut in wartime taxes. Having chosen to remove the main restraints on consumption (and I assume that political realism forbade any other choice), what then? The only way remaining to keep aggregate demand in check would have been drastic monetary restraint on investment. Would this have been desirable policy? I think not. A rapid transition to full peacetime production required massive investment in plant, equipment, and inventories to make good the accumulated shortages caused by the war. It was a choice of the lesser evil. It did indeed mean a price increase percentagewise considerably greater than the increase in aggregate output. But the massive investment laid the groundwork for a large increase in output later and contributed greatly to the slowingdown of the price movement by 1948.

Following the Second World War we had, as we all know, a considerable price rise. There are those who regard this as simply due to war and postwar mismanagement. I cannot agree. Granted that the controls had to be removed and that taxes had to be cut—that, politically speaking, they could not be continued for a year or so longer—then I think it follows that some considerable price rise was inevitable. This is true because of the accumulated backlog of unfulfilled demand and of postwar shortages. The closets were empty, the shelves were bare; consumers' stocks and business inventories had to be replenished. Under these circumstances price stability could not have been achieved unless indeed we had been prepared to cut employment and income sufficiently to reduce demand to the level of the then available flow of consumers' goods. And a severe cut of this character would have been necessary even though there had been no widespread holdings of liquid savings, since people were quite prepared, in view of the backlog of demand for clothing, household furnishings, automobiles, etc., to spend all of their current income. Any net investment in excess of corporate net saving would under these circumstances have created inflationary pressures.

The path we chose was much to be preferred. It brought indeed a considerable rise in prices, but it gave us full employment and it stimulated a tremendous outpouring of goods which already by the middle of 1947 had drenched the inflationary fires.

Periods of rapid growth have usually also been periods of moderate price increases. In the usual case the price system tends to respond in this manner to rapid expansion. It is not probable that we can achieve in the next twenty years anything like the growth of which we are capable, without some moderate increases in wholesale and consumer prices.

Economists generally tend to exaggerate the evils of moderate price increases. The accumulated savings, it is said, are eaten into. Inflation, it is said, tends to eliminate the sturdy middle class, and it concentrates income in the hands of the lucky few.

These things have indeed always happened in the great astronomical inflations. And conclusions based on these undoubted facts are then erroneously applied to such price increases as we have experienced in the United States during the last half-century.

The alleged evils which are typically cited are, in fact, based on abstractions that have no relevance to conditions as we actually find them in the United States. We have indeed experienced a considerable price upheaval both in the first quarter and again in the second quarter of the current century. But private property continues firmly in the saddle. Savings per family (after correcting for price changes) are more than twice as large as in 1925. Urban home ownership has increased from 45 to 55 percent. Farm ownership has increased from 58 percent to 75 percent. The middle class is stronger than ever before in our history. There is less inequality in the distribution of income. Adjustments in social-security benefits can be made and have been made when price changes occur.

In this connection it is well to remember that nothing eats so dangerously into family savings as deflation and unemployment. On the other hand, even the considerable price increases we have had since the end of the Second World War have not wiped out family savings. According to the Home Loan Bank Board, the accumulated savings, per family, in life insurance, savings accounts, United States savings bonds, and savings and loan associations have risen from $2,500 in 1944 to $4,200 in 1954, an increase (after correction for consumer price changes) of 10 percent in real purchasing power. I do not say that we might not have done better had not the aftermath of the war brought the price increases. But I do say we have not suffered the serious effects on family savings that are so often quite irresponsibly alleged.

Thus I conclude that if in the pursuit of rigid price stability we permit, and even foster, a considerable amount of unemployment, we shall then fail to achieve the growth of which we are capable. If, fearful of short-run instability, we fail to place the economy under the pressure of an aggregate demand adequate to produce full employment, we shall not even discover what our potentialities for growth are. Under these circumstances we could gradually drift into a condition of stagnation.

The Case against High-pressure Economics

HENRY C. WALLICH

Henry C. Wallich, who coined the phrase "high-pressure economics," criticizes it in an article entitled "Postwar United States Monetary Policy Appraised," which was written for the American Assembly in 1958. Mr. Wallich is professor of economics at Yale University and was a member of the Council of Economic Advisers from 1959 to 1961.

AGAINST THE SPECTRE of unemployment in a low-pressure economy, the defenders of [price stability] can raise the equally serious vision of inflation in an economy running at high pressure. Unemployment hurts a limited number of people severely, but for the most part temporarily. Inflation hurts large numbers, usually less severely, but the damage done to savings and relative income position tends to be permanent. If inflation should ultimately lead to severe depression we shall end up with the worst of both worlds. Yet it must be conceded that the public seems to enjoy most of the manifestations of inflation and, unlike unemployment, does not regard it as an evil demanding immediate redress.

Finally, the partisans of [price stability] can argue that full employment and growth are not indivisible. It is at least conceivable that an economy running at a slightly lower rate of employment and output for a time may in the end enjoy the same or a larger average rate of growth as would a high pressure economy. If a low pressure economy grows at the same rate as a high pressure economy, it will not lose very much by leaving an extra one or two percent of its labor force unused. At an annual growth rate of four percent, the loss of output from one percent unemployment will be the equivalent of three months' growth. At this rate, the low pressure economy would fall behind the high pressure economy only very little.

Whether or not the same rate of growth can be expected in the two economies depends principally on the kind of pressure prevailing in the high pressure system. It may be the kind that results from high investment financed by bank credit, creating large profits and imposing "forced savings" on the consumer by preventing him from consuming as much as he would like. This kind of inflationary pressure probably accelerates growth, at least for a while. The inflationary pressure may also be of the type known as cost push, however. In that case, consumption rather than investment will be the expanding force. Whether growth can much accelerate in this type of situation is doubtful, and what will happen eventually if inflation should gain momentum or be brought to a sudden halt is quite obscure. The recent inflation in the United States has had many of the earmarks of cost-push inflation, although it has also featured an expansion of investment.

It is on the longer-run consequences of inflation that the defenders of stable prices must fundamentally rest their case. In the short run all sorts of good things can be promised and performed by the high pressure economy—fuller employment, more output, more growth. What will happen in the long run?

The United States has no experience of a prolonged inflation consciously felt as such. Prolonged upward price movements have occurred—from 1896 to 1940, or even from 1933 to the present. But when those who think inflation is relatively harmless point to these periods as evidence, they overlook one basic distinction: those price increases were not viewed by the public as a continuing process. An inflation that is expected to continue, one that everybody tries to stay ahead of, is a new phenomenon. Consequently, we cannot appeal to experience in trying to forecast the long-run results of inflation. We depend upon surmises. That is the great uncertainty in the debate over inflation.

It has been argued that permanent inflation must inevitably accelerate from a creep to a run. As its victims learn to defend themselves, by obtaining quicker wage and salary adjustment or through escalation, the beneficiaries must move their own demands ahead faster and faster to preserve their gains. Galloping inflation, however, is obviously unsustainable; it must end in collapse or it will be stopped in some other, probably drastic manner.

This chain of reasoning is plausible but not compelling. If inflation is fought vigorously, it may well be held to a permanent or intermittent creep. Perhaps the best one can say is that acceleration constitutes a serious risk.

But even if it does not accelerate, continuing inflation will, in the view of those who oppose it, do increasing harm. The distortion of investment decisions, the discouragement of saving, the compulsion to speculate, the misallocation of resources, the strengthening of the monopoly position of firms owning old and low cost equipment—all are familiar dangers that have been pointed out many times. The inherent instability of an economy in which everything is worth what it is only because it is expected to be worth more next year; the fluctuations in the value of "inflation hedges" produced by the uncertain speed of the inflation; the need to concentrate all efforts on staying ahead of the game—all this does not add up to a satisfactory picture of a stable and rapidly growing economy. And, as the moralistically inclined may feel tempted to add, a society in which all contracts and financial promises are made with the afterthought that they will be partly cancelled by inflation, does not offer a morally-elevating picture either.

Few of the critics of inflation would claim that they can foresee its ultimate consequences. It may lead to collapse into deep depression, or simply to more inflation with stagnating growth. Or more likely, it will lead to price controls imposed under the pressure of impatient citizens and politicians. The immediate sacrifices that a policy of stable prices demands seem preferable to any of these.

I have presented here what I believe to be the main points of view in the debate over the objectives of policy, a debate that has gained urgency ever since the recent boom seemed to open a chasm between the objectives of price stability on one side and growth and full employment on the other. In this debate, the inflationists enjoy one great advantage: in the short run, they are usually right. More can be got out of an economy over a few months or years by running it at high pressure instead of at low. The chickens take some time to come home to roost—if they do come.

The supporters of stable prices labor under a corresponding difficulty. Theirs is a long-run case, in a world where experience consists of a succession of short runs. At best they can argue that the period during which inflation may help growth has become shorter, because everybody is watching the price index.

Inflation anticipated holds fewer promises and far more threats than inflation noted only after the event. Their case could be proved only, if at all, over a prolonged period and at great ultimate cost. One may hope that this form of proof will never have to be supplied. But one must realize also that so long as it has not, the inflationists will always have a plausible argument.

The Cruel Dilemma

James Tobin, Sterling Professor of Economics at Yale University, was a member of President Kennedy's Council of Economic Advisers in 1961–1962. This selection is an adapted version of his presentation to a University of Pennsylvania conference in 1966. It was originally published in Prices: Issues in Theory, Practice, and Public Policy, *edited by Almarin Phillips and Oliver Williamson, 1967.*

WE IN THE UNITED STATES are rediscovering that the terms of trade our economy offers us between inflation and unemployment are not to our liking. If we have as little as we would like of one, we have more than we want of the other. This is an unpleasant fact of life, not only here but in all non-communist industrial economies. It does no good to ignore it. Critics of federal economic policy want the government to check inflation by curtailing aggregate demand. They may be right. But many of them do not see, or do not say, that cutting demand will lower employment and production at the same time as it slows the rise in prices. Other critics find the present rate of unemployment too high; they would expand demand in order to reduce it further. Many do not see, or do not say, that the same expansion of demand would raise both prices and the rate of increase of prices. Both 4 percent per year inflation and 4 percent unemployment are too high. But the fact is that the government has at its command no simple way to reduce one figure without raising the other.

Much discussion of current policy is based on an overly simple model which my generation of economists learned and taught— both perhaps too well—thirty and twenty years ago. The model did double duty, applying both to full-scale war mobilization and to large-scale unemployment. In this model, full employment and the productive capacity of the economy are well defined. If aggregate demand, in real terms, exceeds this capacity, there is "excess demand," or an "inflationary gap." Prices, if uncontrolled, will rise continuously—without inducing any gains in output—until events or policies lop off the excess demand. Eliminating excess demand is economically painless, though it may be politically painful; it stops inflation without touching employment or output. On the other hand, if aggregate real demand is less than the economy's full-employment capacity, there is insufficient demand, a "deflationary gap." However large or small the departure from full employment, so long as it stays the same, prices are stable. An increase in demand, moving the economy toward full employment, may mean a one-shot increase in the price level, necessary to induce employers to expand output and employment. But it does not set off a *continuing* inflation. We hear the echoes of this doctrine in diagnoses of the current situation as one of clearly excess demand.

The mid-fifties did not fall easily into either of these patterns. Prices rose rapidly in 1955–58 while unemployment was constant or rising. Yet it was hard to attribute the inflation to generalized excess demand, since unemployment hovered at 4 percent plus, whereas it had been as low as 2.9 percent in 1953. This popularized the concept of cost inflation, and the dichotomy of cost-push and demand-pull became commonplace. The new inflation, as it was called, supposedly originated in the setting of higher wages by unions or higher mark-ups by managements.

Subsequent discussion has pretty much obliterated the notion of a simple, well-defined, full-employment capacity, and therefore at the same time fuzzed up the distinction between the two kinds of inflation. We now think of a zone of unemployment rates, each one associated with a certain rate of continuing inflation—the less the unemployment the higher the rate of inflation. There is presumably some rate of unemployment at which prices would be stable. But higher demand can obtain more employment and output as well as inflation. Such inflation is neither demand-pull nor cost-push, or, rather, it is both. It could not happen without the pressure of higher demand, which gives individuals and groups more power to obtain increments in their rates of money income. Their use of this power may be called "cost-push," but its strength is not independent of the state of demand.

This approach, of course, is summarized in the Phillips curve,

which relates the rate of increase of money wages—and thus in-
directly the rate of increase of prices—inversely to the unemployment rate. We could redefine "demand-pull" to mean increases
in the speed of inflation associated with demand-induced reductions in the rate of unemployment, and redefine "cost-push" to
mean unfavorable upward shifts in the Phillips curve so that
we get faster inflation at any given rate of unemployment. But
this greatly alters the significance of the terms and of the dichotomy between them. It is better to abandon them.

The Phillips curve approach forces us to confront squarely the
fact that our goals for prices and employment are not wholly reconcilable. That is, they are not wholly reconcilable by government management of aggregate demand through fiscal and
monetary policies. The first question that arises, therefore, is how
bad the situation is. What are the terms of trade in our economy
between inflation and unemployment?

It is hard to infer reliable associations between inflation and
unemployment from the data. There are few relevant observations, and we know that observed movements of price level are
influenced by many things besides the contemporaneous level
of unemployment.[1] A fundamental problem is that the economy
has not settled down long enough at a steady unemployment
rate to permit us to observe the corresponding permanent rate
of inflation, if there is one. We should not forget one lesson of
the first and simpler model—namely, that movement toward
fuller employment is likely to cause a once-for-all rise in the
price level. To some unknown extent recent rises in prices are
from this source—in the early sixties the price level was not
high enough to induce full employment output even with stable
labor costs.

It is plausible that larger increases, both in money wages
and in mark-ups, are required to effect a given increase in the
rate of utilization of the economy's capital and labor resources
when the shift occurs quickly than when it occurs slowly. If so,
some of the recent and current speed of inflation is attributable
to the surge of the economy in the winter of 1965–66. But we do

1. Figures 1 and 2 (which were not part of Mr. Tobin's original article)
show the observations of 1954–69 on the relationship of price and wage
movements to unemployment in the United States—*Editor.*

not know how much of the current rate of inflation to attribute to these sources and how much to regard as a permanent by-product of 4 percent unemployment.

Nor do we know the answer to the even more basic question of whether continuation of 4 percent unemployment would, so long as it generates any inflation, generate an accelerating inflation. The orthodox prediction would be: Wages and other incomes rise because people want real gains, and the bargaining power of individuals and groups depends on the real situation. If they find that they are cheated by price increases, they will simply escalate their money claims accordingly. On this view the Phillips curve would blow up if growth at a steady utilization rate were maintained. Only cyclical interruptions in the learning process have saved us from accelerating inflation. On this interpretation, the only true equilibrium full employment is the degree of unemployment that corresponds to zero inflation—any higher rate of utilization can be called excess demand. This is a dismal conclusion, if true, because it appears to take a socially explosive rate of unemployment—more than 6 percent in the United States —to keep the price level stable.

The Phillips curve idea is in a sense a reincarnation in dynamic guise of the original Keynesian idea of irrational "money illusion" in the supply of labor. The Phillips curve says that increases in money wages—and more generally, other money incomes—are in some significant degree prized for themselves, even if they do not result in equivalent gains in real incomes. Empirical support for this view is found in statistical variants of the Phillips curve where the elasticity of money-wage increase with respect to price increases is generally found to be smaller than 1.0. A number of institutional reasons can be advanced to explain this phenomenon. (1) Annual money-income gains are a symbol of continuing success and status for unions, individuals, managements. (2) Even in relatively weak sectors, reductions in money wages and prices are opposed by a host of psychological, legal, and institutional barriers. Minimum-wage laws provide one floor. But even when they are inoperative, money-wage rates and salaries are seldom reduced; such drastic action would be a real judgment of failure on the employee or the employer, or both. The same barriers do not apply to reductions in relative *real* wages and

FIG. 1 *Price Performance and Unemployment, 1954–69*

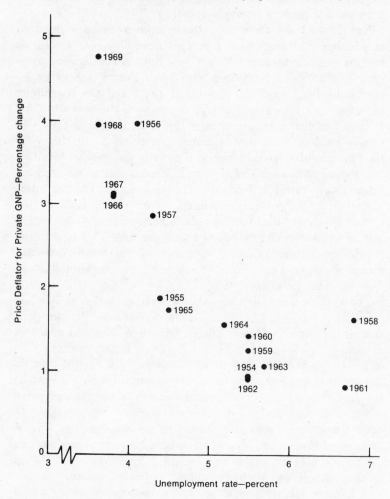

SOURCES: U.S. Department of Commerce and U.S. Department of Labor
  1. Change during year calculated from end of year deflator (derived by averaging fourth quarter of a given year and first quarter of subsequent year).
  2. Average for the year.

FIG. 2 *Wage Behavior and Unemployment, 1954–69*

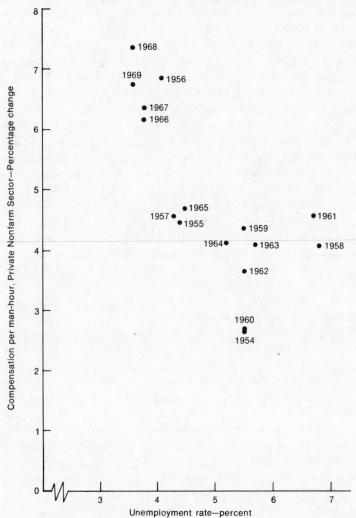

SOURCES: U.S. Department of Commerce and U.S. Department of Labor

1. Change during year calculated from end of year wage (derived by averaging fourth quarter of a given year and first quarter of subsequent year).

2. Average for the year.

prices so long as they are accomplished by wage and price increases elsewhere. This means that the changes in wage and price structure needed to induce resource shifts impart an upward bias to the over-all price level.

If we do not like the terms of trade our economy now offers us between inflation and unemployment, what can we do about it? There are two general strategies. One is to try to make the terms less severe. The other is to make them easier to live with, by reducing the social costs of inflation or unemployment or both. I will speak of these two strategies in turn.

The first is to try to shift the Phillips curve down—so that less inflation is associated with low unemployment. This strategy has both long-run and short-run aspects. One fairly uncontroversial set of long-run measures concerns the improvement of the labor market and of labor mobility. The better the labor force is adapted in advance to geographical and industrial shifts in the composition of demand, the smaller the wage and price increases needed to accomplish such adaptations. In general, expansion of demand both reduces unemployment and increases unfilled vacancies. By manpower and labor-market policies we need to reduce the number of unfilled vacancies associated with any given rate of unemployment.

A second and more controversial class of long-run measures are those directed to making labor and product markets more competitive. According to the orthodox diagnosis of the problem, this is the only fundamental solution. On that diagnosis, the problem is that high levels of demand enable the various groups in the economy to claim in total more output than is being produced. For example, strategically placed unions and industries become able, when demand is high, to improve their terms of trade against the rest of the economy. Other groups must either accept lower real incomes or unemployment or fight back in kind. If they won't accept lower real incomes, they give the inflationary spiral another twist. To the extent that this is a correct diagnosis of the problem, the only eventual solution is to eliminate these mutually inconsistent concentrations of power. We should not let a general tightening of markets to unemployment rates of 4 percent or less provide any groups with the power to levy extortionate claims.

Of course it is easier to make this diagnosis than to prescribe a realistic remedy—realistic either economically or politically. I will not be foolhardy enough to invade the provinces of anti-trust and labor legislation. I do observe that the bargaining powers of unions are in considerable degree granted to them by federal legislation. In return for these privileges, it seems to me, the public could require unions to be effectively open to new members and apprentices. It is especially important to eliminate racially discriminatory barriers to entry.

A third fundamental remedy is an increase in the capital-labor ratio. Observe that at present preferred industrial operating rates, around 92 percent of capacity, are reached concurrently with 4 percent unemployment. We would have more control of price increases if there were more excess capacity. Over the long run we could induce this result by mixtures of monetary and fiscal policy favorable to investment. Another way of making the same point is the following: The more rapid the growth of productivity, the less inflationary is the course of prices. This often-asserted proposition makes sense if the Phillips curve makes sense but not necessarily otherwise. If money wages have a trend of their own, they will not automatically rise faster when the growth of productivity speeds up. We know, of course, that in the distant long run we cannot make productivity grow faster than the natural rate of improvement of technology. But we can buy time in the intermediate long run by deepening and modernizing capital. More orthodox analysis would be that increases in (marginal) productivity mean equivalent increases in labor's bargaining power. They do nothing to resolve the fundamental excess of claims over resources.

These are long-run measures. In the short run we cannot improve the labor market, break up concentrations of economic power, or increase the ratio of capacity to labor force. That leaves us with incomes policy or guideposts, what Paul Samuelson has described as "talking the Phillips curve down." In spite of my complicity in the origins of the guideposts, I do not intend to discuss or defend them (unless you regard a canvass of the obstacles to other approaches as a defense). But I will make the following point, because it is too little appreciated:

One principal purpose of guideposts is to guide the government. For a variety of reasons unconnected with macroeconomic policy, the government is involved in the setting of certain prices and wages. In national emergency labor disputes, the government will not tolerate a stoppage and it attempts to substitute some other mechanism of settlement for industrial warfare to the bitter end. The guideposts set standards of public interest in the terms of the settlement. Too often, previously, the government—aided and abetted by the industrial relations fraternity and their mystique that the results of collective bargaining are always good because the process is good—was interested solely in the fact of a settlement, not in the content. Under the guideposts, the government seeks peace but not peace at any price level. Other ways in which the government is involved in wage and price decisions are minimum-wage legislation, management of stockpiles, pay scales of government employees, agricultural price supports, utility regulation, and regulations regarding wages and prices in government contract work. Not all these policies follow the guideposts, but they should.

I have sketched various approaches to improving the trade-off of inflation for unemployment. The second strategy is to mitigate the social costs of falling short of one or both goals. On the side of unemployment, one obvious step is to extend the coverage of unemployment compensation and improve the size and duration of its benefits. Likewise, the costs of unemployment would be smaller if it were more evenly distributed and if long-term unemployment were diminished. We certainly need improvements in the employment service, the better to match the beneficiaries of unemployment insurance with available vacancies. But many of the unemployed do not have previous work experience and for many young people the important thing, individually and socially, is the work experience rather than the money. Moreover, there is no national recompense for the loss of output from operating the economy at higher rather than lower rates of unemployment.

The ill effects of inflation could be mitigated in a number of ways: balance-of-payment troubles can be eased by flexibility of exchange rates; internal inequities can be lessened by making available purchasing-power bonds, variable annuities, and other enrichments of the menu of financial assets. Those who regard every inflation as symptomatic of a basic real disequilibrium, who therefore disbelieve in the Phillips curve except as a descriptive device of solely transient stability, will regard such measures as futile and perhaps dangerous. They do nothing to remove the real causes; they only accelerate the inevitable explosion. Those who believe in the Phillips curve world will acknowledge that measures to protect potential victims of inflation will sometimes lead to more inflation. But the process is not explosive, and once the sting is removed from inflation, there is nothing wrong with having more of it.

My only conclusion can be that we must take all three approaches at once. In the short run, the guideposts, battered as they are, are the only tool we have. I very much agree with suggestions that the wage–price canons for the year be divorced from the permanent and eternal guideposts, and also that labor and management representatives must participate in the formulation of the canons. The political and ideological climate may be more favorable for such cooperation now than it was in 1961–62. Certainly the Council of Economic Advisers cannot be in the business of judging every wage contract and price change, not to mention the surveillance of the invisible sins of omitted price cuts which are as damaging as visible price increases.

A series of short runs becomes a long run, and someday we must start on the difficult structural reforms needed to dissolve the cruel unemployment–inflation dilemma or to make it less painful.

The Workings of the Multiplier

COUNCIL OF ECONOMIC ADVISERS

*The Economic Report of the President for 1963 contained this
exposition of the multiplier process following from tax reduction.
It was part of the Annual Report of the Council of Economic
Advisers, which then consisted of Walter W. Heller, chairman,
and Gardner Ackley.*

TAX REDUCTION will directly increase the disposable income and
purchasing power of consumers and business, strengthen incentives and expectations, and raise the net returns on new capital
investment. This will lead to initial increases in private consumption and investment expenditures. These increases in spending will set off a cumulative expansion, generating further increases in consumption and investment spending and a general
rise in production, income, and employment. This process is discussed in some detail in this section.

INITIAL EFFECTS: CONSUMPTION

Effects on Disposable Income · The proposed reduction in personal income tax rates will directly add to the disposable income
of households. In addition, the reduction in corporate tax rates
will increase the after-tax profits of corporations as a result of
which corporations may be expected to increase their dividend
payments. The initial direct effect on the disposable income of
households resulting from the entire program of tax reductions
should be approximately $8½ billion, at current levels of income.

Consumer Response to Increase in Disposable Income · The

ratio of total consumption expenditures to total personal disposable income has in each recent calendar year fallen within the range of 92 to 94 percent. Although there are lags and irregularities from quarter to quarter or even year to year, the change in personal consumption expenditures has in the past, after a few quarters, averaged roughly 93 percent of any change in personal disposable income. On this basis, the initial addition to consumer expenditures associated with tax reductions would be on the order of $8 billion, although all would not be spent at once.

Additions to after-tax incomes resulting from tax reduction are likely to be spent in the same way as other additions to income. The largest part of the proposed tax reduction will be reflected in reduced withholding of taxes from wages and salaries, and therefore in larger wage and salary checks; thus, it will be indistinguishable from additional income arising from wage or salary increases, greater employment, or longer hours of work. Similarly, part of the reduced corporate taxes will be passed along to stockholders in increased dividend checks. Stockholders will not be able to identify the source of their additional dividends. Tax reduction dollars carry no identifying label, and there is no reason to expect recipients to treat them differently from other dollars.

Recent experience with tax reduction demonstrates clearly that additions to disposable income from this source are spent as completely as any other additions. Taxes were reduced by about $4.7 billion on May 1, 1948, retroactive to January 1, with resulting large refunds in mid-1949. Again taxes were cut, net, by about $6 billion, effective January 1, 1954, with further cuts later that year. The table shows that the percentage of disposable income spent by consumers remained within the normal range of quarterly fluctuation during the periods following the enactment of each of these tax reductions.

It is sometimes suggested that tax reductions which add only a few dollars to the weekly pay check of the typical worker would do little good even if the money was spent, since the amounts involved would not be large enough to permit major expenditures—say on washing machines or automobiles. Instead, the money would be "frittered away" on minor expenditures and would do little good for the economy. But all purchases lead to production which generates income and provides employment.

Personal Consumption Expenditures as a Percentage of Disposable Personal Income during Two Postwar Periods of Tax Reduction

1948–1949		1953–1955	
Quarter	*Percent*	*Quarter*	*Percent*
1948: I	97.3	1953: IV	91.5
II	94.0	1954: I	91.8
III	92.6	II	92.8
IV	93.2	III	93.0
1949: I	93.9	IV	93.2
II	95.2	1955: I	94.5
III	95.7	II	93.5

Based on seasonally adjusted data.
SOURCE: Department of Commerce.

Therefore, the purpose of tax reduction is achieved when the proceeds are spent on any kind of goods or services.

Actually, of course, tax reduction which expands take-home pay even by a relatively small amount each week or month may induce recipients to purchase durable goods or houses of higher quality, since the increased income would permit them to handle larger monthly installment payments. It may even induce a re-arrangement of expenditure patterns and thus bring about purchases of durable goods that would not otherwise be made.

INITIAL EFFECTS: INVESTMENT

Investment is a more volatile element than consumption in national expenditure. The timing and magnitude of its response to tax changes is less predictable. But a cut in tax rates on business income will stimulate spending on new plants and new machinery in two ways. First, it will strengthen investment incentives by increasing the after-tax profits that businessmen can expect to earn on new productive facilities. Second, it will add to the supply of internal funds, a large part of which is normally reinvested in the business. . . .

Since the largest part of business investment is made by corporations, the proposed cuts in the corporate income tax are especially significant. But investments of unincorporated businesses will also be encouraged by cuts in personal income tax rates, especially in the upper brackets. The impact of the 1963 proposals to reduce taxes on business will, of course, differ from company to company and industry to industry, depending in part on the adequacy of their internal funds and their levels of capacity utilization. Though the speed of response may vary, industry after industry will begin to feel pressure on its capital facilities and funds as markets for its products are expanded by the 1963 tax program.

Furthermore, there are many individual companies for which the supply of internal funds is a constraint on investment, and many others that do not have excess capacity. Moreover, it is estimated that some 70 percent of the investment in plant and equipment is for modernization and replacement rather than expansion, that is, it is designed to produce new or better products, or to reduce production costs rather than primarily to expand productive capacity. For this large segment of capital spending, the stronger inducement to invest provided by business tax changes will translate much more readily into actual purchases of plant and equipment.

As production expands and existing capacity is more fully utilized, business tax reductions will provide an even stronger stimulus to investment.

CUMULATIVE EXPANSION: THE CONSUMPTION MULTIPLIER

Tax reduction will start a process of cumulative expansion throughout the economy. If the economy is already undergoing slow expansion, this cumulative process will be superimposed upon it. The initial increases in spending will stimulate production and employment, generating additional incomes. The details and timing of this process will vary from industry to industry. The first impact may be to draw down inventories rather than to expand production. But as inventories are depleted, retailers will quickly expand orders. As manufacturers' sales rise in response and their own inventories of finished goods decline, they will activate idle production lines, hire additional workers, place orders for materials and components. Thus the expansion will spread to other industries, leading to further expansion of production, employment, and orders.

Expanded sales mean increased profits. Increased employment means greater wage and salary income. Each additional dollar's worth of gross production necessarily generates a dollar of additional gross income.

But expansion does not proceed without limit. A considerable fraction of the value of gross production is shared with governments or becomes part of corporate retained earnings and does not become part of consumers' after-tax income. Some of the increase goes to pay additional excise and other indirect business taxes. Typically, when GNP is rising toward potential, corporate profits increase by about one-fourth of the rise in GNP. But a substantial part of this increase in profits is absorbed by Federal and State corporate income taxes, and another part is ordinarily retained by the corporations. Only the remainder is passed on to the households in dividend payments. Part of the additional wage and salary incomes associated with added production is absorbed by higher social security contributions. At the same time, increased employment means a drop in payments for unemployment insurance benefits.

When all of these "leakages" are taken into account, a little less than two-thirds of an additional dollar of GNP finds its way into the before-tax incomes of consumers in the form of wages, dividends, and other incomes. Part is absorbed by personal taxes, Federal, State, and local. The increase in personal disposable income is 50 to 55 percent. Of this amount a small fraction—about 7 percent—is set aside in personal saving, and the remainder—about 93 percent—is spent on consumption, as indicated earlier. Thus, out of each additional dollar of GNP, initially generated by the tax cut, roughly half ends up as added consumption expenditure. But the process does not stop here.

The additional expenditure on consumption that is brought about by the rise in GNP generates, in its turn, further production, which generates additional incomes and consumption, and so on, in a continuous sequence of expansion which economists call the "multiplier process." The "multiplier" applicable to the initial increase in spending resulting from tax reduction, with account taken of the various leakages discussed above, works out to roughly 2. If we apply this multiplier only to the initial increase in consumption (about $8 billion), the total ultimate effect will be an increase in annual consumption—and in production (and GNP)—of roughly $16 billion. Lags in the process of expansion will spread this increase in GNP over time, but studies of the relationships between changes in disposable income, consumption, and production of consumer goods suggest that at least half of the total stimulus of an initial increase in disposable income is realized within 6 months of that increase.

CUMULATIVE EXPANSION: THE INVESTMENT RESPONSE

Tax reduction will also have important cumulative indirect effects on investment in inventories and in fixed productive facilities. These effects are much more difficult to predict than the induced effects on consumption.

Inventory Investment · The stocks of goods that businessmen wish to hold depend upon current and expected rates of sales and production and the volume of new and unfilled orders, as well as on price expectations and other factors. An expansion of aggregate demand can be expected to raise business inventory targets. Production for inventory will generate further increases in demand and income over and above the multiplier effects discussed above, and will in turn induce further increases in consumption spending.

Inventory investment is volatile, and induced inventory accumulation can add significantly to the expansionary effects of tax reduction within a few months. At the same time, it should be recognized that inventory investment is exceedingly difficult to forecast. As the increase in production and sales tapers off, stocks and the rate of inventory investment will be correspondingly adjusted.

Business Investment in Plant and Equipment · A tax reduction large enough to move the economy toward full employment will also stimulate business investment in plant and equipment. General economic expansion will reinforce the initial stimulus to investment of cuts in business taxes. In the first place, narrowing the gap between actual and potential output—now estimated at $30-40 billion—will increase the utilization of existing plant and equipment. As excess capacity declines, more and more businesses will feel increasing pressure to expand capacity. At the same time, increases in the volume of sales and in productivity will raise corporate profits—in absolute terms, relative to GNP, and as a rate of return on investment. Internal funds available for investment will rise, while at the same time higher rates of return on existing capital will cause businessmen to raise their estimates of returns on new investment. When investment incentives are strengthened by rising demand, internal funds are more consistently translated into increased investment than when markets are slack.

Residential Construction · The demand for housing depends on growth in the number of families, on the existing stock of houses, and on the cost and availability of mortgage credit. But housing demand also responds, to some extent, to changes in disposable income. Thus, tax reduction will have some direct effect on residential construction. And as production, employment, and income generally expand, the demand for new homes can be expected to increase further. This increase will, in turn, reinforce the other expansionary effects of tax reduction.

STATE AND LOCAL GOVERNMENT EXPENDITURES

State and local government units have found it difficult to finance the needed expansion of their activities. Given the present importance of income and sales taxes in State and local tax systems, government revenues at the State and local level expand automatically as GNP rises. The additional State-local revenues generated by economic expansion will assist these governments to meet their pressing needs. Moreover, since Federal tax liabilities are deductible under many State income tax laws, reduction in Federal tax rates will automatically generate some further addition to State-local tax revenues. Finally, a reduction in Federal taxes will enlarge the tax base available to State and local government units and may make it easier for them to raise rates or impose new taxes.

Undoubtedly, some of the added State-local tax revenues will be used either to retire existing debt or to reduce current borrowing rather than to increase expenditures. Whether the net result will be expansionary will depend upon whether the proportion of additional tax revenues spent on goods and services by State and local government units is greater or smaller than the proportion which would have been spent by the taxpayers from whom they collect the additional taxes. But whether or not the response of State and local government units is such as to strengthen the aggregate impact of Federal tax reduction on income and employment, the Federal tax program will ease, to some extent, the problems of these units in obtaining revenues needed to finance urgent public activities, such as education, transportation facilities, and urban development.

SUMMARY OF EFFECTS ON GNP

Tax reductions for consumers will have initial direct effects on the demand for goods and services, as consumers raise their spending level to reflect their higher after-tax incomes. Corporate tax reductions and the lower tax rates applicable to the highest personal income brackets will stimulate investment directly, through raising the rate of return on new investments and providing additional funds for their financing.

These direct or initial effects on spending would occur even if total output, employment, and incomes remained unchanged. But the increased spending cannot fail to increase total output, employment, and incomes. And as activity responds to the initially increased level of spending, cumulative impacts begin to develop in which the several elements interact to carry the expansion far beyond its initial point.

The higher incomes which consumers receive from the added production of both consumer and capital goods will lead to a further step-up in the rate of spending, creating further increases in incomes and spending. The same expansion process raises rates of capacity utilization, thereby interacting with the initial impact of tax reduction on business incomes to make investment both for modernization and expansion more profitable. This in turn generates higher consumer incomes and more spending, helping to provide the added demand which justifies the higher investment.

If there were no investment stimulus—either initially, or as a result of the cumulative process of expansion—we could expect that GNP would ultimately expand by about $16 billion. If the result were no more than this, the tax reduction would still be abundantly rewarding in terms of greater production, employment, purchasing power, and profits. What will really be given up to produce added output will be only unwanted idleness of workers (whose families have reduced neither their needs nor aspirations) and incomplete utilization of plant and machinery (which have continued to depreciate).

But the pay-off is much more than this purely consumption impact. There is also an investment impact, and each extra dollar of investment that is stimulated should bring roughly another dollar of added consumption and encourage still further investment.

Weak Links in the Multiplier Chain

MILTON FRIEDMAN

Milton Friedman is Paul S. Russell Distinguished Service Professor of Economics at the University of Chicago. Friedman's criticisms of multiplier analysis appeared in his book, Capitalism and Freedom *(1962).*

I SHOULD LIKE to discuss the view, now so widely held, that an increase in governmental expenditures relative to tax-receipts is necessarily expansionary and a decrease contractionary. This view, which is at the heart of the belief that fiscal policy can serve as a balance wheel, is by now almost taken for granted by businessmen, professional economists, and laymen alike. Yet it cannot be demonstrated to be true by logical considerations alone, has never been documented by empirical evidence, and is in fact inconsistent with the relevant empirical evidence of which I know.

The belief has its origin in a crude Keynesian analysis. Suppose governmental expenditures are raised by $100 and taxes are kept unchanged. Then, goes the simple analysis, on the first round, the people who received the extra hundred dollars will have that much more income. They will save some of it, say one-third, and spend the remaining two-thirds. But this means that on the second round, someone else receives an extra $66⅔ of income. He in turn will save some and spend some, and so on and on in infinite sequence. If at every stage one-third is saved and two-thirds spent, then the extra $100 of government expenditures will ultimately, on this analysis, add $300 to income. This is the simple Keynesian multiplier analysis with a multiplier of three. Of course, if there is one injection, the effects will die off, the initial jump in income of $100 being succeeded by a gradual decline back to the earlier level. But if government expenditures are kept $100 higher per unit of time, say $100 a year higher, then, on this analysis, income will remain higher by $300 a year.

This simple analysis is extremely appealing. But the appeal

is spurious and arises from neglecting other relevant effects of the change in question. When these are taken into account, the final result is much more dubious: it may be anything from no change in income at all, in which case private expenditures will go down by the $100 by which government expenditures go up, to the full increase specified. And even if money income increases, prices may rise, so real income will increase less or not at all. Let us examine some of the possible slips 'twixt cup and lip.

In the first place, nothing is said in the simple account about what the government spends the $100 on. Suppose, for example, it spends it on something that individuals were otherwise obtaining for themselves. They were, for example, spending $100 on paying fees to a park which paid the cost of attendants to keep it clean. Suppose the government now pays these costs and permits people to enter the park "free." The attendants still receive the same income, but the people who paid the fees have $100 available. The government spending does not, even in the initial stage, add $100 to anyone's income. What it does is to leave some people with $100 available to use for purposes other than the park, and presumably purposes they value less highly. They can be expected to spend less out of their total income for consumer goods than formerly, since they are receiving the park services free. How much less, it is not easy to say. Even if we accept, as in the simple analysis, that people save one-third of additional income, it does not follow that when they get one set of consumer goods "free," two-thirds of the released money will be spent on other consumer goods. One extreme possibility, of course, is that they will continue to buy the same collection of other consumer goods as they did before and add the released $100 to their savings. In this case even in the simple Keynesian analysis, the effect of the government expenditures is completely offset: government expenditures go up by $100, private down by $100. Or, to take another example, the $100 may be spent to build a road that a private enterprise would otherwise have built or the availability of which may make repairs to the company's trucks unnecessary. The firm then has funds released, but presumably will not spend them all on what are less attractive investments. In these cases, government expenditures simply divert private expenditures and only the net excess of government expenditures is even available at the outset for the multiplier to work on. From this point of view, it is paradoxical that the way to assure no diversion is to have the government spend the money for something utterly useless—this is the limited intellectual content to the "filling-holes" type of make-work. But of course this itself shows that there is something wrong with the analysis.

In the second place, nothing is said in the simple account about where the government gets the $100 to spend. So far as the analysis goes, the results are the same whether the government prints extra money or borrows it from the public. But surely which it does will make a difference. To separate fiscal from monetary policy, let us suppose the government borrows the $100 so that the stock of money is the same as it would have been in the absence of the government expenditure. This is the proper assumption because the stock of money can be increased without extra government expenditure, if that is desired, simply by printing the money and buying outstanding government bonds with it. But we must now ask what the effect of borrowing is. To analyze this problem, let us assume that diversion does not occur, so in the first instance there is no direct offset to the $100 in the form of a compensating drop in private expenditures. Note that the government's borrowing to spend does not alter the amount of money in private hands. The government borrows $100 with its right hand from some individuals and hands the money with its left hand to those individuals to whom its expenditures go. Different people hold the money but the total amount of money held is unchanged.

The simple Keynesian analysis implicitly assumes that borrowing the money does not have any effects on other spending. There are two extreme circumstances under which this can occur. First, suppose people are utterly indifferent to whether they hold bonds or money, so that bonds to get the $100 can be sold without having to offer a higher return to the buyer than such bonds were yielding before. (Of course, $100 is so small an amount that it would in practice have a negligible effect on the required rate of return, but the issue is one of principle whose practical effect can be seen by letting the $100 stand for $100 million or $100 ten-million.) In Keynesian jargon, there is a "liquidity trap" so people buy the bonds with "idle money." If this is not the case, and clearly it cannot be indefinitely, then the government can sell the bonds only by offering a higher rate of return on it. A higher rate will then have to be paid also by other borrowers. This higher rate will in general discourage private spending on the part of would-be borrowers. Here comes the second extreme circumstance under which the simple Keynesian analysis will hold: if potential borrowers are so stubborn about spending that no rise in interest rates, however steep, will cut down their expenditures, or, in Keynesian jargon, if the marginal efficiency schedule of investment is perfectly inelastic with respect to the interest rate.

I know of no established economist, no matter how much of a Keynesian he may regard himself as being, who would regard either of these extreme assumptions as holding currently, or as being capable of holding over any considerable range of borrowing or rise in interest rates, or as having held except under rather special circumstances in the past. Yet many an economist, let alone non-economist, whether regarding himself as Keynesian or not, accepts as valid the belief that a rise in governmental expenditures relative to tax receipts, even when financed by borrowing, is *necessarily* expansionist, though as we have seen, this belief implicitly requires one of these extreme circumstances to hold.

If neither assumption holds, the rise in government expenditures will be offset by a decline in private expenditures on the part either of those who lend funds to the government, or of those who would otherwise have borrowed the funds. How much of the rise in expenditures will be offset? This depends on the holders of money. The extreme assumption, implicit in a rigid quantity theory of money, is that the amount of money people want to hold depends, on the average, only on their income and not on the rate of return that they can get on bonds and similar securities. In this case, since the total stock of money is the same before and after, the total money income will also have to be the same in order to make people just satisfied to hold that money stock. This means that interest rates will have to rise enough to choke off an amount of private spending exactly equal to the increased public expenditure. In this extreme case, there is no sense at all in which the government expenditures are expansionary. Not even money income goes up, let alone real income. All that happens is that government expenditures go up and private expenditures down.

I warn the reader that this is a highly simplified analysis. A full analysis would require a lengthy textbook. But even this simplified analysis is enough to demonstrate that any result is possible between a $300 rise in income and a zero rise. The more stubborn consumers are with respect to how much they will spend on consumption out of a given income, and the more stubborn purchasers of capital goods are with respect to how much they will spend on such goods regardless of cost, the nearer the result will be to the Keynesian extreme of a $300 rise. On the other side, the more stubborn money holders are with respect to the ratio they wish to maintain between their cash balances and their income, the closer the result will be to the rigid quantity theory extreme of no change in income. In which of these respects the public is more stubborn is an empirical question to be judged from the factual evidence, not something that can be determined by reason alone.

Before the Great Depression of the 1930s, the bulk of economists would unquestionably have concluded that the result would be nearer to no rise in income than to a $300 rise. Since then, the bulk of economists would unquestionably conclude the opposite. More recently, there has been a movement back toward the earlier position. Sad to say, none of these shifts can be said to be based on satisfactory evidence. They have been based rather on intuitive judgments from crude experience.

In co-operation with some of my students, I have done some fairly extensive empirical work, for the United States and other countries, to get some more satisfactory evidence.[1] The results are striking. They strongly suggest that the actual outcome will be closer to the quantity theory extreme than to the Keynesian. The judgment that seems justified on the basis of this evidence is that the assumed $100 increase in government expenditures can on the average be expected to add just about $100 to income, sometimes less, sometimes more. This means that a rise in government expenditures relative to income is not expan-

1. Some of the results are contained in Milton Friedman and David Meiselman, "The Relative Stability of the Investment Multiplier and Monetary Velocity in the United States, 1896–1958," in *Stabilization Policies* (Commission on Money and Credit, 1963).

sionary in any relevant sense. It may add to money income but all of this addition is absorbed by government expenditures. Private expenditures are unchanged. Since prices are likely to rise in the process, or fall less than they otherwise would, the effect is to leave private expenditures smaller in real terms. Converse propositions hold for a decline in government expenditures.

These conclusions cannot of course be regarded as final. They are based on the broadest and most comprehensive body of evidence I know about, but that body of evidence still leaves much to be desired.

One thing is however clear. Whether the views so widely accepted about the effects of fiscal policy be right or wrong, they are contradicted by at least one extensive body of evidence. I know of no coherent or organized body of evidence justifying them. They are part of economic mythology, not the demonstrated conclusions of economic analysis or quantitative studies. Yet they have wielded immense influence in securing widespread public backing for far-reaching governmental interference in economic life.

The Need for Balanced Federal Budgets

MAURICE H. STANS

Maurice H. Stans, President Nixon's Secretary of Commerce, was President Eisenhower's Director of the Budget when he presented this paper to the American Academy of Political and Social Science in 1959.

THE FEDERAL government should have a balanced budget; its expenditures, especially in times like these, should not exceed its income. Of this I am deeply convinced.

As a matter of fact, I find it difficult to understand why there are still some people who do not seem to agree. Even though I have now been an official of the government almost four years and know by hard experience that there are at least two sides to all public questions, on this, one the facts speak eloquently for themselves. And the arguments that are marshalled in opposition to show that a balanced budget is unimportant—or that it can be safely forsaken for lengthy periods of time—certainly seem unsound. It is true that we as a nation have been extremely fortunate in maintaining our fundamental strengths thus far despite the heavy deficit spending of the past thirty years. But we cannot count on being lucky forever, and more and more the consequences of past profligacy are now catching up with us.

Let us look at some of the facts:

1. It is a fact that in 24 of the last 30 years the federal government has spent more than it has received.

2. It is a fact that last fiscal year the federal government had a deficit (12.5 billion dollars) larger than ever before in time of peace.

3. It is a fact that the federal government debt is now 290 billion dollars and that the annual cost of carrying that debt is more than 10 percent of the budget income of the government—and has been going up.

4. It is a fact that our economy is operating at a higher rate of activity than it ever has before and that the standard of

living it is producing for all America is far beyond that of any other country in the world.

5. It is a fact that in times of high economic activity there is competition among business, consumers, and government for the productive resources of the country; if government, by indulging in high levels of spending in such times, intensifies that competition, it openly invites inflation.

6. It is a fact that with an unbalanced budget, federal borrowings to raise the money to spend more than income tend to add to the money supply of the country and therefore are inflationary.

7. It is a fact that the purchasing power of the dollar has declined more than 50 percent in the last twenty years. Today we spend more than $2.00 to get what $1.00 would buy in 1939.

8. And finally, it is a fact that all too often in history inflation has been the undoing of nations, great and small.

In my view, the facts that I have recited clearly demonstrate the need for:

1. Containing federal expenditures within federal income—which means balancing the budget.

2. Establishing the principle of a balanced budget—including some surplus for reduction of the national debt—as a fiscal objective for the prosperous years ahead.

These are the standards on which fiscal integrity for the nation should rest. These are the standards by which the force of inflation induced by reckless fiscal policy can be averted. Yet in 24 of the last 30 years we have not been able to attain them.

Let us look at some of the circumstances which have caused heavy federal spending in the past and have, perhaps, made us insensitive to the dangers of deficits.

LOOKING BACK

Over the last three decades the federal government has spent 264 billion dollars more than it has received. The six years in which there was an excess of income over expense produced negligible surpluses in relation to the deficits of the other years.

We need hardly be reminded of the cause of most of those deficits. In the earlier years it was depression; in the middle years it was war; in recent years it has been war again and then recession.

In the depression years it was not possible to balance the budget; while government services and costs were growing by popular demand, federal revenues declined as a result of economic inactivity. The efforts made to balance the budget by increasing tax rates in 1930 and 1932 and in 1936 to 1938 were apparently self-defeating.

As for the expenditure side of the budget, the decade of the 1930s produced a great deal of talk about "pump-priming" and "compensatory spending"—federal spending which would compensate in poor times for the decline in business and consumer demand and thus lend balance and stability to the economy. The theory was, of course, for the federal government to spend proportionately larger amounts during depression times and proportionately smaller amounts during good times—to suffer deficits in poor years and enjoy surpluses in prosperous years, with the objective of coming out even over the long pull.

Then, in the early 1940s came World War II. During the war years, the federal government's expenditures vastly exceeded its income, and huge further deficits were piled up. In retrospect, most students of wartime economic developments now agree that we did not tax ourselves nearly enough. We did not pay enough of the costs of war out of current income. We created a large debt while suppressing some of its inflationary consequences with direct economic controls, but the suppression was only temporary.

Depression and war, although major factors, were not the only reasons for increased federal expenditures and deficits during the past thirty years. It was more complex than that. In the 1930s the national philosophy of the responsibilities of the federal government underwent a major change. The country's needs for economic growth and social advancement were gradually given increased recognition at the federal level.

The aim of economic growth, of social advancement, and of "compensatory" economic stability became intertwined. Many federal activities of far-reaching implications were established in ways which affected federal expenditures for very long periods of time—if not permanently. Social security, greatly increased support for agriculture, rural electrification, aids to homeowners and mortgage institutions, public housing, public power developments like the Tennessee Valley Authority and other multi-purpose water resource projects, and public assistance grants are just a few examples. All of them, however, remained as federal programs after World War II. And we were actually fighting in that war before federal spending for work relief could be stopped.

The immediate postwar period was marked by dramatic demobilization. Nevertheless, many of the major costs of war lingered on. The maintenance in the postwar period of even the reduced and relatively modest structure of our Armed Forces was far more costly than anything that existed in the way of the machinery of war prior to 1940. The war also left us with greatly increased expenditure commitments for interest on the public debt, for veterans, and for atomic energy. The Marshall Plan and the mutual security program followed in succession. It became obvious, next, that the cold war was going to be expensive. Then, with the Korean aggression, it became necessary to rearm and, even after the shooting stopped, the peacetime striking force and defensive machinery we had to maintain continued expenditures at levels that far exceeded in cost anything we had earlier imagined.

Thus, the postwar growth of the budget has been partly in the area of national security, partly deferred costs of World War II, and partly the inheritance of activities and ways of thinking that characterized the depression of the 1930s. We have now learned that many of the programs the federal government initiated in the 1930s were neither temporary nor "compensatory" in character. Moreover, we have not only retained many of them, but we have also greatly expanded them in the postwar period. Since World War II we have seen large increases in federal expenditures for urban renewal, public health, federal aid for airports and highways, new categories and a higher federal share of public assistance grants, aid to schools in federally impacted areas, great liberalization in aid to agriculture, as well as new programs for science, education, and outer space.

THE PRESENT

What can we conclude from all of this?

It seems to me that in the first place we must recognize that the compensatory theory of federal spending has failed thus far and offers little hope for the future unless we exert a more forceful and courageous determination to control the growth of federal spending. The major spending programs which originated in the depression years have in most cases persisted in the following decades. A work relief project could be turned off when we started to fight a war, but most of the programs established in the 1930s developed characteristics of a far more permanent sort.

An example can be found in the program of the Rural Electrification Administration (REA). This program was started in 1936 when only a minority of farm families enjoyed the benefits of electricity. Today, 95 percent of our farms receive central station electric service. We have invested 4 billion dollars in this program, at 2 percent interest. Nonetheless, indications are that future demands for federal funds will be even greater as the REA co-operatives continue to grow.

The startling fact is that three out of four new users currently being added are nonfarm users. About one-half of REA electric power goes to industries, communities, or nonfarm families. The reasonable approach is that rural electric co-operatives should now be able to get some of their financing from other than government sources, especially for nonfarm purposes that compete with taxed private industry. . . .

Inability to turn off expenditures is not all that is wrong with the compensatory theory of the prewar period. Initially, it dealt largely with the spending side of the fiscal equation whereas the income side now appears to be playing a more important part. Today—with corporate income tax rates at 52 percent—any substantial reduction of corporate earnings produces an immediate proportionate and large loss to the federal treasury. Personal income taxes also respond, though less sharply, to a fall in national production and employment. Thus, when times take a turn for the worse, federal revenues decline promptly and substantially.

Couple this with enlarged social obligations in times of recession or depression—unemployment compensation, public assistance, and so on—and you have substantial leverage of a more or less automatic character for the production of federal deficits in times of depressed economic activity. To do more than this—

to deliberately step up expenditures still more, for public works and other construction, as was done last year—runs grave risks. There is, first, the risk that an antirecession expenditure program cannot be turned off after the recession, but instead represents a permanent increase in the public sphere at the expense of the private. Second, it is difficult to start programs quickly, so the major impact may come long after the need for the economic stimulation has passed. Both of these risks mean that anti-recession actions can well represent an inflationary danger for the postrecession period. The danger is there even if, as some believe, positive governmental intervention is required to counter recessions. It is more grave, however, if—and I believe this was proved true in 1958–59—the economy is vigorous and resilient enough to come out of a temporary recession and to go on through a revival period to new prosperous peaks without any direct financial federal interference.

I think we may conclude that it is inevitable that our nation will be faced with large budgets in the years ahead. This is particularly true for the defense obligations which our country has assumed, for its international undertakings to provide economic and military assistance to other free nations, and as a result of many programs which have been started over the years —major programs for water resource development, agriculture, veterans' benefits, low-cost housing, airways modernization, and space exploration—all these and many others have taken on a permanent quality which makes it clear that federal budgets will be large budgets in our lifetimes.

There is still another conclusion which springs from this short recitation of the history of the last thirty years. It is that the federal government has assumed more and more responsibility for activities which formerly were regarded as being under the jurisdiction of state and local governments. More and more the federal government has assumed responsibility for public assistance, housing, urban renewal, educational aid to areas with federal installations, and many other programs that are now supported by federal grants-in-aid to the states. All this, of course, contributes to the conclusion that these federal programs are not only large at the present time, but have a built-in durability—a staying power with which we must reckon as a fact of life.

I think these thoughts are well summarized in the words of Mr. Allen Sproul, former president of the New York Federal Reserve Bank, who recently said:

Government, in our day, touches upon the economic life of the community in an almost bewildering variety of ways, but its overall influence comes into focus in the consolidated cash budget and, in a subsidiary way, in the management of the public debt. When we abandoned the idea of taxation for revenue only and admitted, as we must, a more important role of Government in economic affairs, we thought up a tidy little scheme called the compensatory budget. This envisaged a cash budget balanced in times of real prosperity, in deficit in times of economic recession, and in surplus in times of inflationary boom. What we have got is a budget that may throw up a shaky surplus in times of boom, but that will surely show substantial deficits in times of recession. The bias, over time, is toward deficits, with only wobbly contracyclical tendencies.

LOOKING AHEAD

It seems to me that as we move into another decade it will be essential to recognize that unless we have a more positive program for operating our federal government within its income, the forces that have gained such tremendous momentum in the past will perpetuate the tradition of deficits—to the great disadvantage of the country as a whole.

Assuming a continuous, but not uninterrupted, economic growth for the country, accompanied by ever-increasing, but not uninterrupted, growth of federal revenues, we should nevertheless expect that the growth of programs started in the past will have a strong tendency to absorb the expected additional revenues—unless aggressive controls are exercised by an alert administration and a statesmanlike Congress during those years. . . .

The lesson is clear. We should pay as we go, and if we are to look for debt reduction or tax reduction on a sound footing—as we should—we must do more than this. We must plan for substantial budgetary surpluses in good years—or we will surely contribute to further dangerous inflation in the years ahead.

The Full Employment Budget

COUNCIL OF ECONOMIC ADVISERS

This discussion of concepts and measures of fiscal policy was included in the 1971 Annual Report *of the Council of Economic Advisers, which consisted of Paul W. McCracken, Chairman, Hendrik S. Houthakker, and Herbert Stein.*

WHEN THE EFFECTS OF budget policy on the overall economy first came to general attention in 1936, the expansiveness of the budget was commonly measured by changes in the actual deficit or surplus. This measure can be grossly misleading, however. Even if existing tax and spending legislation remains unchanged, the actual budget balance will rise and fall, as changes in incomes influence tax receipts and call for different unemployment and welfare payments. In fact, the actual deficit can rise in the face of restrictive policy actions of government. For example, a fall in tax revenues can coincide with an increase in tax rates if incomes decline sufficiently. A given change in the actual deficit (or surplus) between two years has a very different significance if economic activity is rising between those two years than if it is falling.

Clearly, a need has existed for a better measure of government budget policy and its effects—one that would show what effects were the result of tax and expenditure decisions and what effects the economy itself had exerted on the budget. There are a number of possible solutions to the problem. Econometric models, for example, can be used to estimate the impact of various combinations of tax rate and expenditure changes on the level of economic activity. Different models utilize different assumptions regarding the nature and relative importance of various determinants of economic behavior, and therefore they provide different estimates of the economic impact of various fiscal policy changes. Consequently, fiscal policy analysts cannot place too much reliance on the results of a particular model, although the distribution of estimates provided by a variety of available models is a useful guide.

For the purposes of public discussion, it is convenient to use simple measures of the stance of fiscal policy which summarize the more complicated policy changes used in the complex models. As noted below, however, considerable care must be exercised in using simple measures of changes in fiscal policy to estimate the effects of these policies on economic activity.

One simple measure of changes in policy can be obtained by calculating the effect of changes in revenue and expenditure legislation at a particular level of economic activity. This technique abstracts from the effect of changes in economic activity on the budget and provides a clearer view of purely discretionary policy changes. For example, at the level of economic activity prevailing in 1970, changes in tax rates occurring during 1970 reduced revenues by roughly $9 billion while expenditures increased by about $15 billion. In other words, exogenous policy actions during 1970 provided a fiscal stimulus of $24 billion.

While changes in the surplus or deficit at a given level of money GNP provide a convenient measure of discretionary policy changes, fiscal policy planning requires a measure containing somewhat more information. Because the labor force and productivity normally rise and prices rarely fall, money GNP normally grows. Consequently revenues also rise and over time the budget surplus would tend to grow rapidly if spending and tax rates remained unchanged. Spending and tax programs that would yield an unchanged surplus in an economy with a constant GNP would thus tend to hold down growth at the normal rate by generating larger and larger surpluses.

It has been found of interest to ask how the surplus or deficit would change if the economy moved along a specific path. Conceptually, any number of growth paths could be selected for this purpose; it is the change in the budget position along the assumed path that will indicate whether the budget policy has been or will be restrictive relative to that path—that is, whether the budget is tending to push the economy above or below the assumed path.

In order to give the measure more relevance it is common to select a growth path that has some normative significance. The full-employment growth path has been used most frequently since the concept of a full-employment budget was developed and publicized by the Committee for Economic Development in 1947. Changes in the full-employment surplus measure changes in spending and tax legislation as well as the effect of full-employment growth on revenues. The difference between the full-employment budget balance and the actual balance reveals the effects of short-run variations in economic activity around the full-employment growth path.

A particular target growth path could serve as an alternative to the full-employment path. Sometimes this path is identical to the full-employment path, but in 1970 it was necessary to be below full employment temporarily in order to moderate the inflationary pressures which had become excessive in 1969 and early 1970. In other circumstances the desired path may be steeper than the full-employment growth path, if it is necessary to regain full employment from a less than full-employment position. The target path budget would reveal the effect of discretionary tax and spending changes and the effect of target growth on tax revenues, but would abstract from the effect on the budget of deviations of economic activity away from the target.

METHOD OF COMPUTATION

The figures for the full-employment budget provided in Table 1 are computed in the following manner: First, the full-employment growth path is estimated in terms of the real value of production. Second, the real growth path is converted into current dollar terms using the actual rate of price inflation. This step suffers from the difficulty that a revenue change resulting from price changes would alter the estimate of the full-employment surplus even though there were no changes in discretionary tax and expenditure policies. One way out of this difficulty might be to convert real output to money income using the inflation rate that would have occurred if the economy had actually been at full employment. But this figure is so difficult to estimate, if indeed there is any unique rate, that the actual inflation rate, despite its shortcomings, is used as a convenient approximation.

Next, full-employment income must be distributed into various tax bases, such as corporate profits, personal income, and other categories. The calculations used in this chapter are based on an estimate of the distribution which would emerge if the economy were actually operating continuously at full employment. For the purposes of comparing full-employment budgets at different points of time it is important that a constant distribution pattern be used. Otherwise the estimates would shift with distributional changes that are unrelated to fiscal policies.

Average tax rates are then estimated for different types of income under current legislation. On the basis of these estimates full-employment revenues can then be calculated. Full-employment expenditures are estimated by adjusting actual expenditures to allow for the difference between actual outlays on unemployment compensation and those that would occur at full employment.

It is clear that the full-employment estimate depends on numerous assumptions and that these create the possibility of error. This problem should not, however, be exaggerated. For most purposes interest focuses on changes between years, and if the assumptions are consistent between years, the errors in the estimated changes in the budget position are likely to be small. Moreover, estimates of the full-employment budget for the future are probably subject to less error than estimates of the actual budget, because the actual future path of the economy is more variable and uncertain than the full-employment path.

THE FULL-EMPLOYMENT BUDGET AS A MEASURE OF FISCAL IMPACT

The absolute level of the full-employment surplus or deficit is of limited significance for indicating how much restraint or stimulus the budget would exert on the economy if it followed the full-employment path, or indeed for indicating which of these directions its influence would take. Changes in the full-employment surplus from period to period are much more important indicators of how much fiscal policy is moving toward contraction or expansion. The fact that the full-employment budget has a surplus does not imply that the budget is not having an expansionary impact on the economy; the effects may be expansionary if the surplus is declining. Similarly a budget with a deficit may be restrictive if the deficit is declining.

Although changes in the full-employment budget balance provide a convenient summary measure of changes in fiscal policy, they do not tell the whole story. A given change in the balance may exert a different force, depending on whether the change stems from a change in transfer payments, purchases of goods and services, corporate taxes, personal taxes, or other instruments of fiscal policy. Results vary because different policy changes affect economic behavior differently, even though the same amounts of money are involved. Some of the most important differences can be considered in complex models of the economy, but no model can capture all of the subtle effects of fiscal policy. For example, virtually identical policy changes may have different results depending on circumstances. A long-anticipated increase in Social Security benefits may have a different consequence from that of an unexpected increase. Similarly, a permanent cut in income taxes probably has a more powerful impact than an equivalent reduction that is known to be temporary. Conceptually, models could be constructed to take account of such differences, but they would be extremely difficult to manage.

RECENT CHANGES IN THE FULL-EMPLOYMENT BUDGET

The table below illustrates changes in the full-employment budget during the last decade. If fiscal policy changes are measured by the annual change in the surplus relative to full-employment GNP, the largest stimulus of the decade came with the tax cut of 1964. The largest shift toward restraint came in 1969, or on a two-year basis, in 1968 and 1969.

The full-employment budget can be computed by using either national income accounting concepts or the concepts applied in deriving the unified budget, which appears in the President's annual budget statement. Economists generally favor the national income accounting approach in the belief that on balance it provides a more accurate measure of fiscal effects; but both concepts have advantages and disadvantages.

On both the expenditure and revenue sides these concepts

embody important differences of timing. In the national accounts budget, purchases of goods and services are recorded when delivery is made. The unified budget records them when checks are issued for payment; this might occur before or after delivery. It is sometimes argued that neither method of timing truly captures the fiscal impact and that for such a purpose the timing of orders should be used.

TABLE 1. *The Full-Employment Receipts and Expenditure Estimates, National Income Accounts Basis, 1960–70 (billions of dollars)*

Calendar year	Receipts	Expenditures	Surplus or deficit (−)	Change in surplus from preceding year	Change as a percent of full-employment GNP
1960	105.0	92.0	13.0	8.3	1.5
1961	109.2	100.4	8.8	−4.2	−.7
1962	113.8	109.4	4.4	−4.4	−.7
1963	121.8	112.8	9.0	4.6	.7
1964	119.2	117.5	1.8	−7.2	−1.1
1965	124.2	123.2	1.0	−.8	−.1
1966	139.3	142.9	−3.6	−4.6	−.6
1967	153.1	163.6	−10.5	−6.9	−.9
1968	175.7	181.7	−6.0	4.5	.5
1969	203.3	191.7	11.7	17.7	1.9
1970	212.0	205.3	6.7	−5.0	−.5

NOTE: Detail will not necessarily add to totals because of rounding.
SOURCE: Council of Economic Advisers.

On the revenue side the unified budget again uses cash receipts. In the national income accounts budget most receipts, such as corporate income and excise taxes, are recorded on an accrual basis, but personal income taxes are recorded when paid by individuals. Steps are now being taken to put the unified budget more on an accrual basis.

The national accounts budget omits the direct lending activities of government except for Commodity Credit Corporation (CCC) "nonrecourse" commodity loans, which are treated as expenditures rather than loans. The unified budget also treats as expenditures CCC loans as well as foreign loans made on noncommercial terms and domestic loans where repayment may be waived. A unified-budget deficit can be computed for the expenditure account alone, or it can be defined to include the net lending not already considered in the expenditure account. In fiscal 1970 such lending amounted to $2.1 billion.

Neither budget considers the loan guarantee and insurance programs of government, and besides these there are a number of government-sponsored lending institutions which operate outside of the budget. During fiscal 1971 it is expected that government net guaranteed and insured loans will increase by about $13 billion, while the increase in the net lending of government-sponsored institutions will be about $8 billion.

Toward a Flexible Tax Policy: Automatic and Discretionary Stabilizers

COMMISSION ON MONEY AND CREDIT

The Commission on Money and Credit showed prophetic vision in stressing its major recommendation for presidential powers to vary income tax rates, subject to congressional veto. The proposal is spelled out in this discussion of tax policy, taken from the commission's report, Money and Credit *(1961).*

AUTOMATIC STABILIZERS

WITH A GIVEN tax and expenditure structure, changes in total output and income result in automatic changes in tax yields and in certain outlays, the first changing in the same direction as income and the latter in the opposite direction. For example, as personal incomes fall, the yield of the personal income tax falls along with them, while payments for unemployment compensation rise. Consequently, the absolute decline in income available for personal spending is less than the absolute decline in national income. As personal incomes increase, tax yields rise, and unemployment compensation payments decline. These and other similar cushioning effects on fluctuations in the amount of income available to the private sector of the economy occur without legislative or administrative changes in tax and expenditure programs and are thus called *automatic stabilizers*.

The higher the tax rates, the more progressive the rate structure, and the more sensitive the tax base to swings in the cycle, the more will changing tax yields absorb variations in national income, and the smaller will be the remaining change in income available for private spending. The more closely unemployment compensation payments approximate the wage the employee loses, the less will unemployment reduce disposable income. But because tax rates are much less than 100 percent at the margin, and because unemployment compensation is less than the lost wages, changes in national income are only partially offset by the tax and transfer-payment changes. Nevertheless automatic fiscal stabilizers do cushion the fall in income. As a result, private expenditures fall less than they would otherwise. Thus, automatic stabilizers aid recovery by reducing the cumulative deterioration in economic outlook that would otherwise take place and facilitate the forces of recovery contributing to an early upswing. Although the built-in stabilizers are very useful when the economy contracts, they are a mixed blessing when it expands. When business conditions recover from a recession, the federal tax system automatically cuts the growth in private spendable incomes, and hence the expansion tends to proceed more slowly. If the recovery is strong, the automatic stabilizers provide an important and desirable curb to the inflationary pressures that may ensue.

The very size of government expenditures and tax receipts relative to gross national product today, compared with the period before the 1930s, greatly increases the potential cushioning effect of the automatic stabilizers. Whatever the merits or demerits of large government expenditures and tax receipts may be on other grounds, it is clear that the larger they are in relation to the total level of economic activity, the stronger is the impact of the automatic stabilizers. If taxes are equal to 30 percent of GNP, it is apparent that the decline in tax yield with a given fall in GNP will be greater than when taxes account for 10 percent of GNP, and as a consequence the reduction in income available for private expenditures will be less severe. . . .

The effectiveness of the automatic stabilizers does not, however, depend exclusively on the relative size of government expenditures and the level of tax rates. It also depends on the degree to which the tax base (the particular incomes or expenditures subject to tax) fluctuates with changes in the national income and on how tax yields vary with changes in the tax base.

The major portion of federal revenues is derived from the corporation and personal income taxes, both of which (especially the former) are highly sensitive to change in national income. In contrast, local tax receipts, primarily from property taxes, vary little with income. State governments have a wide variety of revenue sources, a large proportion representing general sales taxes or sales and excise taxes levied on particular commodities or services. State tax revenues are therefore much less sensitive to changes in national income than are federal revenues but more so than local revenues.

In addition, state and local governments are less able to borrow than the federal government. Thus, no individual state or local unit of government, acting by itself, has the same capability as the federal government to take countercyclical actions. In addition, since the effects of its fiscal actions are not contained within its own borders but spill over to other areas, they do not have the same incentives.

It follows from the above discussion that the task of maintaining the strength of the automatic stabilizers must be undertaken at the federal level. So long as the major fraction of total government expenditures continues to be made by the federal government, largely because of the size of national security and related outlays, the automatic stabilizers will remain relatively strong. If, however, an improvement in international conditions should permit a substantial reduction in the share of the gross national product required for defense, the power of the automatic stabilizers would be weakened.

In this eventuality the strength of the automatic stabilizers could be partially maintained by modifications which would permit a substitution of the more flexible components of the federal revenue system for the less flexible components of the state and local systems. One means would be to expand the use of federal grants to state and local governments, thereby enabling taxes to be collected at the federal level and spent at the state and local level.

It is impossible to estimate precisely the effectiveness of existing automatic stabilizers. The best available evidence indicates that during the postwar period the built-in flexibility of the federal budget offset between one-third to two-fifths of the fall (or increase) in the gross national product. This is a sizable fraction, far greater than that prevailing before World War II. Recent experience with recurrent and moderately severe recessions raises the question whether the automatic stabilizers can and should be strengthened to play a greater role in reducing the amplitude of cyclical fluctuations. Possible means of increasing the strength of the automatic stabilizers might take the form of greater reliance on more cyclically responsive types of tax revenue and a revision of unemployment insurance.

DISCRETIONARY FISCAL MEASURES

Even if the automatic stabilizers can be improved, discretionary fiscal measures will remain an important instrument of stabilization policy. Consequently, the advantages and disadvantages of possible discretionary actions must be considered. Two major objections are commonly raised against [them].

The first is that economic forecasts are necessarily so inaccurate that there is always the possibility that discretionary action taken on the basis of such forecasts may do more harm than good. However this objection is applicable to all discretionary stabilization policies, monetary or fiscal. It is a serious objection, for much is yet to be learned before we can assess the economic outlook as well as we need to. Nevertheless, the Commission is convinced that judicious use of discretionary measures, including fiscal policy, cannot be dispensed with.

Secondly, it is frequently alleged that the time required by Congress to enact discretionary measures and by the executive to put them into effect may rule them out. For instance, the time required by Congress to enact tax changes is frequently alleged to rule out such changes as a desirable means of discretionary stabilizing action. It is claimed, for example, that the time necessary to enact tax reductions to combat a recession is so long that they are not likely to take effect until the subsequent recovery is well underway and that consequently these reductions, enacted to cut short a recession, may in fact feed a subsequent boom.

The alleged inability of Congress to act promptly is usually based on the fact that the passage of major revenue legislation has been typically an extended process. This was true in the case of the Revenue Act of 1942, the Revenue Act of 1951, and the Internal Revenue Code of 1954, all of which took the major part of a year to enact into final form. These measures, however, dealt with complicated long-run structural reforms rather than with short-run problems of economic stabilization. In certain instances, when emergency conditions dictated a need for speed, even complicated reforms were put through in a shorter time. For example, the Revenue Act of 1950 was halted halfway through its passage as a tax reform measure and sped to enactment as a substantial tax increase in only 60 days. The Excess Profits Tax of 1950 was passed within 49 days of a presidential message.

Of more relevance as a measure of congressional legislative

speed are the simple tax extension measures, such as those in the postwar period covering the excise and corporate income tax rates. They have generally consumed less than a month's time from the initial action by the Ways and Means Committee. Even the highly controversial extension of the excess profits tax in 1953 required less than 50 days. The temporary extension of unemployment compensation in 1958 was enacted in 73 days, and its extension in 1959 took only 18 days. Debt ceiling increases are the same type of legislation. Prompt hearings and prompt reports could reasonably be expected because of the compelling nature of arresting a boom or stopping a recession.

In sum, when Congress has had straightforward changes before it which it wished to enact, ways have been found to accelerate the legislative process. Fear that action will be delayed by legislative lags, therefore, provides no valid excuse for executive failure to recommend action. These precedents indicate that there is no technical or institutional barrier to a discretionary fiscal policy designed to promote economic stabilization and growth *provided* that the need for such policy is recognized by Congress and the executive and that appropriate discretionary measures are proposed. This conclusion, however, rests on the acceptance of the following basic proposition.

Discretionary fiscal policy requires speed of decision and effect and can only be successful if temporary and reversible fiscal changes for stabilization purposes are dissociated from permanent and structural changes. Techniques should be developed by which taxation and expenditure policies can be applied more flexibly, and the first step in this direction lies in a sharp demarcation between short-run cyclical changes and long-run structural changes. . . .

The tax structure and expenditure programs do change from time to time and must be changed periodically as the growth of the economy alters the tax revenue-expenditure relationship. The periodic reassessment of the relationship between tax revenues and expenditures is necessary. When reassessment indicates the need for changes, it would be helpful for stabilization purposes if these basic changes could be timed to coincide with stabilization needs. However, stabilization policies and programs must not be dependent on basic changes in tax and expenditure programs.

TAX POLICY CHANGES

What component of private demand should bear the brunt of fiscal adjustments to promote short-run stability? Should it be consumption or investment, and what kind of expenditures within these broad groups? It would be helpful if investment outlays could be pushed up in recessions and pulled down in booms, since they are the primary short-run destabilizer. Such a result would provide a more steady level of capital formation and more sustainable rate of growth. Yet this sector is probably more difficult to affect than any other. Consequently, it would appear that at present the best policy is to consider both investment and consumption as potential candidates for stabilization adjustments.

To be able to alter taxes or transfers for this purpose, they must meet certain criteria. Changes must be easy to make without creating uncertainty in the administration of, and compliance with, the tax law. They must be promptly effective and easily reversible. And they must not create uncertainty in business output, planning, and efficiency.

The personal income tax ranks high in satisfying these criteria, with cyclical varying of the starting rate preferable to varying personal exemptions. The tax is not a major factor in business planning; it is broadly based; and the rate can be easily varied and changes can take effect promptly through withholding. Variation in personal exemptions might create uncertainty from year to year for many taxpayers about whether they needed to file.

Excise taxes can be easily raised or lowered, but their initial effect on demand is perverse. Advance notice of changes must be given. Therefore, if rates are to be raised because demand is excessive, taxpayers are put on notice that their purchases will shortly cost them more. This encourages them to speed up purchases and increases demand. Similarly, if demand is deficient, a coming reduction in excise tax rates can lead to the postponement of purchases, further weakening demand. . . .

Temporary changes in social security contributions have some of the same advantages as changes in the starting rate of the personal income tax, but the employer contribution is a cost item and changes in it may disturb costs and prices. Furthermore, countercyclical variation in contributions may not be readily compatible with the nature of the old age insurance system; the government tries to maintain a schedule of contribution rates that matches actuarial estimates of costs in the long run. Also, the unemployment compensation system is state administered and might not be readily subject to variation. The federal payroll tax for unemployment compensation might be varied, with excess collections going into a federal fund to provide emergency relief in recessions.

Countercyclical adjustments in the corporation income tax rate, the remaining important tax to be considered, would almost surely create the most uncertainty for business. This holds for changes in the tax rate, as well as for changes in depreciation allowances or in investment credits.

As in the proposal for formula flexibility, the most appropriate choice for short-run discretionary changes in taxes is the first-bracket rate of the personal income tax. They are least likely to open up controversial questions of income tax structure. The legislative and administrative problems in making such changes would be relatively simple. No uncertainty would be encountered in complying with such changes. They could be made effective with very short notice to taxpayers through the withholding mechanism. They would be easily reversible. They would have a minimum of adverse side-effects such as causing uncertainty in business planning or speculation in commodities. Moreover, small changes in the tax rate would provide large amounts of additional spendable funds to consumers. A one-percentage point reduction in the tax rate would provide consumers with additional disposable income at an annual rate of well over $1 billion. . . .

If this rate reduction were expected to continue in effect for some time, the best evidence indicates that consumer expenditures would rise by a very large fraction of the increase in disposable income, probably by upwards of 80 cents on the dollar within a year of the date of tax reduction. In fact, more than half this response would probably occur in the first quarter following the tax reduction. It seems reasonable to suppose that the response in spending would be somewhat lower if the tax reduction were clearly understood to apply for only a brief period of six months or less, but almost no empirical evidence exists on which to base a quantitative estimate for such tax reductions. Conversely, tax increases would cause a fall in consumption as disposable income was reduced.

A variation of this procedure would be to make a percentage reduction in all rates and thus a percentage adjustment in final liabilities. In principle this is the same kind of device as a change in the starting rate alone, but it would apply to upper-brackets rates as well as to the starting rate.

Clearly, as a stabilization instrument, the first-bracket rate adjustment is superior to proportional adjustments in the entire rate structure in stimulating consumption, since for each dollar of income tax reduction the lower income groups would receive a proportionately larger share of the reductions.

The Commission therefore concludes that when discretionary tax adjustments are used to promote short-run economic stabilization, they should consist of variations in the first-bracket rate of the personal income tax.

Such variations should be regarded strictly as temporary departures from a permanent tax structure. Under such a plan the starting rate could be shifted to a temporary level, either up or down, for as long a period as is believed desirable, with a corresponding adjustment provided in the final tax liabilities for the year depending upon the length of time over which the temporary rate was in effect. For example, if the first-bracket rate were cut two percentage points to 18 percent for six months, the annual liability would be based on a 19 percent starting rate, rather than on the present annual rate of 20 percent. Obviously, there are many possible variants of this illustration.

The main point to emphasize here is that short-run stabilization adjustments are not the place to make basic changes in the tax structure. The permanent rate structure should be governed by such considerations as tax equity, investment incentives, and economic growth. Full consideration of all these factors is not really relevant to this section on short-run stabilization policy.

Because of the vicissitudes attending the consideration of ordinary legislation, the President's responsibilities for prompt and decisive action under the Employment Act warrant a limited delegation of power to initiate a tax rate change as an instrument of countercyclical fiscal policy. Any proposal to vest the President with stand-by power to alter tax rates for any reason under any circumstances runs counter to the long-established tradition, jealously guarded, that gives the House Ways and Means Committee exclusive jurisdiction to originate revenue measures. The Congress since 1934, to be sure, has acquiesced in a delegation of power to the President, within specified limits and conditions, to change tariff rates under the Reciprocal Trade Agreements Acts, but only because tariffs vitally affect our foreign policy—traditionally a primary concern of the President, and a field in which he is otherwise accorded a wide latitude of discretion—and because the trade agreements can hardly be negotiated without the offer of firm commitments. Even in this case the Ways and Means Committee, not the Committee on Foreign Affairs, initiated the basic legislation.

The delegation should specify the particular rate to be changed and limit the maximum amount and duration of the changes, as well as the conditions under which it is to be made. Finally, the delegation should be accompanied by an opportunity for a congressional veto of its application in particular cases, along lines currently employed when executive reorganization plans are authorized. This procedure protects the opportunity for timely action by assuring that a tax adjustment, once formally proposed, will not get lost in a shuffle of alternative proposals; it must be acted upon, in the form submitted, within a limited time. Moreover, it minimizes the disturbance in the balance of executive-legislative power.

The position of the Commission on discretionary changes in tax rates is summarized below.

1. One obstacle to stabilizing tax policy has been the failure to disassociate temporary and reversible changes for stabilization purposes from permanent and structural changes. It is the Commission's view that techniques must be developed by which tax policy can be applied more flexibly, and that the first step in this direction lies in the separation of short-run cyclical tax changes from long-run structural changes in the tax system.

2. Among various alternative taxes, the personal income tax lends itself best to countercyclical variation, and adjustments in the first-bracket rate are recommended as the best type of change.

3. In order to provide maximum flexibility for stabilizing tax changes, the Commission recommends that Congress grant to the President limited conditional power to make temporary countercyclical adjustments in the first-bracket rate of the personal in-

come tax, the grant to be accompanied by the following qualifications and safeguards:

(a) The power should be available for exercise only when the President has issued a statement that in his judgment economic conditions are running significantly counter to the objectives set forth in the Employment Act as amended.

(b) The range of permissible adjustment should be limited to five percentage points upward or downward, that is, one-quarter of the present 20 percent rate.

(c) The duration of the adjustment should be limited to six months subject to renewal by the same process, unless Congress acts sooner by law to extend or supplant it.

(d) The exercise of the conditional power by the President should be subject to a legislative veto by a concurrent resolution of both houses of Congress before any tax adjustment takes effect, in accordance with the procedures made familiar by the recent Reorganization Acts. To this end the President should be required to lay before the Congress any proposal to adjust the tax rate, the proposal to lie there up to 60 days, unless a concurrent resolution of disapproval is sooner voted on and rejected, and to take effect only if no such resolution is adopted in that time. In the same law that authorizes the adjustment, the parliamentary rules of the two houses should be amended ad hoc in a manner to ensure that a concurrent resolution of disapproval may be introduced and voted upon within a 60-day period.

PART THREE

Monetary Tools and
Their Uses

Organization for Monetary Policy

G. L. BACH

*These views on the appropriate relationships of the Federal
Reserve to the President and to the Congress were stated in the
concluding chapter of* Making Monetary and Fiscal Policy (1970).
*G. L. Bach is Frank E. Buck Professor of Economics and Public
Policy at Stanford University.*

FEDERAL RESERVE INDEPENDENCE

*The present degree of "independence" from the White House
is about right—though the Federal Reserve should become a
somewhat more active participant in top-level policymaking.*

The issue of Federal Reserve independence is central to the
problem of macroeconomic policymaking. Today it is widely
agreed that Federal Reserve goals should be part of, and substantially the same as, the goals of overall national macroeconomic policy. Moreover, the growing interdependence of
monetary, fiscal, and debt policies and increasingly high performance standards for the economy require a close working relationship between the Federal Reserve and the other main arms
of government economic policy—the Treasury, the Council of
Economic Advisers, and the White House. Complete separation
of the Federal Reserve from the President and his administration would threaten confusion and conflicts in monetary-fiscal
policy. The past half century, encompassing depression, war, and
inflation, has demonstrated beyond reasonable doubt that no
modern central bank can, or should, be completely independent

of, or isolated from, the executive branch of the government in times of stress. The nation cannot brook a divided, obstructionist monetary-fiscal policy in crisis periods.

Thus, the old concept of central bank independence, based on a narrow view of central bank responsibilities, has been swept away by the realities of modern, large-scale government financial operations in war and peace, and by recognition that government fiscal and monetary policies are powerful stabilization instruments. Only in periods when general economic conditions are relatively normal is it realistic to conceive of Congress and the administration acquiescing in central bank behavior that threatens the government's macoreconomic policies. Tied into macroeconomic policy as monetary policy is, proposals to keep money and monetary policy "out of politics" and "out of the government" are unrealistic, except in the narrow sense of keeping monetary policy as free as possible from narrowly partisan, day-to-day political pressures. In this sense, there is little ground for distinguishing between monetary policy and other macroeconomic policies. The real problem is how to obtain the most reasoned, deliberative judgment as to optimal policy for achieving the nation's macroeconomic goals.

The Case for Independence • What, then, is the case for Federal Reserve "independence"? There are two powerful arguments:

First, dispersion of power is fundamental in the U.S. system of government. Control of the nation's money stock is a vital economic function. A partially independent Federal Reserve may contribute to a significant broadening of the total base of macroeconomic decision making in the federal government. The President and his aides have substantial power over other macroeconomic policies. To center more control over macroeconomic policy in the White House would further concentrate power in the hands of the President and his administration. Thus, Congress chose to disperse this power by making the Federal Reserve responsible for one significant part of U.S. macroeconomic policy.

Second, history warns that governments tend to err on the side of inflation when war or other factors create strong pressures for government spending. Treasuries frequently turn to money-issue through the banking system to pay their bills when taxes are inadequate. The modern world's major inflations have all come when large government deficits were covered by the issue of new money (currency or bank deposits). Although legislators vote the expenditures, treasuries must pay the bills, and they feel pressed to do so at low interest rates when they must borrow. Thus, heads of government and their treasuries have a predictable inflationary bias, however well-intentioned and generally conservative their treasury secretaries may be. Against this bias, central bankers have tended to hold stability of the monetary unit in higher esteem.

Indeed, the entire American democratic political process has an inflationary bias. It is always easier for Congress to spend money than to raise taxes; some say "politicians" are inherently irresponsible financially. An independent Federal Reserve is needed to call a halt on the overspending politicians who may respond too readily to demands for jobs and booming prosperity, even though these may generate inflation.

Stated bluntly, this second argument for Federal Reserve independence is that it allows the System to stand against inflation, providing a buffer, or temporary inertial force, against the inflationary bias of U.S. democratic political processes. The Second World War and modern fiscal policy have led to increasing expectations that the government will maintain high employment and good times. Thus, the wage, price, and income expectations of all participants (laborers, businessmen, farmers, citizens) persistently exceed the economy's real productive potential. These pressures for higher wages and prices must be validated by expansionary monetary-fiscal policy if they are not to create recession and unemployment. Elected government officials repeatedly feel compelled to give in to these excess-income claims with inflationary macroeconomic policy in order to avoid recession and unemployment. The need for a strong "stable money" voice in government macroeconomic councils is perhaps greater now than ever before. At least, a system that ensures a thorough questioning of inflationary government policies is better than one that does not.

Independence From Whom? · Federal Reserve independence *from Congress* makes little sense in the democratic system of government in the United States. Congress established the Federal Reserve. Congress can change it whenever it wishes or call it to account for any of its actions. Federal Reserve officials readily acknowledge their responsibility to Congress. Fortunately, however, Congress has been reluctant to intervene directly in Federal Reserve operations. Nor does the System need to go to Congress for appropriations to conduct its affairs. Thus, in practice, Federal Reserve monetary policy is substantially insulated from day-to-day congressional pressures, although there is no doubt that Congress has ultimate authority to control the System and its policies.

Domination of the Federal Reserve *by the Treasury* has repeatedly brought inflationary monetary policy (as during the 1940s), when the central bank has been called on to help assure low-interest-cost financing of the government debt. The System's independence from the Treasury, as was argued above, rests firmly on the evidence of history.

But this is not an argument for Federal Reserve isolation. The Treasury is a crucial operating branch of the government. The Secretary of the Treasury is inevitably in close contact with the White House; often he is a personal confidant and adviser of the President. Given these Treasury responsibilities, Federal Reserve officials feel obliged to work closely with the department, especially on debt-management issues. Conflict between the Treasury and the Federal Reserve on debt-management issues would threaten inefficiency and confusion. Indeed, the times when the Federal Reserve has been least effective have been when the chairman has been most isolated from the President and the Treasury, not the contrary—with the spectacular exception of 1951. The problem is to assure reasonable Federal Reserve participation in fiscal and debt-management decisions, so that it is not faced with the de facto necessity of working with administration and Treasury policies made without its participation.

In principle, the Treasury or some other administration agency like the Council of Economic Advisers could provide the strong stable-money voice needed in government stabilization councils. Indeed, in many nations the central bank is formally subservient to (or part of) the treasury and the government. Such arrangements have advantages. If all monetary-debt policy responsibility were concentrated in the Treasury, "buck passing" would be far more difficult than it is now.

But the counterarguments are stronger. Consolidation of debt and money-creating powers in the Treasury would give the powers to spend and to create money to the same agency. History warns that this would probably lead to too-easy reliance on money creation, to too-easy inflation, and to too little emphasis on sound fiscal and monetary policies when they call for heavier taxation, restricted government expenditures, and deflationary monetary management.

The central issue is should, or can, the Federal Reserve be independent from *the President?* Control over the nation's money supply is a vital governmental operating responsibility. Monetary policy is inextricably intermingled with fiscal policy and with debt management policy. The President must ultimately be responsible for recommending and executing the nation's basic macroeconomic policy. This logic leads clearly to the conclusion that the Federal Reserve must work closely with other agencies under the general responsibility of the President for carrying out national economic policy. To give an independent Federal Reserve the power to negate at will the basic policies of the federal government would be intolerable for any administration, Republican or Democratic. But independence, looked at practically, is a matter of degree. The real question, thus, concerns the *terms* on which the Federal Reserve participates in government policymaking and execution.

ROLE OF THE FEDERAL RESERVE CHAIRMAN

To be most effective, the Federal Reserve must be in a position to work closely with the other major government agencies responsible for national economic policy—especially the White House, the Council of Economic Advisers, and the Treasury. As the main spokesman for the System, the chairman of the Federal Reserve Board must be a man respected by the President and one with whom he can work personally. Federal Reserve influence and power have waned with its increasing isolation (independence) from other top government macroeconomic officials. This was substantially the case in the much-discussed decade of the 1940s, when the Federal Reserve was most subservient to Treasury debt-management needs. Secretaries Henry Morgenthau and John Snyder were close personal confidants of Presidents Roosevelt and Truman; during the 1940s, top Federal Reserve officials seldom saw either President. On the other hand, when Marriner Eccles worked closely with Roosevelt, and William McChesney Martin, Jr., with the administrations of Eisenhower, Kennedy, and Johnson, Federal Reserve influence was clearly greater than during the 1940s. Making the Federal Reserve completely independent of, and operationally separate from, the administration is likely to produce less, not more, Federal Reserve power. As a practical matter, complete independence is likely to mean splendid isolation from most of the decisions that matter.

The influence of the Federal Reserve for the stable-money point of view can best be assured if the Reserve is an active, continuous participant in the day-to-day processes of government economic policy formation. Cooperation is a two-way street. The Federal Reserve cannot expect to exert strong influence on policy formation unless it plays ball a good share of the time.

To implement this relationship, the term of office of the chairman of the Federal Reserve Board should be made roughly coterminous with that of the President. This would give each President power to nominate his own chairman. To insist that a new President accept a Federal Reserve chairman to whom he seriously objects would serve little purpose and would be far more likely to reduce the effectiveness of the federal Reserve than to increase it. It is significant that both Martin and Eccles, the two men who dominated the Federal Reserve for nearly forty years, vigorously support this recommendation.

But this is not to say that the Federal Reserve or its chairman should be, like the Treasury, directly subservient to the President. On the contrary, experience suggests that there is substantial benefit to be had from giving the Federal Reserve a partially independent status in the government. Realistically, this permits the Federal Reserve to serve as a buffer—to resist the pressures of excess-income-claims inflation more easily than can the President himself, Congress, or any of the regular cabinet agencies. The indirect impact of monetary policy, and its partial insulation from direct political pressures, make it a more flexible weapon against inflation than are other macroeconomic controls.

The President has great power, if he chooses to exercise it, over all agencies, including the Federal Reserve. On the other hand, even his power is limited. He does not have control over fiscal policies; this has been tightly held by Congress, on both the tax and the expenditure sides. Congress has been willing to delegate power over monetary policy only under special conditions—to a board rather than an individual, and to a board significantly insulated from the day-to-day pressures of partisan politics. This reflects a widespread American distrust of centralized power. . . .

The danger that an appropriate degree of independence for the Federal Reserve will be overridden by a President who is displeased with its monetary policies is easy to overstate. There is little doubt that Presidents have exercised informal influence over the so-called "independent agencies" throughout their existence. But here again the power of the President is far from complete. . . .

Even in appointing a Federal Reserve chairman, no President is likely to exercise his power lightly. It was rumored, for example, that Presidents Kennedy and Johnson both would have liked to appoint replacements for William McChesney Martin, Jr., but Martin's high standing in domestic and international financial and business circles made this infeasible, as a practical matter. On balance, the Federal Reserve needs more independence from the Treasury than it has often had in the past (for example, during the bond-pegging period of the 1940s), but probably somewhat less independence (isolation) from the presidency and basic governmental macroeconomic policymaking.

CONGRESS AND THE FEDERAL RESERVE

Congress's primary role in monetary policymaking should be to specify goals and general rules for the operating agencies— not to prescribe a rigid rule or detailed operating procedures.

A bicameral legislative body of 535 members, with widely diverse interests and backgrounds, and representing fifty different states, is inherently incapable of directing in detail intricate monetary policy operations like those often involved in combating private-sector or international disruptions. This conclusion rests firmly on the repeated lessons of history. Having passed governing legislation, Congress's further role properly lies in investigative surveillance of the Federal Reserve and the other agencies executing monetary policy, not in active intervention in the administrative process.

Congress has wisely chosen to delegate operating monetary stabilization responsibilities in large part to the Federal Reserve, specifying only broad goals—mainly through the Federal Reserve Act and the Employment Act of 1946. More congressional intervention in day-to-day Federal Reserve operations is not needed, nor would it be productive. Such intervention is more likely to impede than to improve the effectiveness of the Federal Reserve in carrying out the duties assigned it by Congress. Congress exerts many (often conflicting) pressures on the System in connection with individual issues, through committee hearings and other public criticism. With these powers and the always-present threat of new legislation, Congress already exercises substantial influence over the short-run operations of the Federal Reserve. It does not need more.

What Monetary Policy Can Do

MILTON FRIEDMAN

This selection is a portion of Professor Friedman's presidential address to the American Economic Association presented in December 1967 and published in the American Economic Review *of March 1968.*

THE MONETARY AUTHORITY CONTROLS nominal quantities—directly, the quantity of its own liabilities. In principle, it can use this control to peg a nominal quantity—an exchange rate, the price level, the nominal level of national income, the quantity of money by one or another definition—or to peg the rate of change in a nominal quantity—the rate of inflation or deflation, the rate of growth or decline in nominal national income, the rate of growth of the quantity of money. It cannot use its control over nominal quantities to peg a real quantity—the real rate of interest, the rate of unemployment, the level of real national income, the real quantity of money, the rate of growth of real national income, or the rate of growth of the real quantity of money.

Monetary policy cannot peg these real magnitudes at predetermined levels. But monetary policy can and does have important effects on these real magnitudes. The one is in no way inconsistent with the other.

My own studies of monetary history have made me extremely sympathetic to the oft-quoted, much reviled, and as widely misunderstood, comment by John Stuart Mill. "There cannot . . . ," he wrote, "be intrinsically a more insignificant thing, in the economy of society, than money; except in the character of a contrivance for sparing time and labour. It is a machine for doing quickly and commodiously, what would be done, though less quickly and commodiously, without it: and like many other kinds of machinery, it only exerts a distinct and independent influence of its own when it gets out of order."

True, money is only a machine, but it is an extraordinarily

efficient machine. Without it, we could not have begun to attain the astounding growth in output and level of living we have experienced in the past two centuries—any more than we could have done so without those other marvelous machines that dot our countryside and enable us, for the most part, simply to do more efficiently what could be done without them at much greater cost in labor.

But money has one feature that these other machines do not share. Because it is so pervasive, when it gets out of order, it throws a monkey wrench into the operation of all the other machines. The Great Contraction [of the 1930s] is the most dramatic example but not the only one. Every other major contraction in this country has been either produced by monetary disorder or greatly exacerbated by monetary disorder. Every major inflation has been produced by monetary expansion— mostly to meet the overriding demands of war which have forced the creation of money to supplement explicit taxation.

The first and most important lesson that history teaches about what monetary policy can do—and it is a lesson of the most profound importance—is that monetary policy can prevent money itself from being a major source of economic disturbance. This sounds like a negative proposition: avoid major mistakes. In part it is. The Great Contraction might not have occurred at all, and if it had, it would have been far less severe, if the monetary authority had avoided mistakes, of if the monetary arrangements had been those of an earlier time when there was no central authority with the power to make the kinds of mistakes that the Federal Reserve System made. The past few years, to come closer to home, would have been steadier and more productive of economic well-being if the Federal Reserve had avoided drastic and erratic changes of direction, first expanding the money supply at an unduly rapid pace, then, in early 1966, stepping on the brake too hard, then, at the end of 1966, reversing itself and resuming expansion until at least November, 1967, at a more rapid pace than can long be maintained without appreciable inflation.

Even if the proposition that monetary policy can prevent money itself from being a major source of economic disturbance were a wholly negative proposition, it would be none the less important for that. As it happens, however, it is not a wholly negative proposition. The monetary machine has gotten out of order even when there has been no central authority with anything like the power now possessed by the Fed. In the United States, the 1907 episode and earlier banking panics are examples of how the monetary machine can get out of order largely on its own. There is therefore a positive and important task for the monetary authority—to suggest improvements in the machine that will reduce the chances that it will get out of order, and to use its own powers so as to keep the machine in good working order.

A second thing monetary policy can do is provide a stable background for the economy—keep the machine well oiled, to continue Mill's analogy. Accomplishing the first task will contribute to this objective, but there is more to it than that. Our economic system will work best when producers and consumers, employers and employees, can proceed with full confidence that the average level of prices will behave in a known way in the future—preferably that it will be highly stable. Under any conceivable institutional arrangements, and certainly under those that now prevail in the United States, there is only a limited amount of flexibility in prices and wages. We need to conserve this flexibility to achieve changes in relative prices and wages that are required to adjust to dynamic changes in tastes and technology. We should not dissipate it simply to achieve changes in the absolute level of prices that serve no economic function.

In an earlier era, the gold standard was relied on to provide confidence in future monetary stability. In its heyday it served that function reasonably well. It clearly no longer does, since there is scarce a country in the world that is prepared to let the gold standard reign unchecked—and there are persuasive reasons why countries should not do so. The monetary authority could operate as a surrogate for the gold standard, if it pegged exchange rates and did so exclusively by altering the quantity of money in response to balance of payment flows without "sterilizing" surpluses or deficits and without resorting to open or concealed exchange control or to changes in tariffs and quotas. But again, though many central bankers talk this way, few are in fact willing to follow this course—and again there are persuasive reasons why they should not do so. Such a policy would submit each country to the vagaries not of an impersonal and automatic gold standard but of the policies—deliberate or accidental—of other monetary authorities.

In today's world, if monetary policy is to provide a stable background for the economy, it must do so by deliberately employing its powers to that end. I shall come later to how it can do so.

Finally, monetary policy can contribute to offsetting major disturbances in the economic system arising from other sources. If there is an independent secular exhilaration—as the postwar expansion was described by the proponents of secular stagnation—monetary policy can in principle help to hold it in check by a slower rate of monetary growth than would otherwise be desirable. If, as now, an explosive federal budget threatens unprecedented deficits, monetary policy can hold any inflationary dangers in check by a slower rate of monetary growth than would otherwise be desirable. This will temporarily mean higher interest rates than would otherwise prevail—to enable the government to borrow the sums needed to finance the deficit—but by preventing the speeding up of inflation, it may well mean both lower prices and lower nominal interest rates for the long pull. If the end of a substantial war offers the country an opportunity to shift resources from wartime to peacetime production, monetary policy can ease the transition by a higher rate of monetary growth than would otherwise be desirable—though experience is not very encouraging that it can do so without going too far.

I have put this point last, and stated it in qualified terms—as referring to major disturbances—because I believe that the potentiality of monetary policy in offsetting other forces making for instability is far more limited than is commonly believed. We simply do not know enough to be able to recognize minor disturbances when they occur or to be able to predict either what their effects will be with any precision or what monetary policy is required to offset their effects. We do not know enough to be able to achieve stated objectives by delicate, or even fairly coarse, changes in the mix of monetary and fiscal policy. In this area particularly the best is likely to be the enemy of the good. Experience suggests that the path of wisdom is to use monetary policy explicitly to offset other disturbances only when they offer a "clear and present danger."

HOW SHOULD MONETARY POLICY BE CONDUCTED?

How should monetary policy be conducted to make the contribution to our goals that it is capable of making? I shall restrict myself here to two major requirements for monetary policy that follow fairly directly from the preceding discussion.

The first requirement is that the monetary authority should guide itself by magnitudes that it can control, not by ones that it cannot control. If, as the authority has often done, it takes interest rates or the current unemployment percentage as the immediate criterion of policy, it will be like a space vehicle that has taken a fix on the wrong star. No matter how sensitive and sophisticated its guiding apparatus, the space vehicle will go astray. And so will the monetary authority. Of the various alternative magnitudes that it can control, the most appealing guides for policy are exchange rates, the price level as defined by some index, and the quantity of a monetary total—currency plus adjusted demand deposits, or this total plus commercial bank time deposits, or a still broader total.

For the United States, in particular, exchange rates are an undesirable guide. It might be worth requiring the bulk of the economy to adjust to the tiny percentage consisting of foreign trade if that would guarantee freedom from monetary irresponsibility—as it might under a real gold standard. But it is hardly worth doing so simply to adapt to the average of whatever policies monetary authorities in the rest of the world adopt. Far better to let the market, through floating exchange rates, adjust to world conditions the 5 percent or so of our resources devoted to international trade while reserving monetary policy to promote the effective use of the 95 percent.

Of the three guides listed, the price level is clearly the most important in its own right. Other things the same, it would be much the best of the alternatives—as so many distinguished economists have urged in the past. But other things are not the same. The link between the policy actions of the monetary authority and the price level, while unquestionably present, is more indirect than the link between the policy actions of the authority and any of the several monetary totals. Moreover, monetary action takes a longer time to affect the price level than to affect the monetary totals, and both the time lag and the magnitude of effect vary with circumstances. As a result, we cannot predict at all accurately just what effect a particular monetary action will have on the price level and, equally important, just when it will have that effect. Attempting to control directly the price level is therefore likely to make monetary policy itself a source of economic disturbance because of false stops and starts. Perhaps, as our understanding of monetary phenomena advances, the situation will change. But at the present stage of our understanding, the long way around seems the surer way to our objective. Accordingly, I believe that a monetary total is the best currently available immediate guide or criterion for monetary policy—and I believe that it matters much less which particular total is chosen than that one be chosen.

A second requirement for monetary policy is that the monetary authority avoid sharp swings in policy. In the past, monetary authorities have on occasion moved in the wrong direction —as in the episode of the Great Contraction that I have stressed. More frequently, they have moved in the right direction, albeit often too late, but have erred by moving too far. Too late and too much has been the general practice. For example, in early 1966, it was the right policy for the Federal Reserve to move in a less expansionary direction—though it should have done so at least a year earlier. But when it moved, it went too far, producing the sharpest change in the rate of monetary growth of the post-war era. Again, having gone too far, it was the right policy for the Fed to reverse course at the end of 1966. But again it went too far, not only restoring but exceeding the earlier excessive rate of monetary growth. And this episode is no exception. Time and again this has been the course followed—as in 1919 and 1920, in 1937 and 1938, in 1953 and 1954, in 1959 and 1960.

The reason for the propensity to overreact seems clear: the failure of monetary authorities to allow for the delay between their actions and the subsequent effects on the economy. They tend to determine their actions by today's conditions—but their actions will affect the economy only six or nine or twelve or fifteen months later. Hence they feel impelled to step on the brake, or the accelerator, as the case may be, too hard.

My own prescription is still that the monetary authority go all the way in avoiding such swings by adopting publicly the policy of achieving a steady rate of growth in a specified monetary total. The precise rate of growth, like the precise monetary total, is less important than the adoption of some stated and known rate. I myself have argued for a rate that would on the average achieve rough stability in the level of prices of final products, which I have estimated would call for something like a 3 to 5 percent per year rate of growth in currency plus all commercial bank deposits or a slightly lower rate of growth in currency plus demand deposits only. But it would be better to have a fixed rate that would on the average produce moderate inflation or moderate deflation, provided it was steady, than to suffer the wide and erratic perturbations we have experienced.

Short of the adoption of such a publicly stated policy of a steady rate of monetary growth, it would constitute a major improvement if the monetary authority followed the self-denying ordinance of avoiding wide swings. It is a matter of record that periods of relative stability in the rate of monetary growth have also been periods of relative stability in economic activity, both in the United States and other countries. Periods of wide swings in the rate of monetary growth have also been periods of wide swings in economic activity.

By setting itself a steady course and keeping to it, the monetary authority could make a major contribution to promoting economic stability. By making that course one of steady but moderate growth in the quantity of money, it would make a major contribution to avoidance of either inflation or deflation of prices. Other forces would still affect the economy, require change and adjustment, and disturb the even tenor of our ways. But steady monetary growth would provide a monetary climate favorable to the effective operation of those basic forces of enterprise, ingenuity, invention, hard work, and thrift that are the true springs of economic growth. That is the most that we can ask from monetary policy at our present stage of knowledge. But that much—and it is a great deal—is clearly within our reach.

Doubts About Monetarism

WALTER W. HELLER

Walter Heller, Regents' Professor of Economics at the University of Minnesota, was Chairman of the Council of Economic Advisers in 1961–1964. He expressed his skepticism about monetarism in a debate with Professor Friedman that was subsequently published as Friedman and Heller, Monetary vs. Fiscal Policy *(1969).*

LET ME REVIEW WITH YOU the factors that say "stop, look, and listen" before embracing the triple doctrine that only money matters much; that control of the money supply is the key to economic stability; and that a rigid fixed-throttle expansion of 4 or 5 percent a year is the only safe policy prescription in a world of alleged economic ignorance and human weakness and folly. . . .

I group doubts, unresolved questions, and unconvincing evidence into eight conditions that must be satisfied—if not completely, at least more convincingly than they have been to date —before we can even consider giving money supply sovereignty, or dominance, or greater prominence in economic policy. These conditions center on such questions as: Which money-supply indicator do you believe? Can one read enough from money supply without weighing also shifts in demand and interest rates—that is, don't both quantity *and* price of money count? Don't observed variations in monetary time lags and velocity cast serious doubt on any simple relation between money supply and GNP? Can a rigid monetary rule find happiness in a world beset with rigidities and rather limited adjustment capabilities? That is, is the rigid Friedman rule perhaps a formula made in heaven, that will work only in heaven?

The first condition is this: The monetarists must make up their minds which money-supply variable they want us to accept as our guiding star—M_1, the narrow money supply, just currency and bank deposits; M_2, adding time deposits; or perhaps some other measure like the "monetary base?" And when will the monetarists decide? Perhaps Milton Friedman has decided; but if he has, his disciples do not seem to have gotten the word.

Let me give you an example. Last spring [1968] M_1 (the money stock) was all the rage. It spurted for four months in a row, from April through July. But when that slowed down, most of the alarmists switched horses to M_2 (money plus time deposits), which quite conveniently began rising sharply in July. And listen to the latest release from the St. Louis Federal Reserve Bank—the unofficial statistical arm of the Chicago School —which very carefully throws a sop to all sides: "Monetary expansion since July has decelerated as measured by the money stock, accelerated as measured by money plus time deposits, and remained at about an unchanged rate as measured by the monetary base. As a result, questions arise as to which monetary aggregate may be currently most meaningful in indicating monetary influence on economic activity." Precisely.

It doesn't seem too much to ask that this confusion be resolved in some satisfactory way before putting great faith in money supply as our key policy variable.

Second, I would feel more sympathetic to the money-supply doctrine if it were not so one-track-minded about money stock —measured any way you wish—as the *only* financial variable with any informational content for policy purposes.

As Lyle Gramley has noted, for example, if we look at money stock alone for 1948, it would indicate the tightest money in the post-war period. Yet, the rate on Treasury bills was 1 percent, and on high-grade corporates 2¾ percent. But isn't it curious that we had tight money by the money-supply standard side by side with 1, 2, and 3 percent interest rates? We were swamped with liquidity—so interest rates do seem to have been telling us something very important.

Or, if we look at 1967 *only* in terms of the money stock, it would appear as the easiest-money year since World War II. M_1 was up 6 percent, M_2 was up 12 percent. Yet there was a very sharp rise in interest rates. Why? Probably because of a big shift in liquidity preference as corporations strove to build up their protective liquidity cushions after their harrowing experience the previous year—their monetary dehydration in the credit crunch of 1966. Again, the behavior of interest rates is vital to proper interpretation of monetary developments and guidance of monetary policy. Interest rates are endogenous variables and cannot be used alone—but neither can money stock. Either interest rates or money stock, used alone, could seriously mislead us.

I really don't understand how the scarcity of any commodity can be gauged without referring to its price—or, more specifically, how the scarcity of money can be gauged without referring to interest rates. It may, strictly speaking, be wrong to identify any market interest rate as the price of money. In the United States, no interest is paid either on demand deposits or on currency. But this is quibbling. The point is that a change in the demand for money relative to the supply, or a change in the supply relative to demand, results generally in a change in interest rates. To insist that the behavior of the price of money (interest rates) conveys no information about its scarcity is, as James Tobin has noted, an "odd heresy."

Third, given the fluctuations in money velocity, that supposedly inexorable link between money and economic activity has yet to be established. We should not forget this, however sweet the siren song of the monetarists may sound. We should not forget the revealing passage from that monumental Friedman-Schwartz volume, A Monetary History of the United States, that makes my point:

. . . the observed year-to-year change in velocity was less than 10 percent in 78 out of 91 year-to-year changes from 1869, when our velocity figures start, to 1960. Of the 13 larger changes, more than half came during either the Great Contraction or the two world wars, and the largest change was 17 percent. Expressed as a percentage of a secular trend, velocity was within the range of 90 to 110 in 53 years, 85 to 115 in 66 years. Of the remaining 26 years, 12 were during the first 15 years, for which the income figures are seriously defective, and 17 during the Great Contraction and the two wars.[1]

Clearly, velocity has varied over time—some might say "greatly," others "moderately." Let me sidestep a bit and say, for

1. Milton Friedman and Anna Jacobson Schwartz, A Monetary History of the United States: 1867–1960 (Princeton, N.J.: Princeton University Press, 1963), p. 682.

purposes of this discussion, "significantly." For I would remind you that the income velocity of money rose roughly 28 percent during the 1960–68 period. Had velocity been the same in 1968 as it was in 1960, nominal GNP would have been not some $860 billion, but only $675 billion.

What Friedman and Schwartz report, then, about the behavior of velocity suggests that there are other factors—strangely, such fiscal actions as tax cuts or budget changes come to mind —that influence the level of economic activity. Velocity has changed, as it were, to accommodate these other influences and will go on doing so, I have no doubt, in the future.

The observed changes in velocity underscore the broader point I was hinting at a moment ago: The Friedman-Schwartz study did not find anything like a near-perfect correlation—a rigid link—between money and economic activity. And such correlation as they did find was based on complex and often quite arbitrary adjustments of their raw data. It was Tobin who noted that the regularities which Professor Friedman claims to have detected in his data are quite esoteric!

This reminds us again that Friedman and Schwartz use an incomplete model of the U. S. economy in testing the potency of money supply. Perhaps, had they used a more complete model, they might have found not only less potency but greater precision in the effects of changes in the money supply (and hence, by the way, less need for a rigid monetary rule). Before succumbing to their massive and impressive array of data, observers in general and policy makers in particular should be clear that the Friedman-Schwartz findings neither prove that "only money matters much" nor disprove that fiscal policy matters a great deal.

Fourth, it would help us if the monetarists could narrow the range on *when* money matters. How long *are* the lags that have to be taken into account in managing monetary policy? Here, I quote from Professor Friedman's tour de force, *A Program for Monetary Stability:*

In the National Bureau study on which I have been collaborating with Mrs. Schwartz we found that, on the average of 18 cycles, peaks in the rate of change in the stock of money tend to precede peaks in general business by about 16 months and troughs in the rate of change in the stock of money to precede troughs in general business by about 12 months. . . . For individual cycles, the recorded lag has varied between 6 and 29 months at peaks and between 4 and 22 months at troughs.[2]

So the Friedman-Schwartz study found a long average lag, and just as important it would seem, a highly variable lag. But why this considerable variance? No doubt there are several possible answers. But again, the most natural one is that the level of economic activity, or total demand for the nation's output, is influenced by variables other than the stock of money—possibly even by tax rates and federal spending and transfer payments!

Suppose I told you that I had checked and found that in repeated trials, it required from 100 to 300 feet for a car going so and so many miles an hour to stop. That is quite a range. But would you be surprised? I think not. You would simply remind me that the distance it takes a car to stop depends, among other things, on the condition of the road surface. If I had allowed for the condition of the road surface, I would not have ended up with such a wide range of stopping distances.

Just so. If Professor Friedman and Mrs. Schwartz had taken account of other variables that influence total demand, or if they had estimated the lag of monetary policy using a complete model of the U. S. economy, they would not have found the lag of monetary policy to be quite so variable. Again, then, one correctly infers that their findings are quite consistent with fiscal policy mattering, and mattering a great deal. Nor is it necessarily relevant, as some have suggested, that in the middle of the nineteenth century, the government sector was relatively small. Variables other than changes in tax rates and government expenditures and transfers can "distort" the money-income lag.

Professor Friedman has also used this finding of (a) a long average lag and (b) a highly variable lag in support of his plea for steady growth of the money supply. With so long an average lag, the argument goes, forecasters are helpless; they cannot see twelve or fifteen months into the future with any accuracy. And even if they could, they would be at a loss to know how far ahead

2. Milton Friedman, *A Program for Monetary Stability* (New York: Fordham University Press, 1959), p. 87.

to appraise the economic outlook. But I doubt that he can properly draw this inference from his finding of a long and highly variable lag.

It seems to me misleading to estimate a discrete lag as the Friedman-Schwartz team did. It's reasonable to suppose, given the research findings of other investigators, that the effect of a change in monetary policy cumulates through time. To begin, there's a slight effect; and as time passes, the effect becomes more pronounced. But insofar as the feasibility of discretionary monetary policy is at issue, what matters *most* is whether there is some near-term effect. If there is, then the Federal Reserve can influence the economy one quarter or two quarters from now. That there are subsequent, more pronounced, effects is not the key question. These subsequent effects get caught, as it were, in subsequent forecasts of the economic outlook, and current policy is adjusted accordingly. At least this is what happens in a non-Friedmanic world where one enjoys the benefits of discretionary policy changes.

Lest I leave any doubt about what I infer from this: If there is a near-immediate effect from a change in policy, then discretionary monetary policy does not impose an unbearable burden on forecasters. For six or nine months ahead, they can do reasonably well. But given the too-discreet way Friedman-Schwartz went about estimating the lag of monetary policy, I see no way of determining the shape of the monetary policy lag. Until they know more about the shape of this lag, I don't see how they can insist on a monetary rule.

Fifth, I'd be happier if only I knew which of the two Friedmans to believe. Should it be the Friedman we have had in focus here—the Friedman of the close causal relationship between money supply and income, who sees changes in money balances worked off gradually, with long lags before interest rates, prices of financial and physical assets, and, eventually, investment and consumption spending are affected? Or should it be the Friedman of the "permanent-income hypothesis," who sees the demand for money as quite unresponsive to changes in current income (since current income has only a fractional weight in permanent income), with the implied result that the monetary multiplier is very large in the short run, that there is an immediate and strong response to a change in the money stock? As Tobin has noted, he can't have it both ways. But which is it to be?

Sixth, if Milton's policy prescription were made in a frictionless Friedmanesque world without price, wage, and exchange rigidities—a world of his own making—it would be more admissible. But in the imperfect world in which we actually operate, beset by all sorts of rigidities, the introduction of his fixed-throttle money-supply rule might, in fact, be destabilizing. Or it could condemn us to long periods of economic slack or inflation as the slow adjustment processes in wages and prices, given strong market power, delayed the economy's reaction to the monetary rule while policy makers stood helplessly by.

A seventh, and closely related, concern is that locking the money supply into a rigid rule would jeopardize the U.S. international position. It's quite clear that capital flows are interest-rate sensitive. Indeed, capital flows induced by interest-rate changes can increase alarmingly when speculators take over. Under the Friedman rule, market interest rates would be whatever they turned out to be. It would be beyond the pale for the Fed to adjust interest rates for balance-of-payments adjustment purposes. Nor is it clear that by operating in the market for forward exchange (which in any event Milton would presumably oppose) the system could altogether neutralize changes in domestic market rates.

Milton has heard all of this before, and he always has an answer—flexible exchange rates. Yet, suffice it to note that however vital they are to the workings of his money-supply peg, floating exchange rates are not just around the corner.

Eighth, and finally, if the monetarists showed some small willingness to recognize the impact of fiscal policy—which has played such a large role in the policy thinking and action underlying the great expansion of the 1960s—one might be a little more sympathetic to their views. This point is, I must admit, not so much a condition as a plea for symmetry. The "new economists," having already given important and increasing weight to monetary factors in their policy models, are still waiting for signs that the monetarists will admit fiscal factors to theirs.

The 1964 tax cut pointedly illustrates what I mean. While the "new economists" fully recognize the important role monetary policy played in facilitating the success of the tax cut, the monetarists go to elaborate lengths to "prove" that the tax cut—which came close to removing a $13 billion full-employment surplus that was overburdening and retarding the economy—had nothing to do with the 1964–65 expansion. Money-supply growth did it all. Apparently, we were just playing fiscal tiddlywinks in Washington.

It seems to me that the cause of balanced analysis and rational policy would be served by redirecting some of the brilliance of Friedman and his followers from (a) single-minded devotion to the money-supply thesis and unceasing efforts to discredit fiscal policy and indeed all discretionary policy to (b) joint efforts to develop a more complete and satisfactory model of how the real world works; ascertain why it is working far better today than it did before active and conscious fiscal-monetary policy came into play; and determine how such policy can be improved to make it work even better in the future.

In a related asymmetry, as I've already suggested in passing, some Friedmanites fail to recognize that if fiscal policy actions like the 1964 tax cut can do no good, then fiscal policy actions like the big budget increases and deficits associated with Vietnam can also do no harm. Again, they should recognize that they can't have it both ways.

Now, one could lengthen and elaborate this list. But enough—let's just round it off this way: If Milton Friedman were saying that (as part of an active discretionary policy) we had better keep a closer eye on that important variable, money supply, in one or more of its several incarnations—I would say well and good, by all means. If the manifold doubts can be reasonably resolved, let's remedy any neglect or underemphasis of money supply as a policy indicator relative to interest rates, free reserves, and the like. But let's not lock the steering gear into place, knowing full well of the twists and turns in the road ahead. That's an invitation to chaos.

Suppose for a moment that a conservative president, heeding—as indeed the Republican candidate seemed to in 1964—the counsel of the monetarists, (a) persuaded the Federal Reserve

Board to set monetary policy on a rigid path of 4 or 5 percent annual increases in monetary supply, and (b) persuaded the Congress to freeze tax policy into a pattern of once-a-year income tax cuts.

With the controls thus locked into place—I started to say, "with the controls thus on automatic pilot," but that's the wrong figure of speech because the automatic pilot adjusts for changes in the wind and other atmospheric conditions—one can imagine what would happen when the economy encountered the turbulence of recession with its downdrafts in jobs, profits, and incomes. How long could Richard Nixon, for example, stand idly by and deny himself and the country the proven tonic of tax cuts, spending speedups, and easier money? Economic common sense and political sagacity—and he has both—would soon win out, I am sure, over the rigid and static rules that so ill befit an ever changing and dynamic economy. So as a practical matter, I don't expect the country to fall into the trap of lockstep economics in the Nixon Administration or any other administration of the foreseeable future. I fully expect the new administration to practice active discretionary fiscal and monetary policy.

This may put me, I realize, in the strange position of defending the Nixon Administration against one of its own advisors. But, as the lady psychiatrist at a convention of psychiatrists said to herself when she was about to slap a male colleague sitting next to her who was taking certain liberties—"Why should I? That's *his* problem!"

Some Issues of Monetary Policy

COUNCIL OF ECONOMIC ADVISERS

This Keynesian discussion of the channels and impacts of monetary policy was included in the 1969 Annual Report of the Council of Economic Advisers which then consisted of Arthur M. Okun, Chairman; Merton J. Peck; and Warren L. Smith.

THE RECORD OF the past eight years demonstrates that flexible, discretionary monetary policy can make an effective contribution to economic stabilization. The economy's gradual return to full productive potential in the early 1960s was partly attributable to a monetary policy which kept ample supplies of credit readily available at generally stable interest rates. And in early 1967, the prompt recovery of homebuilding after the 1966 slowdown was the direct result of timely and aggressive easing of credit conditions by the Federal Reserve.

The most dramatic demonstration of the effectiveness of monetary policy came in 1966, however, when a dangerously inflationary situation was curbed primarily by a drastic application of monetary restraint. Credit-financed expenditures at the end of that year appear to have been as much as $8 billion below what they might have been had monetary policy maintained the accommodative posture of the preceding five years. And there were substantial further "multiplier" effects on GNP as these initial impacts reduced income and consumption spending.

THE CONDUCT OF MONETARY POLICY

The primary guides for monetary policy are the various broad measures of economic performance, including the growth rate of total output, the relation of actual to potential output, employment and unemployment, the behavior of prices, and the nation's balance-of-payments position. Extensive research, together with the experience of the last few years, has increased our knowledge of the complex process by which monetary policy influences these measures. While there are still major gaps in our knowledge of the precise chain of causation, some conclusions seem well established.

Like fiscal policy, monetary policy affects economic activity only after some lag. Thus actions by the Federal Reserve must be forward-looking. In considering the prospects ahead, however, an assessment must be made of both the expected behavior of the private sector and of the likely future course of fiscal policy. As noted earlier, the inherent flexibility in the administration of monetary policy permits frequent policy adjustments to take account of unexpected developments in either the private or the public sector.

Sectoral Impacts · Monetary policy can affect spending through a number of channels. To some extent it works by changing the terms of lending, including interest rates, maturities of loans, downpayments, and the like, in such a way as to encourage or discourage expenditures on goods financed by credit. There may also be market imperfections or legal constraints and institutional rigidities that change the "availability" of loans as monetary conditions change—that is, make it easier or more difficult for borrowers to obtain credit at given terms of lending. Under some circumstances, purchasers of goods and services may finance their expenditures by liquidating financial assets, and changes in the yields on these assets produced by a change in monetary policy may affect their willingness to engage in such transactions. Changes in monetary policy may also, on occasion, change the expectations of borrowers, lenders, and spenders in ways that affect economic conditions, although these expectational effects are rather complex and dependent upon the conditions existing at the time policy is changed.

Monetary policy affects some types of expenditures more than others. The extent of the impact depends not only on the economic characteristics of the activity being financed but, in many instances, on the channels through which financing is obtained and the legal and institutional arrangements surrounding the financing procedures.

The sector of the economy most affected by monetary policy is residential construction. Although the demand for housing—and for mortgage credit—does not appear to be especially responsive to mortgage interest rates, the supply of mortgage funds is quite sensitive to several interest rate relationships.

The experience of 1966 clearly demonstrated how rising interest rates can sharply affect flows of deposits to banks and other thrift institutions and thereby severely limit their ability to make new mortgage loans. In the first half of that year, the net deposit gain at savings and loan associations and mutual savings banks was only half as large as in the preceding six months. These institutions could not afford to raise the rates paid on savings capital to compete with the higher rates available to savers at banks and elsewhere because of their earnings situation—with their assets concentrated in mortgages that earned only the relatively low rates of return characteristic of several years earlier. Commercial banks experienced a similarly sharp slowing in growth of time deposits in the second half of the year, as the Federal Reserve's Regulation Q prevented them from competing effectively for liquid funds. This forced banks to make across-the-board cuts in lending operations. . . . Savings and loan associations and mutual savings banks together supplied less than 10 percent of total funds borrowed in 1966, well below their 22 percent share in the preceding five years. This was the main factor limiting the availability of household mortgage loans. The effect on homebuilding was quick and dramatic, as the seasonally adjusted volume of new housing units started fell by nearly half between December 1965 and October 1966.

In 1967, as interest rates in the open market retreated from their 1966 highs, the thrift institutions were able to regain their competitive position in the savings market. A good part of their funds was fairly quickly channeled into the mortgage market. By fall, housing starts had recovered nearly to the level of late 1965. Many factors—including several significant institutional reforms, sharply improved liquidity positions, and the widespread expectation that monetary restraint was only temporary pending passage of the tax bill—helped to moderate the adverse effects of renewed monetary restraint on mortgage lending in

1968. But the thrift institutions again experienced some slowing of deposit inflows when market interest rates rose to new heights, and mutual savings banks switched a good part of their investments away from the mortgage market to high-yielding corporate bonds.

State and local governments also felt the effects of monetary restraint in 1966. These governments cut back or postponed more than $2.9 billion, or nearly 25 percent, of their planned bond issues that year.

It is difficult to determine precisely what caused these postponements. In cases involving more than half the dollar volume, the reasons given related to the prevailing high level of interest rates. In some instances, the interest costs simply exceeded the legal ceiling governments were permitted to pay for borrowed funds. In other cases, finance officers decided to delay bond issues for a few months in the expectation that interest rates would decline.

This sizable cutback in borrowings had a relatively small effect on state and local government expenditures. Larger governments apparently were able to continue most of their projects about as scheduled by drawing down liquid assets or borrowing temporarily at short term. Smaller governmental units, however, cut their contract awards by a total estimated at more than $400 million.

Because of the problems state and local governments often face in raising funds, the Administration is proposing the establishment of an Urban Development Bank, which could borrow economically in the open market and then lend in the amounts needed to individual local governments. The Bank could lend at federally subsidized interest rates, with the federal government recovering the cost of the subsidy through taxation of the interest income earned by holders of the Bank's securities.

The 1966 credit squeeze undoubtedly also had some effects on business and consumer spending, though the amount of impact is not easily determinable. Most theoretical and empirical studies find that business firms in some way balance the cost of borrowed capital against the expected returns from their capital projects. Some small firms may also simply not be able to obtain funds during tight money periods. In 1966, bank lending to business did slow sharply during the second half of the year. Many of the larger firms shifted their demands to the open market—and paid record high interest rates for their funds— but some of the smaller ones probably were forced to postpone their projects.

Household spending on durable goods—particularly automobiles—has been shown to be affected by changes in the cost and availability of consumer credit, as reflected in the interest rate, maturity, downpayment, and other terms. While it is difficult to sort out cause and effect, households borrowed only two-thirds as much through consumer credit in the second half of 1966 as in the preceding half year. Capital gains or losses on asset holdings accompanying changes in yields may also induce consumers to spend more or less on goods and services.

Active and Passive Elements · Monetary policy, like fiscal policy, has what might be termed active and passive components. Recognition of this distinction played an important role in formulating the accommodative policy of the early 1960s. In the 1950s, economic expansion had generally been accompanied by rising interest rates, which tended to produce an automatic stabilizing effect somewhat similar to the fiscal drag of the federal tax system. The large amounts of underutilized resources available in the early 1960s made such restraint inappropriate, and credit was expanded sufficiently to prevent it from occurring.

It is especially important to distinguish between these elements in monetary policy at cyclical turning points. If, for example, private demand weakens and causes a decline in economic activity, interest rates will generally fall as credit demands slacken, even without any positive action by the Federal Reserve to push rates down. This induced fall in interest rates can help to check the decline in economic activity but may not, by itself, induce recovery. Similarly, as the economy rises above potential, the induced rise in interest rates may only moderate the expansion but may not bring activity back into line with capacity.

An active monetary policy during such periods requires positive effort by the Federal Reserve to produce further changes in interest rates and in availability of credit beyond those that would occur automatically. Since expectational responses may either accentuate or moderate the effects of the initial action, it is sometimes difficult to know in advance precisely how much of a policy change is needed. But the main point is clear—at such turning points, interest rate movements alone are not likely to provide an accurate reflection of the contribution of monetary policy to economic stabilization. Careful attention must also be paid to credit flows, particularly those to the private sector of the economy.

MONETARY POLICY AND THE MONEY SUPPLY

Examination of the linkages between monetary policy and various categories of expenditures suggests that, in the formulation of monetary policy, careful attention should be paid to interest rates and credit availability as influenced by and associated with the flows of deposits and credit to different types of financial institutions and spending units. Among the financial flows generally considered to be relevant are: the total of funds raised by nonfinancial sectors of the economy, the credit supplied by commercial banks, the net amount of new mortgage credit, the net change in the public's holdings of liquid assets, changes in time deposits at banks and other thrift institutions, and changes in the money supply. Some consideration should be given to all of these financial flows as well as to related interest rates in formulating any comprehensive policy program or analysis of financial conditions.

Much public attention has recently been focused on an alternative view, however, emphasizing the money supply as the most important—sometimes the only—link between monetary policy and economic activity. This emphasis has often been accompanied by the suggestion that the Federal Reserve can best contribute to economic stabilization by maintaining growth in the stock of money at a particular rate—or somewhat less rigidly, by keeping variations in the rate of growth of the money stock within a fairly narrow band.

There are, of course, numerous variants of the money view of monetary policy. The discussion below focuses only on the simple version that has captured most of the public attention.

Money and Interest Rates · In a purely theoretical world, abstracting from institutional rigidities that exist in our financial system and assuming that relationships among financial variables were unvarying and predictable, it would make little difference whether monetary policy were formulated in terms of interest rates or the money supply. The two variables are inversely related, and the alternative approaches would represent nothing more than different paths to precisely the same result. The monetary authorities could seek to control the money stock, with interest rates allowed to take on whatever values happen to result. Or alternatively, they could focus on achieving the interest rates that would facilitate the credit flows needed to finance the desired level of activity, allowing the quantity of money to be whatever it had to be.

But financial rigidities do exist that often distort flows of credit in response to swings in interest rates. And financial relationships have changed steadily and significantly. Just since 1961, several important new financial instruments have been introduced and developed, including negotiable time certificates of deposit and Euro-dollar deposits. Attitudes of both investors and lenders have also undergone marked shifts, with sharp variations in the public's demand for liquidity superimposed on an underlying trend toward greater sensitivity to interest rates.

There is, to be sure, enough of a link between money and interest rates at any given time to make it impossible for the Federal Reserve to regulate the two independently. But this linkage is hardly simple, and it varies considerably and unpredictably over time. The choice between controlling the stock of money solely and focusing on interest rates, credit availability, and a number of credit flows can therefore make a difference. This choice should be based on a judgment—supported insofar as possible by empirical and analytical evidence—as to whether it is money holdings alone that influence the decisions of various categories of spending units.

Money and Asset Portfolios · The Federal Reserve conducts

monetary policy primarily by expanding and contracting the supply of cash reserves available to the banking system. Such actions seek to induce an expansion or contraction in loans and investments at financial institutions, with corresponding changes in the public's holdings of currency and deposits of various kinds. The proportions in which the public chooses to hold alternative types of financial assets depend upon a complex set of preferences, which, in turn, depend upon interest rate relationships.

The process of expansion and contraction of money and credit stemming from Federal Reserve actions is fairly complex. But one aspect of it should be clearly understood: The money so created is not something given to the public for nothing as if it fell from heaven—that is, it is not a net addition to the public's wealth or net worth. There can be an immediate change in public wealth, but only to the extent that changes in interest rates generate capital gains or losses on existing assets.

Any change in the money stock is associated with a change in the composition of the public's balance sheet, as people and institutions are induced to exchange—at a price—one asset for another or to increase (or decrease) both their assets and their liabilities by equal amounts. Since all the items in the public's balance sheet might be changed as a result of these compositional shifts, the change in the public's liquidity is not likely to be summarized adequately in terms of any single category of financial assets.

It is, of course, possible that decisions to spend on goods and services are affected more by the presence of one type of financial asset than another in a spending unit's portfolio. But there is only scattered evidence of such behavior in various sectoral studies that have been undertaken to analyze the factors affecting the spending decisions of consumers, business, or state and local governments. Indeed, to the extent these studies do find spending decisions systematically affected by financial variables, it is often through changes in interest rates and availability of credit.

Money and Income and a Monetary Rule · One problem with the money supply as a guide to monetary policy is that there is no agreement concerning the appropriate definition of "money."

One definition includes the total of currency outside commercial banks plus privately held demand deposits. A second also includes time deposits at commercial banks, and even more inclusive alternatives are sometimes used. On the other hand, there is a more limited definition, sometimes called "high-powered money" or "monetary base," which includes currency in circulation and member-bank reserve balances at the Federal Reserve banks.

These different concepts of money do not always move in parallel with one another—even over fairly extended periods. Thus assertions that the money supply is expanding rapidly or slowly often depend critically on which definition is employed. In the first half of 1968, for example, there was a sharp acceleration in the growth of currency plus demand deposits, but growth of this total plus time deposits slowed considerably.

On the other hand, relationships between movements in GNP and any of the money concepts have been close enough on the average—especially when processed through complex lags and other sophisticated statistical techniques—to be difficult to pass off lightly.

There is, of course, good reason to expect some fairly close relationship between money and income. This would be true even in a completely abstract situation in which it was assumed that the money supply per se had no direct influence on GNP, and that monetary policy worked entirely through interest rates. Since interest rates and the money supply are inversely related, any rise in GNP produced by a reduction in interest rates and increased credit availability would be accompanied by at least some increase in the money supply.

The relationship also exists in a sort of "reverse causation" form—that is, as income goes up so does the demand for money, which the Federal Reserve then accommodates by allowing an increase in the actual money stock. This is precisely what happened during the 1961–65 period of accommodative policy, and it is always present to some extent as the Federal Reserve acts to meet the economy's changing credit needs. The problem of sorting out the extent of causation in the two directions still challenges economic researchers.

A one-sided interpretation of these relationships is sometimes used to support the suggestion that the Federal Reserve conduct policy on the basis of some fixed, predetermined guideline for growth of the money supply (however defined). Given the complex role of interest rates in affecting various demand categories and the likely variations in so many other factors, any such simple policy guide could prove to be quite unreliable.

The experience of the past several years illustrates the kind of difficulties that might be encountered in using the money supply (defined here as currency plus demand deposits) as the exclusive guide for monetary policy. As described previously, high interest rates in 1966 began affecting the nonbank thrift institutions, the mortgage market, and the homebuilding industry soon after the start of the year. But during the first four months of that year, the money supply grew at an annual rate of nearly 6½ percent, well above the long-term trend. Later that year, the financial situation of major mortgage lenders improved somewhat and housing eventually rebounded despite the fact that growth of money supply plus bank time deposits was proceeding at only a snail's pace.

Growth of the money supply in the second quarter of 1968 was at an annual rate of 9 percent. The reasons for this acceleration—to a rate almost double the growth in the preceding quarter—are not fully apparent. The Federal Reserve could have resisted this sizable increase in the demand for money more than it did, but interest rates in the open market would then have risen well above the peaks that were in fact reached in May. Whether still higher rates would have been desirable is another issue, which cannot be settled merely by citing the rapid growth of the money supply.

These illustrations suggest that any simple rigid rule related to the growth of the money supply (however defined) can unduly confine Federal Reserve policy. In formulating monetary policy, the Federal Reserve must be able to take account of all types of financial relationships currently prevailing and in prospect and be able to respond flexibly as changing economic needs arise. In deciding on such responses, careful consideration must be given to likely changes in interest rates and credit availability, in view of the effects of these factors on particular sectors of the economy—especially the homebuilding industry.

A Rule for Monetary Policy?

This middle-of-the-road position on the possible uses and dangers of a monetary rule was set forth in an article in Deutsche Bank Studies (1969).

A NEW FAITH, not to say religion, is gaining converts among practitioners and students of American monetary policy. It holds that the central bank should look at the money supply, not at interest rates. The central bank should increase the money supply at a stable rate, commensurate with the growth rate of the economy. Policy makers should not be deflected from that objective by fluctuations in the economy seeming to call for correction. By doing so, i.e., by abdicating as policy-makers, they will produce a better monetary policy than by using their judgment.

PROGRESS OF THE "RULE"

This unflattering theory has already obtained adherence of the United States Congress, where both the majority and the minority of the Joint Economic Committee have endorsed a version of it. The Federal Reserve has been called upon by the Committee to appear before it whenever the rate of money growth has gone above 6 percent or below 2 percent. The Federal Reserve has agreed to appear and explain.

The Federal Reserve, a many-headed and multi-tongued institution, still is predominantly skeptical, in some cases violently so. But the Federal Reserve Bank of St. Louis is a firm devotee, and its monthly bulletin has captured top readership interest among Federal Reserve System publications. The Bank also supplies data on money supply growth. Thanks to its generous mailing list, everybody can and many people do now know the exact growth rate of money during any recent period. The

Bank gently lampoons official Federal Reserve policy in its reports. Its own version of policy, known within the Federal Reserve Board's marble halls as "brand X" is strictly according to the Rule.

Many academic and some business economists have taken up the new doctrine with greater or lesser seriousness. The chairman of the President's Council of Economic Advisers admits to some sympathy for it. In the light of the very unstable policies followed by the Federal Reserve in recent years, even very differently oriented economists find it hard, in their speeches, to forego some reference to the need for a stabler policy line. The new doctrine has initiated the greatest upheaval in economic policy since the Keynesian Revolution of the 1930s. It is less profound analytically, and also less novel, because its intellectual foundation, the quantity theory of money, has long been known. But it bids fair to engender a similar amount of debate and acrimony. Orthodox Keynesians had believed to have firmly buried the quantity theory. Its revival comes as a shock. The quantity theory's reincarnation is now polarizing into militant Keynesians and anti-Keynesians members of a profession that not long ago believed Keynes to have been well absorbed into history. Evidently they were wrong.

The Philosophy · The principal author of the new doctrine, as everybody knows, is Professor Milton Friedman of Chicago. If his views continue to gain acceptance at their present rate, he will undoubtedly be the most influential shaper of policy since Keynes. In contrast to Keynes, Friedman's views rest not upon abstract reasoning, but upon a large body of historical and quantitative research. Before examining the doctrine in greater detail, however, something needs to be said about the philosophical framework within which it is placed.

Professor Friedman's thought is in the "Chicago tradition," which advocates the rule of law rather than of men. It is essentially a *laissez-faire* tradition, although with some left-wing variants. This Chicago faith in free markets provides another point of conflict with Keynesians who, sometimes for reasons unrelated to Keynesian analysis, lean toward more controls. The affinity between the quantity theory of money and *laissez-faire* on one side, and Keynesianism, government intervention, and preference for a large public sector on the other is not always traceable to the undetached eye, but it clearly exists. Thus, it was undoubtedly gratifying to Professor Friedman that his empirical researches tended to support his philosophical position.

While advocating the widest possible scope for free markets, including schools and the post office, Friedman nevertheless believes that the monetary system must be regulated by government. This follows from the fact that private business, e.g., banks, if allowed to produce paper money without restraint, would overproduce it. But painful need for government intervention can be minimized if the central bank's discretion in creating money can be limited. If government intervention in money cannot be avoided, let it be according to rule. Then markets can adjust, everybody knows what he is at, and government power is curbed. That is the core of the philosophy. . . .

The Lag of Monetary Policy · The quantity theory is not a sufficient basis for the stable money growth rule. At first sight, in fact, it seems to provide grounds for giving *carte blanche* to the central bank. If the central bank can closely influence economic activity by varying the quantity of money, why not let it do so anticyclically? To expand the money supply in recessions, to reduce it or curb its growth in expansions, would seem to be the prescription for stability.

To make a case for a money growth rule, stable through thick and thin, one further premise is needed. Professor Friedman has found that changes in the growth rate of the money supply lead economic activity with a long interval. In the United States, the time distance between peaks in the rate of money growth and peaks in economic activity has ranged from 13 to 24 months, averaging 16 months. Between troughs in money growth and economic activity, the range has been 5–21 months, averaging 12 months.

This means, in effect, that monetary policy works with a long lag. To be well timed, action against recession, for instance, would have to be taken over a year ahead. Even then the instability of the lag makes the impact uncertain. If a central bank acts, not on a one year forecast, but on the current facts, the effects may be felt under totally changed conditions. Restraint exerted to curb a boom may become effective only after the economy has gone into recession. If the swings of the business cycle are relatively short, as they were during the 1950s, monetary policy almost inevitably will act out of phase, aggravating downturns and intensifying upswings.

To operate on a forecast of a year ahead or more, everybody would agree, is out of the question for central banks. There is no such visibility. Ergo, monetary policy is useless for cyclical stabilization. The best it can do is to contribute to long term stability. This can be accomplished by ignoring cycles and ploughing ahead with a stable rate of monetary expansion in keeping with the long-run monetary needs of the economy.

It will be noted that two propositions are involved in Professor Friedman's famous findings. First, it is the money supply that is related to economic activity, not interest rates. A central bank therefore should seek to control the money supply, not interest rates. Second, the money supply affects activity only with a long and, deplorably from the viewpoint of quantity theory, a rather unstable lag. The fixed money growth rule rests upon the second finding. One could accept the first and still favor an activist monetary policy, providing one had evidence, or faith, that the lags were short. . . .

Which Way Causation? · Changes in money growth, to be sure, lead changes in activity very reliably. The statistic is not in doubt. But does this mean money growth is the cause, the level of activity the effect?

Suppose that in fact it were the level of economic activity that determines the level of the money supply, and that this relation were more or less simultaneous. How would the rate of money growth behave? Turning points in the rate of growth of a cyclical variable inevitably precede turning points in its level. In a perfect sine curve, the peak rate of growth leads the peak level by one-quarter of a phase. When the curve is at its peak, its rate of growth is zero. It is therefore quite possible for the rate of money growth to lead economic activity and still to be determined by it, instead of vice versa. Which way causation does in fact predominantly run depends on the action of the central bank or whatever other mechanism governs the money supply. Excellent theoretical and empirical grounds exist for believing that *if* the central bank arbitrarily changes the money supply, economic activity will be affected. That too much money causes inflation is beyond doubt. But what if the central bank does not aim at the money supply, but at interest rates? Suppose that, as central banks do, it seeks to raise and lower interest rates to counteract the cycle, but does so rather moderately. Extreme interest rate fluctuations are distasteful to central bankers. If in an expansion the rate of return that borrowers can earn rises faster than the rate they have to pay, borrowings and the money supply will accelerate. By raising the loan rate less than it should, the central bank would be raising the money supply more than it should. In this way, fluctuations in activity would generate fluctuations in money growth. Put in simplest terms, the supply of money would be governed mainly by the demand for it, which in turn is governed by economic activity. If there is no deliberate or mechanical control of the supply of money, that is of course precisely what would happen.

To disentangle this chicken and egg proposition satisfactorily may be impossible. To claim that the causal sequence runs exclusively from economic activity to money would be to deny any effect of money on activity altogether. That surely would run counter to theory and experience. But given the attachment of the Federal Reserve to what is in effect an interest rate target, very strong impulses particularly in recent years must have run from activity to money supply. That, in fact, is the main point of the critics of the Federal Reserve who allege that the System has aimed too much at interest rates and too little at money supply. . . .

Theoretical Objections · The proponents of the rule do not argue that it will produce the best possible policy. An ideal discretionary policy could always do the same as the rule when that was appropriate, and something else when that was more appropriate. What is claimed is that, given the kinds of discretionary policies that in fact have been and seem likely to be pursued, the rule will do better. In particular, discretionary policies are likely to produce too much variability, and a variability with badly timed cyclical impact. . . .

The rule is vulnerable, however, to criticism arising out of the findings of its own sponsors. Professor Friedman has provided a theoretical statement of the quantity theory of money that he calls a theory of the demand for money. The demand for money, he points out, depends not only on income, but on factors such as interest rates, yield of capital, and inflation. In other words, velocity, the ratio of income to money, is not a magnitude mechanically fixed by payments habits and the like. It is a variable that responds to influences which make the holding of money more attractive or less. Empirically, the existence of a relation between interest rates as well as inflation and the demand for money has been confirmed many times.

A money growth rule that disregards interest rates and price changes, therefore, conflicts with the modern quantity theory. It is what in years gone by students learned to call the "crude" quantity theory. Whether anybody ever subscribed to that theory we need not here examine. Almost forty years ago, Carl Snyder, the statistician of the Federal Reserve Bank of New York, suggested that the business cycle and the price level could be stabilized by increasing the money supply by 4 percent per year. But nevertheless Snyder knew that velocity fluctuated with the business cycle. So did Irving Fisher, an even earlier pioneer of the quantity theory (which is probably as old as economics). Thus, the rule violates the theory upon which it purports to rest in that theory's old as well as modern version. A given growth in the money supply is not the same thing when interest rates are rising and when they are falling, or when prices are rising or falling.

The economic premises of the fixed money growth rule can be challenged, therefore, on at least three grounds:

1. It assumes a degree of influence of money on the economy that rests on probably faulty evidence.

2. It implies a length and variability of the lag between monetary action and the reaction of the economy that likewise is probably exaggerated.

3. It disregards the inverse influence of high interest rates and inflation upon the appropriate rate of money growth. Facts like these, one should think, would caution responsible policy makers

against adoption of a rule of this type. So far, however, they have not blunted the drive of the faithful. On the contrary, it continues to gain strength and acceptance.

MONEY VS. INTEREST RATES

It is of some interest to examine why this has been so. At the theoretical level, greater recognition of the role of the money supply has been overdue. The mechanics of central banking, and the nature of the data reflecting central bank policy, lead almost inevitably to an over-emphasis on interest rates. The discount rate is still the most dramatic and visible of central bank tools. Interest rates in the money and capital markets are plainly observable and published daily. The money supply, in contrast, is a variable published only with a lag, in most countries a long one. Ambiguities of definition—treatment of time deposits, of government deposits, of non-bank deposits with the central bank, deprive it of precision. It must compete with statistics of the volume of bank credit and other credit, which sometimes move in step with the money supply and sometimes not. In short, the money supply is a subtle and not very visible variable that tends to be overlooked in favor of interest rates.

So long as interest rates and money supply throw off the same signals, no great harm is done by orienting monetary policy by only one or the other. Rapidly rising money supply and low interest rates, stagnant money supply and high interest rates, both say the same thing about policy. But what if the two diverge? In early 1966, when the Fed's recent troubles began, interest rates were rising sharply, conveying the impression—to the Fed and many of its observers—that policy was tight. But the money supply was also rising at a rate far above average, suggesting an expansive policy. Soon the incipient inflation made clear which signal was the right one. The false signal thrown off by rising interest rates was due to the simultaneous but unobserved rise in the return on investment. Assuming that this increase exceeded the rise in interest rates, investment was becoming increasingly profitable despite its higher cost. Under such conditions, interest rates can be misleading as an indicator of monetary policy. . . .

Also at the theoretical level, it needs to be observed that if the central bank is to stabilize either interest rates or money supply growth, money supply growth is almost certainly the better variable. It was noted earlier that the Fed, while it rejects with horror any thought of pegging interest rates, is in fact doing something very like that when it moves market rates more gradually than the return on capital probably tends to move. To peg interest rates means to create an explosive situation. Almost inevitably, the pegged rate will not be the equilibrium rate. Suppose it is below the equilibrium rate. Borrowing then will expand, being cheap. The economy becomes inflated, nominal rates of return rise, and the gap between them and the pegged interest rate widens. Borrowing expands faster, and the inflation accelerates.

If the rate of growth of the money supply is pegged, that, too, will probably not be an equilibrium growth rate. But, the side effects noted earlier apart, the damage is not fatal. If the growth rate chosen is too high, prices will trend upwards, but not explosively. Much the same applies, to both interest rates and money supply, on the down side.

Recent developments have strengthened the case, not for a money supply rule, but for giving more weight to money than to interest rates. High rates of inflation have caused the money rate of interest to diverge from the "real," i.e., from the return to the investor after discounting inflation. Since the inflation to be discounted depends on the investor's expectation of future prices, the real rate is a subjective variable that cannot be observed. But at any rate it is bound to be well below the nominal today for investors in the United States.

At the same time, inflation probably tightens the closeness in the relation of money and economic activity. Pockets of idle money are soaked up as investors take advantage of high interest rates. It is true that the precise nature of the relationship may be less predictable. High nominal interest rates reduce the demand for money. Velocity then rises and the appropriate rate of growth of the money supply diminishes. But broadly speaking, money supply and the economy keep each other on a very tight rein right now. We have moved more completely into a quantity theory world, where simple propositions of that theory tend to prevail over the more sophisticated mechanism of Keynes.

There is little assurance, of course, that the quantity theory will continue to be a reliable guide. The trouble with it in the past has not been that it has usually failed, but that it has failed at critical moments. It seems doubtful that when important real variables of the economy combine in an adverse fashion tending to produce recession, an increase in money or a reduction in interest rates can nullify that effect. Total reliance on monetary policy, especially in its quantity theory version, is likely therefore to bring rude awakenings.

ATTRACTIONS OF THE "RULE"

Recent instability of the economy, and the extreme variations in Federal Reserve policy that responded to—or produced?—it, seem to have generated, among theorists and politicians alike, a kind of nostalgia for a stabler environment. Hence perhaps the surprising receptiveness of both to the suggestion of some kind of policy rule. The excited policy switches of the Fed, from overexpansion to crunch in 1966 and back to overexpansion in 1967, followed by renewed overexpansion in 1968 with a subsequent switch to tightness in 1969, have not been successful in stabilizing the economy. Until early 1969, inflation became worse as the Fed tried to get the better of it. None of this is evidence that stable policies would have been better, only that different policies would. But if a panacea was wanted, the proposal for a stable money growth rule supplied it.

Politicians particularly were led by recent events to discover the charms of stable monetary policies. Congress has had a hard time with stabilization measures. During the early 1960s when a tax cut was called for—in a long-run rather than cyclical sense—the decision went along the grain of human nature. But when taxes had to be raised in 1966, it was something else again. At that point, politicians began to see the advantages of monetary policy. If the Federal Reserve could stabilize the economy, why should the legislature do it and accept the political onus? And if the Fed, that troublesome independent body, could simultaneously be curbed by subjecting it to a rule, why would not that be the best of all possible worlds? The temptation to jump on the fixed money rule bandwagon must have been great.

CONSEQUENCES OF A "RULE"

The United States is still some distance away from the adoption of some modified version of the fixed money growth rule, but perhaps not all that much. It is worthwhile considering concretely, therefore, what consequences the rule might produce.

Interest rates principally will feel the effect of the rule. Today, the Federal Reserve's monetary policy consists, very broadly speaking, in keeping interest rates stable or moving them gradually and gently in the direction in which the Fed thinks they should go. This is implied in what the Fed says about being guided by the "feel" of the market. It is implied also in aiming at a given level of "net free reserves." For to stabilize free reserves, positive or negative, means to give the banks added free reserves at any time when, confronted with rising loan demand, they have used up some of those they have. The reverse applies when diminishing demand for funds increases free reserves. Adjustments of central bank credit to fluctuating demand for funds means, of course, that bank assets and hence the money supply are allowed to vary so as to keep interest rates stable.

These variations in money supply reflect the underlying instability of the daily demand for money. The demand for money fluctuates because firms and individuals have larger payments to make on some days than on others. Some of these are predictable, such as interest and dividend rates, tax dates, harvest financing, and the Christmas trade. Others involve a fortuitous bunching of large transactions and are not predictable.

Suppose now that the central bank wants to keep the money supply on a stable growth path, from week to week. Some may doubt that it can do this, and these doubts may have substance. But assuming it succeeds, the result for interest rates is clear— they will fluctuate with daily changes in the demand for money. Some fluctuations will be smoothed out by the market's anticipatory action. But short-run random fluctuations will have their full impact upon the money market. The instability of the Federal funds rate, despite Federal Reserve smoothing, is indicative of what unstable demand and supply can do.

In addition to the random and very short run fluctuations that a stable money growth rule would induce in interest rates, longer and more intensive moves are likely also. Not even the strongest enthusiasts believe that adoption of a rule will end all economic ups and downs. There will be mini-recessions and mini-booms at the very least. A stable money growth rule—if it can be and is implemented—would then cause interest rates to move anticyclically. This would be the right direction; the question is about the extent, and how these moves would impinge upon the various markets and sectors that are susceptible to interest rates. It is quite possible that these moves would be modest much of the time, smaller possibly than under existing policies. But at times they might also be much wider. The latter seems probable especially in recessions. Recent Fed policies have increased the money supply only slightly in contractions or even allowed it to fall. Increasing the money supply stably in recessions may produce much wider rate swings.

The instability of rates induced by a stable money growth rule will be most severe in the money market, at the short end of the interest rate spectrum. But to some extent it will be transmitted to the long end, especially when the move is cyclical instead of seasonal or random short-run. The results of interest rate instability will be felt principally in three areas: the balance of payments, the corporate and municipal bond markets, and Treasury financing.

The Balance of Payments · The balance of payments will respond, of course, to interest rate movements. Rates that move unstably from day to day will cause erratic short term capital flows. These flows will help to keep the interest rate within bounds. But they will also transmit some of its fluctuations from American markets to European and other markets.

Wide cyclical swings of interest rates may have graver consequences. Under the regime proposed the Fed would no longer be able to pay attention to international repercussions. Some countries may find themselves losing, or gaining, more reserves than they like. Principally, however, it is the United States whose reserves would be threatened. If during a recession of some duration the Fed insists in steadily increasing the money supply, interest rates may go very low and American reserves may become depleted. In the extreme case, the Fed may be unable to increase the money supply because gold and other reserves might flow out as fast as Federal Reserve credit is created. This would raise the question of how the dollar could be kept convertible under a stable money growth rule. Professor Friedman's theoretical position is unimpeachable on this score: he favors flexible exchange rates. Very low interest rates thus would depress the international value of the dollar, but would not create a convertibility problem. On the contrary, the dollar's decline would improve the American balance of payments and help end the recession.

But in general the proponents of the rule make their case without insisting on flexible exchange rates. Whether they are consistent is very much open to doubt.

The Bond Market · The corporate and municipal bond markets likewise would suffer. They are being fed by a steady stream of new issues coming from underwriting houses. This underwriting function would be affected if interest rates, particularly long term rates, became significantly unstable. The underwriter takes the risk connected with holding an issue during distribution. If that risk were to become great, he would have to charge a possibly prohibitive price for the function, or else some new method of distributing securities would have to be found.

Treasury Financing · The U.S. Treasury, finally, would find itself deprived of the benefits of the "even keel" on which the Fed now maintains the market during Treasury financings. The Treasury's issues are large and hence difficult to place. They present a particularly delicate problem of pricing. Since the Treasury has no formal underwriter, the function of distribution must be performed, informally, by government bond dealers and commercial banks to the extent that they find it profitable to do so without receiving a commission. The Fed eases the problem of pricing an issue and of distributing it by avoiding changes in monetary policy that would affect securities prices, during a period of 2–3 weeks.

This "even keel" operation interferes, of course, with the Fed's monetary policy. If the Treasury comes to the market often enough, it may be quite hard for the Fed to find a time for initiating a major policy move. The money supply may increase or shrink contrary to the Fed's wishes while the even keel is in effect. A stable money growth rule would compel abandonment of the practice. From the viewpoint of monetary policy alone that would be a good thing whether for the purpose of conducting a stable money growth rule or otherwise. Whether the Treasury could continue to finance in its present form, and if not what new methods might be workable, is an open question. . . .

OUTLOOK

Enumeration of these difficulties suggests what is the most likely evolution of the fixed money growth rule. As the proposal gains in force and becomes more concrete, the obstacles also come increasingly into view. Perhaps some highly modified version may become effective, in the form of some resolution, imposed upon the Fed externally or internally, to forego the extreme swings of policy of recent vintage. Perhaps the Fed will reject even this limitation on the grounds that while in driving a car it is bad to jerk the wheel, it is better to jerk than to crash. If the rule is never adopted, we shall of course never be quite sure that any instability suffered is not due to that failure. But the only way of definitively disproving the rule would be to adopt it and see.

PART FOUR   The Record of
the New Economics

The Fiscal Route to Full Employment

This success story of the early sixties is a portion of Professor Heller's Godkin lectures at Harvard, delivered in 1966 and published as New Dimensions of Political Economy (1967).

STANDARDS OF ECONOMIC PERFORMANCE must be recast from time to time. Recasting them in more ambitious terms was an indispensable prelude to the shaping of economic policies for the 1960s which would be suitable to the tremendous output capabilities of the U.S. economy.

In 1961, once recession had turned into recovery, nothing was more urgent than to raise the sights of economic policy and to shift its focus from the ups and downs of the cycle to the continuous rise in the economy's potential. Policy emphasis had to be redirected from a *corrective* orientation geared to the dynamics of the cycle, to a *propulsive* orientation geared to the dynamics and the promise of growth. For this purpose, it was essential that the Council of Economic Advisers formulate specific, usable models within which to relate prognosis and prescription, economic targets and economic policies.

The main instrument for dethroning the cyclical model and enthroning the growth model has been the *GNP* or *performance gap* and the associated estimates of the economy's potential and growth rate at 4-percent unemployment ("full" or "high" employment). These guides have now passed the rugged test of five years' use as benchmarks for policies to match demand with capacity, culminating in the virtual closing of the gap as the economy reached and broke through the 4-percent unemployment level early in 1966.

Estimating the trend rate of growth for this purpose was a comparatively unemotional—if technically intricate—matter of adding together the growth rates in labor inputs and productivity. When we initiated the "official" calculation in 1961, this growth in potential was running at a rate of 3½ percent a year; it is now nearly 4 percent. . . .

THE NEW LOOK IN FISCAL POLICY

Reorienting policy targets and strategy to the economy's full and growing potential yielded not only new norms but new semantics for stabilization policy, especially in its fiscal aspects.

Gap-Closing and Growth · This, rather than the smoothing of the business cycle, became the main preoccupation of policy, its broader guide to action. As we put it in our January 1962 *Annual Report:* "The mandate of the Employment Act renews itself perpetually as maximum levels of production, employment, and purchasing power rise through time. The weapons of stabilization policy—the budget, the tax system, control of the supply of money and credit—must be aimed anew, for their target is moving."

Fiscal Drag · The moment the upward-moving target was recognized, three things became clear.

First, the traditional thinking that tended to identify prosperity with a rising economy often gave the wrong signals to fiscal policy, calling for a cut-off of its stimulus long before the production gap was closed, long before full employment was reached. Part of the critical barrage that greeted President Kennedy's tax-cut proposal early in 1963 was based on this failure to distinguish between the *direction* of the economy, which was up, and its *level*, which was still far below its capabilities.

Second, the vaunted "built-in flexibility" of our tax system, its automatic stabilizing effect, is a mixed blessing. True, it cushions recessions, which is good. But left to its own devices it also retards recovery by cutting into the growth of private income, which is bad—at least until the production gap is closed and inflation threatens.

Third, in a growth context, the great revenue-raising power of our federal tax system produces a [substantial] built-in increase in federal revenues (net of the automatic increase in transfer payments). Unless it is offset by such "fiscal dividends" as tax cuts or expansion of federal programs, this automatic rise in revenues will become a "fiscal drag" siphoning too much of the economic substance out of the private economy and thereby choking expansion.

Fiscal Dividends · A central part of the job of fiscal policy is precisely this delicate one of declaring fiscal dividends of the right size and timing to avoid fiscal drag without inviting inflation. In an overheated economy, the fiscal drag that develops when fiscal dividends are *not* declared is a welcome antidote to inflation. When recession threatens, an extra dividend is appropriate. But in normal times we must close the fiscal loop by matching the annual revenue growth with tax cuts, increased expenditures (including social security benefits), and more generous support to state and local governments.

Full-Employment (or High-Employment) Surplus · As part of the reshaping of stabilization policy, then, our fiscal-policy targets have been recast in terms of "full" or "high" employment levels of output, specifically the level of GNP associated with a 4-percent rate of unemployment. So the target is no longer budget balance every year or over the cycle, but balance (in the national-income-accounts, or NIA, budget) at full employment. And in modern stabilization policy, as we will see in a moment, even this target does not remain fixed.

To know that the actual budget deficit in 1961 (NIA basis) was $3.8 billion tells us very little about the economic impact of the budget. We cannot tell whether it was expansionary or restrictive, and by how much. Even when we know that $3.8 billion represented a swing of about $7 billion from 1960, when the budget ran a surplus of $3.5 billion, we are not much better off. How much of this swing was the automatic result of changes

in output and income? How much was the purposive result of
changes in fiscal policy? We don't know. But if we put both
years on a comparable basis—specifically, at the GNP levels
that would yield our target level of 4-percent unemployment—
we can immediately judge how big a burden the economy was
carrying in its struggle to get back to full employment, and how
much of that burden was being removed by conscious fiscal
action.

So we have adopted as our fiscal gauge the "full employment
surplus," the excess of revenues over expenditures which would
prevail at 4-percent unemployment. It lifts the veil to tell us that
the budget in 1961 would have been running a surplus of about
$10 billion at full, or high, employment. It tells us also that
federal fiscal action had brought that surplus down from a
huge $13 billion in 1960. What on its face looked like a stimula-
tive budget in 1961 was, in fact, still exerting a strong fiscal
drag on the economy in spite of the removal of about $3 billion
of that drag through federal fiscal action.

Although our budget policy of recent years has been aimed at
approximate balance at full employment, there are times when
we may want to shift its target to a surplus or deficit, depending
on the underlying strength of demand, the stimulative or restrictive effect of monetary policy, and so on. The large swings
in the strength of private demand in the postwar period serve
to remind us that the targets of compensating government
policy have to shift correspondingly. The $13 billion full-employ-
ment surplus in 1960 was an oppressive economic drag, a major force pulling us down into the recession of 1960–61. Yet a
big surplus in the face of surging postwar demand in the late
1940s—at a time when we had tied our monetary-policy hands
behind our backs—represented, not fiscal oppression, but a welcome restraint on inflation.

In other words, the long period of slack private demand relative to the economy's potential after 1957 should not lead us
to the conclusion that it will be ever thus. As fears of recession,
properly, win less of a role in the businessman's investment
calculus and the consumer's saving calculus, both investment
and consumption propensities may shift upward. If so, the fiscal-
policy targets should shift upward to a significant full-employ-

ment surplus. A changing fiscal-monetary mix could have the same implication. Monetary policy may one day be able to shift from its 1961–65 role of accommodating a fiscally spurred expansion as best it could in the face of the conflicting demands of balance-of-payments policy—or its 1965–66 role of damping demands through tight money—to a post-Vietnam role of promoting growth through lower interest rates and easier money. When that day comes, the possibility of combining tighter fiscal policy (a full-employment surplus) with easier money will be back on the stabilization-policy agenda.

Operationally, training our sights on specified full-employment targets led to several significant changes in fiscal strategy.

First, it became more activist and bolder. Feeding fiscal stimulus into a briskly rising economy—typified by the Berlin defense buildup without a tax increase in 1961 and, even more, by the huge tax cut in 1964—is now seen as a prudent response to the needs of an expanding economy that is still operating well below its full potential.

Second, it follows that fiscal strategy has to rely less on the automatic stabilizers and more on discretionary action responding to observed and forecast changes in the economy—less on rules and more on men.

Third, under the new approach, not only monetary policy but fiscal policy has to be put on constant, rather than intermittent, alert. Since 1961, there have been almost continuous official consideration and public debate over tax cuts and expenditure increases to stimulate the economy or, since late 1965, tax increases or expenditure cuts to curb inflation. Clearly, the management of prosperity is a full-time job.

In part, this shift from a more passive to a more active policy has been made possible by steady advances in fact-gathering, forecasting techniques, and business practice. Our statistical net is now spread wider and brings in its catch faster. Forecasting has the benefit of not only more refined, computer-assisted methods, but of improved surveys of consumer and investment intentions. And the advances made in strategic planning and systematic analysis in business are building a better base for forecasting the inventory and capital-spending sector of the GNP.

At the same time, the margin for error diminishes as the economy reaches the treasured but treacherous area of full employment. Big doses of expansionary medicine were easy—and safe—to recommend in the face of a $50 billion gap and a hesitant congress. But at full employment, targets have to be defined more sharply, tolerances are smaller, the line between expansion and inflation becomes thinner. So in a full employment world the economic dosage has to be much more carefully controlled, the premium on quantitative scientific knowledge becomes far greater, and the premium on speed in our fiscal machinery also rises. . . .

THE "NEW ECONOMICS" AT WORK, 1961–1965

Within the foregoing framework of objectives and standards, economic policy moved at first haltingly and then dramatically into the new world of Keynes-cum-growth. Most of the observers of the 1961–65 experience under the new economic policy have focused on the workings and wonders of the 1964 tax cut. Not that it didn't work or that it wasn't wonderful. But I think we have overdone the tax-cut story a bit. To get a balanced view, we must look beyond tax cuts to expenditure increases, and beyond fiscal stimulants and expansion of demand to the companion structural measures designed to increase productivity and maintain price stability.

If 1961–65 policy had been as one-track-minded about expansion as casual critics often picture it, it would stand us in poor stead today. It was only because economic policy gave equal billing to measures for higher productivity and cost-price stability that *sustained* growth was made possible.

Policies for Demand Expansion · To get a bird's-eye view of five years of expansionary fiscal policy, perhaps the best way is to observe how the federal government deployed $48 billion of fiscal dividends (at annual rates) between the second half of 1960 and the second half of 1965. This huge figure embraces not only the offsetting, or absorption, of the $34 billion by which high-employment revenues would have grown if federal tax rates had stayed at their 1960 levels, but also the wiping out of the $14 billion high-employment surplus that existed late in 1960.

The forms of fiscal dividends in this period were as follows (in billions of dollars, rounded):

Tax reductions		Expenditure increases	
Personal income tax	$11	Defense and space purchases	$11
Corporate income tax	6	Personal transfer payments	9
Excise tax	2	Grants-in-aid	5
Payroll tax		Interest and subsidy payments	4
(increase)	−3	Domestic nondefense purchases	3
Net tax reduction	$16	Expenditure increases	$32

Tax cuts of $19 billion, less $3 billion of payroll tax increases, were the major form of dividend. They dwarfed the discretionary increases in federal civilian expenditures, consisting mainly of the $3 billion of domestic nondefense purchases and a small fraction of the transfer, interest, and subsidy payments. Defense and space, plus automatic increases in interest, social security benefits, and grants-in-aid, accounted for the lion's share of the increase in federal spending.

Thus, the big income tax cut in 1964 ($14 billion at 1965, $11 billion at 1963, income levels) is rightfully regarded as the most overt and dramatic expression of the new approach to economic policy. The successful use of the GNP gap and full-employment surplus in fixing the size of the 1964 tax cut deserves brief comment.

The production, or GNP, gap, which had narrowed from about $50 billion in early 1961 to $30 billion in early 1962—and then held stubbornly at that level—was instrumental in setting the proposed net tax cut at roughly $11 billion. On the basis of observed stable relationships between disposable income and consumption, together with not-so-stable investment relationships, the Administration spelled out how the proposed cut would multiply itself into an increment of GNP that could "close or nearly close, the gap between potential and actual output. . . ." The tax cut was also designed to bring the high-employment surplus—which had been reduced to $6½ billion in 1962 but grew to over $11 billion (by the end of 1963) while Congress was debating the tax cut—down to, or close to, zero.

Thus the rationale of the 1964 tax-cut proposal came straight out of the country's postwar economics textbooks. And in turn the tax cut itself—recently described by Dexter Keezer as "a triumph of high-test Keynesian economic therapy"—will richly repay its debt to the textbooks by supplying the classic example of modern fiscal policy and multiplier economics at work. Careful appraisal of the tax cut's impact on GNP shows a remarkably close fit of results to expectations. And until Vietnam intervened, the tax cut *had* brought us back to a "balanced budget in a balanced economy"—in fact, by the first half of 1965, federal receipts had already risen $7½ billion above their pre-tax-cut levels, and the federal budget (NIA basis) was in surplus. So in conception as in delivery, it was a textbook tax cut.

Policies for Productivity and Cost-Price Stability • The 1964 tax cut captured the public's attention and imagination and led to a profound change in public attitudes. Its expansionary melody was quickly and easily learned. Taxpayers were still humming the happy tune in 1965 when nearly $5 billion of excise tax cuts were enacted.

But the harmonics of economic policy for cost-price stability are more subtle and less readily committed to memory. Yet they are equally important—they are a co-requisite of sustained prosperity. The discouraging pattern of recessions every two or three years between 1949 and 1960 has been broken, not by a simple-minded devotion to demand stimulus, but by a tight coupling of measures to boost demand with measures to boost productivity and hold costs in check—a combination designed to bring the demands of full employment into harmony with those of high growth, cost-price stability, and external payments equilibrium.

Indeed, sizable and sustained productivity advances may be thought of as "the great reconciler." From 1961 to 1965, rapidly rising output per unit of input made it possible largely to satisfy the rising income claims of business and labor while holding, or even cutting, unit costs of output. Moderation in wages and prices becomes more bearable when higher productivity, bigger volume, and lower taxes keep take-home pay and profits rising merrily.

The search for ways and means to build a firm base of price-cost stability for expansion began in 1961, long before massive tax stimulants to demand were proposed. A first line of defense against inflation had been provided by the legacy of price stability that grew out of the restrictive monetary-fiscal policies, economic slack, high unemployment, and slow growth that ushered in the 1960s. But the hard task was to maintain that stability while stimulating the economy, taking up the slack, restoring full employment, and doubling the rate of growth. To accomplish it required several important innovations in American economic policy.

Most important among the measures to speed the advances of productivity were $3 billion of tax incentives to investment in plant and equipment recommended in April 1961 and put into effect in 1962. Added to these were another $3 billion of corporate tax rate deductions in 1964. The combination of investment tax credits, more liberal depreciation, and lower corporate rates may be thought of as a $6 billion shift from public to private saving, one that offered direct investment stimulants in the form of expanded cash flows as well as increased profitability of investment projects.

Measures to stimulate physical investment in plant and equipment were accompanied by increased intangible investments in human beings. Manpower development and retraining measures initiated early in 1961 were the forerunners of a long line of programs—including new aids to education and large segments of the war on poverty—which were designed to increase the skills, the quality, and the mobility of the labor force.

Another 1961 innovation was the effort to twist the structure of interest rates so as to hold down the costs of long-term funds for investment in new plant and equipment while raising short-term rates to minimize the outflows of volatile funds to other countries. Successive increases in interest rates payable by commercial banks on time deposits played an important role in redirecting the flow of funds from the short to the longer term end of the spectrum and thus serving the objectives of the twist. Only as the economy began to heat up under the impact of Vietnam was the twist dropped as part of a general monetary tightening to curb overexpansion.

This American counterpart to the "incomes policies" of Europe was introduced early in 1962. The guideposts have been a useful moderating influence in 1961–65. Since they are designed to function as a supplement rather than an alternative to overall fiscal monetary policy, they should not be expected to carry the burden of stabilization—nor should they be judged by the performance of wages and prices—in a period of excessive total demand. . . .

The Economic Record · That these policies met their mark is confirmed by our unmatched record of price and cost stability in the first half of [the sixties]. The rise of only 1.3 percent a year in U.S. consumer prices from 1960 to 1965—and of only 2 percent in wholesale prices for the entire period—is a record no other industrial nation can match. Western European prices, for example, went up two to three times as fast as ours.

The record also shows that from 1960 to 1965, average unit-labor costs in the private economy rose by only 0.6 percent a year, less than one third as rapidly as the rise of 2.1 percent a year from 1953 to 1957, and less than one half the 1.4 percent rise between 1957 and 1960. Unit labor costs in manufacturing actually fell slightly between 1960 and 1965 as output per man-hour rose by an average of 4 percent annually while hourly compensation rose only 3.6 percent.

In weighing this evidence of stability, one must view it in the light of the remarkable advances in output, jobs, and income in the first five years of expansion (specifically, from the first quarter of 1961 to the first quarter of 1966). Gross national product advanced by $218 billion, or by one third in real terms. Over 7 million added jobs were created, bringing the unemployment rate down from nearly 7 percent to under 4 percent. Real per capita income, after taxes, rose by one fifth. The realized growth rate of the economy doubled, rising from 2¼ percent for the period 1953–60 (measured from cyclical peak to cyclical peak) to 4½ percent since 1960.

The Fiscal Fiasco of the Vietnam Period

ARTHUR M. OKUN

This selection is condensed and adapted from The Political Economy of Prosperity *(1970) based on the Crawley Lectures delivered at the Wharton School of the University of Pennsylvania in 1969.*

THE HIGH-WATER MARK OF the economist's prestige in Washington was probably reached late in 1965. At that point, for a brief moment, even congressmen were using the appellation "professor" as a term of respect and approval. There could be no greater tribute to the success of the expansionary policy strategy that had created such a long and strong prosperity.

Even under the best of circumstances, with no defense buildup, the attainment of full utilization would have ushered in a new environment with new challenges to economic policy-making. The growth of output and real incomes was bound to slow down. Once full utilization was attained, the range of tolerance for policy error would have to shrink, as the dangers of both inadequate and excessive demand had to be faced. The problems would be compounded by the difficult compromise between the objective of maximum production and employment, on the one hand, and the objective of price stability, on the other.

As matters developed, these normal challenges of high employment became immensely complicated by the upsurge in defense spending. On July 28, 1965, President Johnson requested additional funds for Vietnam and announced that a further supplemental appropriation would be required in January 1966. That opened a new chapter in the economic expansion. We entered a world of rapidly growing defense spending at a time when we were approaching full utilization of resources. For the next three years Vietnam played the Danish prince in the *Hamlet* of our economic history.

THE PRINCIPLES OF WAR FINANCE

A significant rise in defense outlays necessarily creates problems of economic stabilization and allocation. If fiscal policy is initially on track, an unanticipated increase in defense outlays pulls it off the track. Fiscal policy is made too stimulative and aggregate demand excessive, unless the government takes neutralizing actions. In principle, such actions can take the form of (a) reduced outlays on government nondefense programs; (b) higher taxes to mop up private purchasing power and curtail the total of consumer and business spending; or (c) a more restrictive monetary policy to curb private outlays.

The proper neutralizing dosage—*how much* restraint—depends upon the magnitude and timing of the extra defense outlays. The proper choice among the various instruments of policy—*what kind* of restraint—depends, however, primarily on social priorities about allocation: What types of spending should be squeezed in order to make room for the resources claimed by defense? On any reasonable interpretation of social preferences, acquiring guns at the expense solely—or even primarily—of public sector butter is a grossly irrational trade. Such a decision would make sense only if all the lowest priority items in the entire national shopping list were in the 12 percent of our gross national product (GNP) devoted to federal nondefense outlays. Clearly, that is not the case.

The overhead cost to society of more guns might sensibly be imposed proportionately on private butter and public butter. Most would then fall on private spending just because it is so big. Federal nondefense outlays would carry a 12- or, at most, 15-percent share of the restraint.

Either higher taxes or additional monetary restraint can be used to make private butter share the burden. Of the two, taxes get the higher grade on allocation grounds. A hike in corporate and individual income taxes will have an essentially across-the-board impact in curbing various types of private spending. Monetary restraint, on the other hand, bears down on those sectors that are most dependent on credit financing, like homebuilding, business investment, and consumer durables. There is no obvious premium on restraining these sectors and hence no persuasive case for a particularly restrictive monetary policy during a defense mobilization.

All of this adds up to a straightforward recipe for dealing with the problem of war finance. Take a substantial rise in taxes and a small cutback in federal nondefense outlays so that, in combination, over-all fiscal policy remains about as stimulative as it would have been in the absence of the additional defense spending. Since the stimulus of defense will then be neutralized within the framework of fiscal policy, monetary policy can be left essentially unaltered—whether viewed in terms of interest rates and credit conditions or in terms of the growth of money and other credit flows.

One major difficulty with that recipe is that we never know in advance how big a war is going to be. Decisions on manpower and procurement for defense are made sequentially, and each new important decision creates new economic problems. If the defense budget is scaled up by new military decisions, a further neutralizing stabilization move is required. The tax dog may have to keep chasing the defense rabbit and may not be able to keep up. During the Korean War, we were willing to pursue the rabbit diligently: three major pieces of tax-raising legislation were enacted in 1950 and 1951. But because there are inevitable legislative and economic lags, economic policy is bound to be handicapped in a period of defense mobilization. Some inflationary bias in wartime may be inescapable.

I am convinced nonetheless that the major source of the inflation that gripped the nation in the late sixties was our failure to apply through the political process the principles of war finance set forth above. If the knowledge that economists had and the advice that they were giving had been turned into the law of the land, the Vietnam War need not have turned into a major inflationary episode. In saying that, however, let me emphasize that, in my personal hindsight view, the enormous tragedy of Vietnam must be measured in terms of other costs: human lives; our national sense of unity, purpose, and rectitude; and the material resources that could have been applied to priority social purposes at home. In perspective, the loss of price stability must be regarded as a tiny piece of the overall picture. It just happens to be the one part of the picture that I can speak about with expertise.

THE INITIAL DERAILMENT

As of mid-1965, the price-cost record of the economy was generally reassuring. The average of wholesale industrial prices was within 1 percent of its level a year earlier. Unit labor costs were below their levels of a year earlier, as productivity advanced briskly and the wage rates rose only modestly. Consumer prices were rising at a rate of 1½ percent a year and the price deflation for overall GNP was rising at a 1¾ percent rate. Although this record represented some slight retreat from the exceptional price stability of the early sixties, that was no surprise. It had been recognized all along that when the slack in resource utilization was taken up, some deterioration in our price performance was inevitable. What was occurring seemed relatively small and readily tolerable. This was not inflation by any definition I know.

The brisk growth of the economy during 1964 and the first half of 1965 turned into a dangerous inflationary boom in the second half of 1965. Defense purchases rose abruptly and defense orders jumped, swelling business inventories of materiel. Reflecting in part the impact of the defense buildup on business expectations, investment in plant and equipment soared in the closing months of the year.

The key fiscal decision for the January 1966 budget program was a negative one: A general tax increase was not proposed. The defense program projected in that budget pointed significantly upward, although it later proved to underestimate the magnitude of the escalation by a wide margin. On the basis of the initial budget estimates, the President was told by his economic advisers at the end of 1965 that a general increase in income taxes was desirable to avoid excess demand. The President did propose—and Congress promptly enacted—a significant but clearly inadequate bits-and-pieces revenue package which rescinded excise tax cuts, instituted graduated withholding on individual income taxes, and accelerated the collection of corporate income taxes. Meanwhile, the general tax increase was placed on the back burner with warnings by the President that it might have to be recommended later during the course of 1966.

President Johnson stated publicly in 1968 that "it was evident that it would be impossible to get a tax increase in 1966." He elaborated on this in a speech to the Business Council in December 1968: "We knew we needed action on taxes in 1966. Many of you in this room will remember what happened when, in the month of March 1966, I asked how much support you would give me. Not a hand went up. And I was told that I could get but four votes in the Tax Committee of the Congress out of twenty-five."

This political reality should be clear in retrospect, especially in view of the antagonism to the surcharge proposal in 1967–68. There was much less reason for higher taxes to get a sympathetic hearing at the beginning of 1966. All that time, to the untrained eye, the economy seemed to be doing remarkably well. Anybody who wanted to slow things down was a killjoy. All the favorable consequences of the boom were clear: Profits were soaring; consumer living standards were improving dramatically; poverty was declining sharply; and the promised land of 4-percent unemployment was finally being reached. On the other hand, there was no compelling evidence of acceleration in prices and wages, deterioration of the balance of payments, skyrocketing of interest rates, or acute pressures in financial markets. All these unfavorable consequences of the boom were still forecasts rather than facts.

The economists in the administration watched with pain and frustration as fiscal policy veered off course. The new developments meant they were no longer calling the shots in fiscal policy. The January 1966 budget marked the first defeat of the new economics by the old politics since Kennedy's decision in August 1962 to delay a tax-cut recommendation. Even more important, the new economics could not pass its crucial test because of the defense upsurge and the political paralysis of tax rates. The new economists had insisted repeatedly to their critics that the policy of fiscal stimulus would be turned off in time and would be amended to head off inflation when the economy did reach full employment. For political—not economic—reasons, the skeptics won the debate.

Post-mortems of the 1966 tax decision still make an interesting parlor game. Even though a presidential recommendation for a tax hike would not have been enacted in 1966, might it have paved the way for an earlier victory in 1967? Would a fiscal program on the side of virtue proposed by the President have redounded to his prestige—and incidentally to that of his econo- mists—even if it had been rejected by the Congress? Or would the revelation that the President could not implement an ur- gent economic program have harmed his image and have shaken the confidence of the business and financial community? Would a presidential recommendation for a tax increase have seriously impaired the Great Society legislative program for 1966 and, indeed, was that an important reason why the President de- cided not to undertake the crusade? Such questions are great fun, despite the fact that we can't answer them—maybe, indeed, because we can't answer them.

Undoubtedly, if the level of defense outlays for fiscal 1967 had been accurately foreseen by the administration in January 1966, the case for offsetting fiscal restraining action would have been much more evident. The underestimate of $10 billion may have been an important cause of the political paralysis on taxes. In retrospect it is clear that every dimension of the Vietnam War was underestimated at that time, and it is hardly surprising that the volume of defense expenditures was projected too low.

The underestimate had two distinct parts: (1) the inaccurate translation of the assumed defense program into a dollar estimate of expenditures; and (2) the impact on outlays of decisions made after January 1966 that added to the size and duration of the military effort in Vietnam. The second was by far the more important—accounting for $8 bilion of the $10 billion divergence. The defense estimates were scaled up again and again because the Vietnam conflict turned into a much larger, longer, and more serious war than had been anticipated. Historians face a major task in explaining why we thought the tail we were grabbing belonged to a mouse when in fact it was that of a bear. But that question transcends budget arithmetic and fiscal economics.

SEARCH FOR THE SECOND BEST

The principles of fiscal policy prescribe higher taxes as the best antidote to the stimulative force of extra defense spending.

They do not tell us what to do if that prescription cannot be filled. In 1966, the search for second-best alternatives yielded results, but some of the remedies were not very strong and others had undesirable side effects.

As one way to battle against the inflation that became evident early in 1966, the government significantly stepped up its "jaw-bone" efforts to talk down wages and prices in areas of market power. To a large extent this activity took the form of private communications and meetings between government officials and leaders of business and labor designed to solicit cooperation. In a great many specific instances, the Council of Economic Advisers (CEA) asked firms to exercise restraint in price decisions, including requests for rollbacks of increases already announced. Businessmen were also informed that the administration appreciated a willingness on their part to discuss in advance any price changes that they were contemplating. On several occasions, the Council issued public statements criticizing certain private decisions on prices and wages. In January 1967, the Council noted some successes:

The outcome of these activities cannot be fully known. In a number of cases, it is clear that price increases which were announced or contemplated have been rescinded, reduced in amount or coverage, or delayed. Some companies have indicated that their subsequent price decisions were affected even where their decision in the immediate case was not changed.

Similarly favorable responses by labor leaders in wage decisions could not be reported, but the moral suasion efforts did seem to have considerable effect in stiffening the resistance of management to large wage demands. The efforts on wages and prices were necessarily asymmetrical, since it takes two to sign a wage bargain and only one to make a price decision.

The nature of the appeals for restraint had to be modified in the light of market realities. Once food and service prices began to accelerate, it became patently unrealistic to ask organized labor to accept wage increases that merely paralleled the trend growth of productivity, in line with the earlier Kennedy–Johnson guideposts. By the end of 1966, such settlements would have barely covered the year's increase in consumer prices, thus providing no rise in real income. Some of the rise in the cost of living had to be reflected in wage gains; but, so long as a full escalation was prevented, the wage-price spiral would be moderated.

The Council reports in 1967 and 1968 substituted temporarily for the productivity guide on wages an interim qualitative standard of partial adjustment of negotiated wages to the cost of living. Similarly, once labor and material costs rose, management could not be asked to absorb these increases without adjusting prices to some degree. The Council stressed the need for partial absorption in its plea for restraint in pricing.

While the appeals of the administration could and did make some difference in the nation's price and wage performance, the tides of excess demand could not be talked down. Because of the resulting appearance of failure, the guideposts were badly splintered in the eyes of the American public. The use of the jawbone in 1966–68 had many drawbacks. But, in a period of acute shortage of good anti-inflationary tools, it did help, in my judgment, to slow both the spiral and the spread of inflationary expectations.

Another stabilization weapon of limited potency was the repeated but careful curtailment of the nondefense budget. The federal civilian program in the January 1966 budget and every budget thereafter was a good deal lower than it would have been in the absence of the Vietnam War. The administration supported a considerable initiation and expansion of those domestic social programs which stood at the very top of the President's priority list, especially ones particularly aimed at aiding the poor and improving the environment of the cities. Moreover, major increases in social security programs took effect during the Vietnam period—most notably the initiation of Medicare. But these were financed by additional taxes adopted for the express purpose, and they did not contribute to the inappropriate fiscal stimulus of the era. Apart from social security and higher interest costs on the federal debt, other nondefense outlays rose by $19 billion from mid-1965 to mid-1969. Along a noninflationary, high-employment growth track, with no changes in tax rates, federal revenues (excluding social insurance taxes) would have risen well over $30 billion during that period. Thus federal nondefense expenditures were held well within the bounds that would have been feasible if defense spending had continued on a plateau.

In retrospect and in perspective, there should be no regrets that the civilian public sector was not squeezed to an even greater extent for anti-inflationary purposes.

RELIANCE ON TIGHT MONEY

With only a little help from other policies, the monetary authorities shouldered most of the thankless burden of restraining the booming economy in 1966. The availability of reserves to banks was sharply curtailed at the start of the year, and interest rates moved upward as the demand for credit outstripped supplies provided by the Federal Reserve. Housing starts began to fall at the start of 1966, and by April they were at their lowest rate in three years. As the monetary authorities continued deliberately and gradually to tighten the screws, credit flows fell off markedly during the spring and summer, and the squeeze extended to areas other than home mortgages.

Even on conservative assumptions, tight money in 1966 had a remarkably impressive total effect. As the CEA reported, the impact was as large as one would have expected from a 10-percent surcharge on corporate and individual income tax liabilities. But unlike the results of such a hike in income taxes, the impact on monetary policy was terribly lopsided, imposing a heavy and uneven burden on homebuilding and creating uncertainties and anxieties in credit markets. Still the Council shared the Federal Reserve's judgment that these were a lesser evil than providing the financial fuel for a dangerous inflationary boom.

The Federal Reserve probed, tested, and reacted. It shot in the dark in some instances. Yet the Board put on an outstanding performance in 1966, making wise judgments and, most of all, having the courage to act promptly and decisively on them. The objectives could not have been carried out if the Board had been frozen by timidity or hogtied by rigid rules about the growth of the money supply, the level of interest rates, or any other criterion of monetary policy. With perfect hindsight, one might conclude that the Fed had a little margin to spare and could have been somewhat less tight at the peak of the summer. Such hindsight judgments are analogous to criticisms of an alert driver who has just avoided a jaywalking child because he careened to a halt when he still had three or four feet to spare.

THE WELCOME SLOWDOWN

Once the monetary brakes worked, they took hold rather abruptly. Because of the nosedive in homebuilding and an abrupt weakening of consumer buying, final demand slacked off in the closing months of 1966. When business production schedules were not scaled down correspondingly, inventories piled up. By the beginning of 1967, the boom was no longer a threat. Rather the danger became that of going into a tailspin. Monetary policy had been reversed toward ease late in 1966, and its support of economic activity continued to be appropriate early in 1967.

Even with the weak over-all economic outlook immediately on the horizon at the start of 1967, it seemed likely that the economy would once again need restraint later in the year because of continued increases in defense spending and the gradual working off of the inventory imbalance. With that requirement in view, the January 1967 budget called for a 6-percent tax surcharge on individual and corporate income taxes to take effect later in the year.

The policy strategy was designed essentially to replay the 1966 hand and to do it right the second time. Politically, a tax increase seemed considerably more feasible in 1967, because of the experiences of 1966, which had underlined the costs of inflation and the distortions involved in using monetary brakes to offset a fiscal accelerator. Yet restrictive tax action could not be taken until the immediate economic slowdown had been surmounted and a rebound was visible to the congressional eye. This strategy of shifting the fiscal-monetary mix depended upon accurate forecasting and appropriate timing of policy measures.

As matters developed, the strategy earned a top grade in economics and a failing mark in politics. It was a vintage year for many economic forecasters who relied on a Keynesian income-expenditure approach. As projected, the first half of 1967 did turn out to be sluggish. Dominated by an inventory adjustment, the economy paused, but the recession predicted by a few non-

Keynesian forecasters was clearly avoided. The unemployment rate stayed around 4 percent. Also as predicted, the slowdown —and the accompanying monetary ease—generated considerable benefits: a decline in interest rates, a rebound in housing, and distinct and definite relief in price advances. After rising at a rate of 4 percent during much of 1966, consumer prices increased at a rate of less than 2½ percent in the first half of 1967.

THE SECOND CHANCE

The rebound at midyear was also remarkably true to the script that the economic forecasters had written at the start of 1967. As the CEA had projected in its January report:

By midyear, construction should be recovering with the stimulus of monetary ease; and inventory investment should be leveling off at a moderate rate. In combination, these two sectors should significantly strengthen over-all private demand. A shift toward restraint in fiscal policy is appropriate at that time to assure that demand does not outrun capacity, that movement toward restoration of price stability is maintained, and that monetary policy does not have to be tightened again.

In July it was clear that this forecast had been realized, and the President's economic and financial advisers unanimously recommended that he press his request for higher taxes on the basis of the evidence then at hand. Largely because defense estimates had been marked up again, the surcharge proposal was scaled up to 10 percent. At this point, the nation's excellent second chance to get on the path of noninflationary prosperity depended on prompt congressional enactment of the tax increase.

The Federal Reserve and the administration might have chosen an alternative stabilization strategy that would not have risked a congressional rebuff. It would have involved continued reliance on monetary brakes to offset the budgetary accelerator. Monetary policy had demonstrably curbed inflation in 1966 and there was every reason to believe that it could do so again in 1967 and 1968. But interest rates—as well as prices—were social targets and so was the composition of the restraint among industries and economic groups. A stabilization policy that continued to kick homebuilding while it was down and that once again put enormous pressure on financial markets would not have met social priorities, even if it made prices behave. Therefore, the Federal Reserve and the administration reached a conscious and coordinated decision that the monetary brakes should not be reapplied. The Federal Reserve pursued a monetary policy that was deemed appropriate on the assumption that prompt tax action was forthcoming.

This proved to be a losing bet, as it turned out, because Congress was unwilling to raise taxes in 1967 on the basis of a forecast of acceleration. The main argument against the tax increase was that the case for economic restraint had not been proved: The economy admittedly was not yet going too fast, our price record was better than it had been, and so were financial markets and our international trade surplus. Congress would not act on a forecast; it wanted facts.

The forecast of an acceleration in economic activity was rooted in the facts of the situation. Final sales had advanced rapidly in the first half of 1967, paced by the continued increase of defense expenditures and the rebound in homebuilding. The overall gains in GNP had, however, been very modest because of a record-breaking downswing in inventory accumulation. As of midyear, there was no reason to expect the growth of final sales to slow appreciably and every reason to believe that the inventory adjustment was largely behind us. These two judgments translated into a diagnosis of an accelerating economy.

In response to congressional demands for facts rather than forecasts, CEA Chairman Gardner Ackley pointed out, "It is impossible . . . to have an intelligent economic and fiscal policy without some kind of a forecast. . . . A forecast is always necessary in evaluating a fiscal program."

It was emphasized that inaction on taxes was action to create a major additional fiscal stimulus. That stimulus could be justified only by accepting the implausible forecast that economic activity was not going to speed up. Congress did not have a choice between acting and not acting, between operating on forecasts or waiting for facts; it could only choose among alternative fiscal programs and among alternative forecasts.

Many independent professional economists backed up the administration's verdict and few dissented. But the Congress was not persuaded. On November 30, in adjourning the hearings before the House Ways and Means Committee for the 1967 congressional session, Chairman Wilbur Mills summarized: "I have not seen as yet any evidence that we are currently in any demand-pull inflationary situation which requires immediate action. . . ."

The skepticism of the Congress was buttressed by widespread opposition of the general public to higher taxes. The man on the street has good reason to be skeptical that he can enhance his welfare by sacrificing 1 percent of his income in the form of higher income taxes. The dent in his take-home pay associated with higher taxes is obvious and definite; the prospect that he will thereby get insurance against inflation and high interest rates and a better chance for long-run prosperity is highly speculative and uncertain. The argument sounds to him like a familiar con game: Just give me your money and I'll make you rich.

FISCAL RESTRAINT—AT LAST

The need for economic restraint became clear to the Congress and the public early in 1968 when the horror stories of the economic forecasts began to come true. Prices accelerated to a 4-percent rate of increase; interest rates rose far above their 1966 peaks; and our world trade surplus again shrank. The economy moved into a feverish boom. Once the need for fiscal restraint was generally recognized, controversy centered on the precise mix of budget cutbacks and tax increases to achieve it. There had been a harbinger of this issue in 1967, when a few members of the Congress had expressed their support for a tax increase provided that it was coupled with a sufficient cutback in expenditures. In the spring of 1968, many others in the Congress embraced the spending issue and reversed their earlier opposition to higher taxes.

Even with a general consensus in favor of fiscal restraint, it was not evident whether any coalition on the Hill was large enough to enact any particular package. Some favored a tax increase only if it were linked to an expenditure cutback; others were for higher taxes only if the extra revenues helped to protect expenditure programs; still others argued that a tax reform to improve equity must be coupled with any tax increase.

Secretary Henry Fowler, who brilliantly and tirelessly handled the administration's legislative strategy, convinced the President that an agreement with the budget cutters offered the best hope for enacting a program of fiscal restraint, and President Johnson accepted a ceiling on federal expenditures as part of a tie-in sale with the surcharge.

The Revenue and Expenditure Control Act of 1968 was signed by President Johnson on June 28. It provided at long last the 10-percent surcharge on corporate and individual incomes that had been requested nearly a year earlier; the surcharge was applied retroactively to April 1 on individual incomes and to January 1 on corporate incomes. The surcharge was coupled with a $6 billion cutback in expenditures for fiscal year 1969, exempting special costs of Vietnam and uncontrollable federal outlays. In combination, these measures represented a very marked shift in the federal budget toward restraint.

Thus a tax increase finally ended the period of inappropriate budgetary stimulus—thirty-five months after it started, thirty months after it was first diagnosed by the President's economic advisers, and eleven months after the President urgently requested the Congress to act. By the time the budget was brought back under control, the boom and the wage-price spiral had developed enormous momentum and they proved terribly difficult to stop. The surcharge turned out to be just the first in a long series of anti-inflationary fiscal and monetary measures that proved necessary to achieve even a modest deceleration of prices. By the middle of 1968, inflation had become a raging disease and could no longer be halted by the dose of preventive medicine that could have worked three or even two years earlier.

A Monetarist Critique of
the New Economics

BERYL SPRINKEL

*The author, Senior Vice President and Economist of the Harris
Trust and Savings Bank, Chicago, delivered this criticism in a
speech to the Illinois Chamber of Commerce on October 27, 1967.*

FEW WOULD QUARREL with the objective of the "New Economics"
to conduct monetary-fiscal and related economic policies in such
a manner as to exert a stabilizing influence upon economic activity. Presumably a stabilizing set of economic policies would
encourage high and relatively steady economic growth, low unemployment, and price stability. However, the record, as well as
analysis of the theoretical underpinnings of the "New Economics,"
suggests that instead of providing "a step toward stability," retro-
gression has actually occurred. Negative results have been obtained because of inherent weaknesses in the concept, not because
of lack of dedication or professional competence.

Before arguing the above proposition, let me define what I
mean by the "New Economics." The hallmark of the "New Economics" is that economic policy-makers now know enough to
properly prescribe and frequently adjust economic policies so as
to consistently add just the right amount of economic stimulus or
restraint. Second, the "New Economics," utilizing the Keynesian
analytical framework, places fiscal policy in the king pin role
while minimizing the stabilization role of monetary policy.
Finally, from time to time the "New Economics" argues that the
imposition of wage-price guidelines will lower the inflation
threshold and contribute in a significant way to the attainment of
economic stability.

INHERENT LIMITATIONS

Let us look briefly at the theoretical underpinnings of the
"New Economics." Since "fine-tuning" policy adjustments must

be made in advance of the desired impact, a high degree of preciseness in forecasting must be achieved. Despite significant improvements in data collection and related forecasting techniques, the evidence indicates that humility rather than arrogance is the proper mental attitude when viewing the future.

Even if forecasting were not treacherous, many other complications exist which almost insure defeat for the "fine tuner." For example, monetary-fiscal authorities are not agreed as to the proper measure of policy changes and even if they were, it is impossible to know how much change is necessary to bring about the desired impact on the economy. Monetary policy measurements proposed by various leading authorities include such diverse series as the change in bank credit, change in free reserves, change in interest rates, change in total reserves, and change in the money supply—both broadly and narrowly defined. Fiscal policy measurements fare no better. For many years we were assured by congressional leaders and others that the fiscal impact should be measured by the administrative budget. The "New Economics" taught us that only the full employment budget mattered. Some of us thought that the cash budget was the best measure, but recently the Council of Economic Advisers insisted that the national income budget is the proper budget for measuring fiscal impact. Unfortunately, the above proposed measures of monetary policy do not all yield the same answers and neither do fiscal measures.

But even if we were agreed on forecasting and measurement of policy change, formidable difficulties remain. There are, unfortunately, demonstrable and largely unpredictable lags in policy-making and execution.

There is first the recognition lag. This lag cost many months of time in late 1965 and early 1966 when the administration refused to believe serious inflationary pressures were developing. There is the execution lag following recognition of the problem. Although for monetary policy this lag may be brief, it can be quite long for fiscal policy, as witness the fact that it took over 1½ years to pass the 1964 tax cut, and is now taking many months to reach a decision on the proposed tax increase. Finally, the impact lag before a policy change affects the economy is variable and difficult to forecast.

Furthermore, the "New Economics" emphasis upon fiscal policy rather than monetary policy appears questionable. Rather than treating monetary-fiscal policies as substitutes, as discussion about the "proper mix" implies, the evidence suggests they should be considered as complementary and that monetary policy changes are more frequently the dominant influence. Each recession and economic pause in this century has been preceded by a tight monetary policy in the form of reduced monetary growth just as each renewed expansion has been preceded by rising monetary growth. Quantity theorists argue this relation is causal. Sometimes fiscal restraint preceded recession and fiscal stimulus preceded economic expansion, but not always. In the three post-war tax cuts of 1948, 1954, and 1964 economic expansion followed the last two tax cuts, which were accompanied by monetary expansion, but recession followed the 1948 tax cut, which was accompanied by monetary restraint. The economic pause which characterized the first half of 1967 is readily explained by the monetary restraint of 1966, and the current renewed economic expansion was preceded and accompanied by a sizable monetary increase. But by most measures, fiscal stimulus accelerated throughout 1965 to 1967 and hence cannot explain the pause and renewed expansion.

Finally, implementation of the "New Economics" apparently requires frequent fiscal change, or so it is argued by its practitioners. Yet, frequent changes in tax rates and government spending may well serve to limit confidence in the sagacity of past and present moves while unduly complicating business and consumer planning. Such frequent changes are analogous to changing frequently the rules of a game while it is being played. Sometimes such economic policy changes become necessary due to unanticipated major events such as war, but they should be made infrequently rather than becoming the fulcrum of an activist economic policy.

RESULTS

So much for the apparent weaknesses in the theories underlying the "New Economics." How about the results? Have the policy-makers surmounted these numerous problems and provided economic stability since 1960? A fair answer for the period from 1961 to mid-1965 must be yes; but for recent times—no. From February 1961 to about mid-1965, economic growth accelerated, unemployment declined, and prices were stable. Both monetary and fiscal policies were expansionary and appropriately so. Economic performance in the period 1961 to mid-1965 reflected "gross tuning" at its best. There was much room for error on the expansionary side since the economy was well below capacity production.

But troubles began as the margin for error diminished. One could have dared hope that as the economy approached full employment of resources near mid-1965, a "flexible" monetary-fiscal policy would provide less stimulus. But alas, the stimulus increased! The administration seriously underestimated the rising cost of the Vietnam War so that increased spending on defense and Great Society programs shifted the cash budget from a small surplus in the second quarter of 1965 to a sizable deficit. And, in fact, the cash budget probably underestimated the changing fiscal impact since the surge in government orders, which initiated hiring and production, occurred well in advance of cash payments.

To compound the difficulty, monetary policy also became more expansive. In contrast to the approximate three percent annual growth in the money supply from 1960 to April 1965, monetary growth doubled to 6.1 percent from April 1965 to April 1966. Furthermore, measures of bank reserves and total bank credit reflected similar tendencies. In December 1965 when the Fed raised the discount rate amid great objections by the Administration, who argued that a tighter monetary policy was inappropriate, the money supply actually increased nearly 1 percent, the largest monthly gain in nineteen years. Even though interest rates were tending upward due to sharp increases in demands for funds, monetary policy continued to fuel the flames of inflation by sharply augmenting the money supply.

We can properly ask why policies became more expansive just as the economy approached full employment of resources and inflation became a threat. The administration clearly underestimated the inflation potential. To a considerable extent this was due to the sizable underestimation of government spending.

Congress consequently did not insist on a tax increase nor did it carefully prune nondefense spending. As the demand for credit accelerated, the Federal Reserve sharply augmented credit supplies in the apparent but, in my opinion, mistaken belief that the rising trend in interest rates and declining free reserves meant monetary policy was becoming tighter. In fact, monetary policy became more expansive as the growth in total bank reserves, total bank credit and the money supplied accelerated.

Several unfortunate consequences followed, largely as a result of increased policy stimulus. Current GNP began to rise at a faster rate. Since resources were in tight supply, inflation became a serious problem for the first time during this economic expansion. For example, consumer prices rose 2.9 percent in 1966 while wholesale prices increased 3.3 percent compared to only 1.3 percent and 0.4 percent annual rates of increase from 1960 to mid-1965. As inflation anticipations accelerated and sales and order trends developed strength, there was increased impetus to borrow, and money and credit demands surged ahead. Despite the rapid infusion of reserves and new money, interest rates rose rapidly. The easy money policy in the year ending April 1966 engendered a tight money market by increasing inflationary fears and thereby stimulating credit demands.

In early May 1966, monetary policy abruptly changed gears and the money supply declined at a 1.7-percent annual rate for the next seven months. The abrupt change in monetary policy, accompanied by an unwillingness of regulatory authorities to permit financial institutions to compete effectively for time money, resulted in a near monetary crisis in August 1966.

Following August, interest rates receded significantly for a few months. Just as an excessively easy money policy stimulated the economy and the demand for funds, a policy of monetary restraint eventually had the opposite effect. Demand for credit began to abate by the fall of 1966, and finally late in that year monetary policy became expansive again. To compound the economic difficulties, on September 8, 1966, the President asked Congress to suspend until January 1, 1968, the 7-percent investment credit. Of all fiscal tools available, this one was probably the most cumbersome since its major effect could not be felt until well into 1967 when it was not clear that restraint would be needed. In 1967, this action was rescinded as it became clear the economy was slowing.

For the first nine months of 1967, the money supply has risen at an 8-percent annual rate and the economy is now rising rapidly, adjusted for the auto strike. Since unemployment is only 3¾ percent and industrial plant utilization is already 85 percent, there is little room to accommodate rapid spending increases without serious inflation. In fact, during the spring and summer of 1967, the price rise has accelerated with consumer prices rising at more than a 4-percent annual rate, and during the summer wholesale prices of industrial commodities have also resumed their advance. Combined monetary-fiscal policies are now the most expansive since World War II, and present indications suggest that even if the surcharge is adopted, inflation is looming as a very serious problem in the months ahead. Once again, an activist economic policy is destabilizing the economy.

During the earlier period when price stability reigned, much was made of the wage-price guidelines and their contribution to stability. Once inflation really became a problem, the guidelines were necessarily abandoned. Nor was this result unexpected since the guidelines affect only symptoms and not causes. The cause of the current inflation is clearly overly-expansive government policies rather than greedy actions by businessmen and laborers.

For more than two years the economy has been subjected to over-stimulus, followed by over-constraint, and now over-stimulus. Economists and policy-makers, unfortunately, do not know enough about the ultimate impact of monetary-fiscal changes to use these policies effectively for "fine tuning" the economy. The record prior to mid-1965 does suggest that "gross tuning" is feasible with the present state of economic knowledge and political will. Rather than using frequent changes in monetary-fiscal policies, which may well affect the economy in a perverse way, a more stable framework is preferable. There is a tendency among economic policy-makers to characterize the private economy as a very unstable system constantly threatening to shift either into recession or depression on the one hand, or into inflation on the other. A contrary view which I believe to be more nearly correct is that the economy tends to be quite stable, but frequent alteration in the degree of stimulus or restraint is likely to destabilize activity.

AN ALTERNATIVE

Looking to the future, how can policy-makers use their limited, tested knowledge, and demonstrated technical abilities to assure better economic performance? Continued empirical research may eventually expand our knowledge to the point where "fine tuning" of the economy with flexible monetary-fiscal policies will be possible, even though it is not now feasible. In the meantime, let us play the more cautious and prudent role of avoiding destabilizing action while providing moderate increases in total spending in line with the growth in the capacity of the economy to produce. A stable growth in the money supply of about 3 percent per year, similar to the 1961–April 1965 period, accompanied by a federal budget designed to attain approximate balance at full employment, is probably the best we can do at present. Application of this more stable monetary-fiscal framework would almost certainly have reduced the degree of instability which has characterized our economy in the recent past.

In conclusion, the recent gross mistakes in economic policy-making and execution have convinced me that until our knowledge is substantially improved, an activist monetary-fiscal policy is quite likely to destabilize an inherently stable economy, especially once full employment has been achieved. It has been demonstrated that a little knowledge can be a dangerous thing when ambitiously applied to economic affairs.

Economic Policy and
the Lessons of Experience

PAUL W. MC CRACKEN

Paul W. McCracken, President Nixon's Chairman of the Council of Economic Advisers from 1969 to the beginning of 1972, wrote this piece in 1968 while still a private citizen. It was published that year in The Republican Papers, *edited by Melvin Laird.*

HIGH ON THE LIST OF deficiencies which economists share with Americans generally is inattention to the lessons of history. While we use statistics and other raw material of experience prodigiously, we are not much inclined to read the minutes of earlier meetings in order to gain some historical perspective about how we got to where we are. This is a pity because the record of our experience with the operation of economic policy provides us with some useful, and even surprising, lessons.

As we examine this record, one conclusion stands out sharply. Fiscal and monetary policies have themselves been a major source of erratic movements in the economy, and the first requirement for improving our economic performance is that these policies themselves be operated in a more even-handed and steady manner. Far from automating fiscal policy, this view of the problem will, if it is correct, require considerably more sophistication and precision than we have yet applied to the task.

The prevailing concept about the nature of the problem of economic instability is itself a manifestation of our disinclination to examine history. We have tended to assume that ours is an economy with strong indigenous tendencies to ricochet from boom to bust, from overheating to unemployment, unless these inherent tendencies are neutralized by stabilizing economic policies. Our strategy, then, would be for these policies to zig or zag vigorously as the economy zags and zigs.

There is a good deal of historical evidence to suggest that this conception of the problem is close to being 180 degrees off course. It would be more in accord with the evidence of history to say that we have had an economy with an impressive capacity to follow a course of vigorous and orderly expansion—except when it has been deflated by a miscarriage of economic policy. Suppose that we explore this a bit to see whether it seems to square with the facts of history.

For several reasons it is useful here to begin with the pre-1929 era, specifically the four decades from 1889 to 1929. The period has certain natural advantages for our point. Annual data are reasonably available. We did not even have a central banking system for two-thirds of these years. During most of these four decades the federal budget was equal in magnitude to about 3 percent of GNP, so its inherent capacity to keep an erratic economy on a short leash would have been severely limited. In any case the concept of fiscal policy had not even been invented at this time. Thus we have here a segment of history during which we should be able to observe the private economy "in the raw" before the instruments of economic stabilization were really available to exert their "restraining" effects on its natural instability.

The National Bureau of Economic Research has decreed that there were twelve identifiable cyclical swings in this span of four decades. And there were eight years during which real output fell below that of the previous year. When we examine the data more closely, however, we discover some interesting things. The median decline for the recedence years was only 2.6 percent in real output. And in eight of the twelve recessions real output in the year containing the low point of the recession was higher than that for the year containing the previous peak.

The four more serious recessions were 1894, 1908, 1914, and 1921. The recession of 1908 was clearly associated with a major monetary panic, and the collapse of 1921 arose out of an overly expansionist set of policies through 1919, followed in 1920 by a drastic reversal of both monetary and fiscal policies. The $13.7 billion swing from a large deficit in FY 1919 to a small surplus in FY 1920 was equal to 16 percent of GNP in 1919 (the equivalent of a $120 billion year-to-year restrictive budgetary swing at 1968 levels). And in three moves the Federal Reserve pushed the discount rate to an all-time high of 7 percent by mid-1920, forcing a 5.2 percent contraction in the money supply from mid-1920 to mid-1921. The remarkable thing here is not that there was a 1921 recession but that our economic system even survived this massive fiscal and monetary whipsaw.

Here clearly what we are observing is not an economy with some endemic case of the shakes, inherently tending to dash from the cellar to the penthouse. It is a record of surprisingly orderly and sustained expansion, except when our foot was pressed too heavily on the accelerator or on the brake (often in quick succession).

The final decade of this period (i.e., 1922–29) is particularly instructive here. Indeed, it is one of the ironies of history that this vastly underrated economic performance tends so often to be characterized as the one that landed us in the ditch of the Great Depression. Actually it was a period that lived up well to Section 2 of the Employment Act of 1946. Real output rose at the average rate of 4.7 percent per year, and each year saw a rise. The price level was steady. And the unemployment rate averaged 3.6 percent.

This good economic performance was no accident. The money supply rose quite steadily at the average rate of 5.1 percent per year, and fiscal policy was also turning in an impressive performance. The full-employment surplus (the difference between federal outlays and the receipts that the revenue system would produce at full employment) for fiscal years 1923 to 1930 apparently ranged from a low of about $0.7 billion in 1926 and 1929 to a high of just under $1 billion in 1930. The full-employment surplus, in short, varied within a narrow range that was equal to roughly 0.3 percent of GNP. Thus this calibration of fiscal policy (which is, of course, analytically superior to actual surpluses as a measure of fiscal policy) shows a remarkable stability with a full-employment surplus of somewhat less than 1 percent of GNP during this period.

Though it has required about three decades to get the point in focus, we do now see that the Great Depression itself was also the result, particularly in the critical 1930 to 1933 phase, of our doing things wrong in the field of public policy virtually whenever there was an opportunity to do so. And we also now see that the catastrophe had nothing to do with any inherent or natural tendency of our economic system to operate at underemployment levels. What we had here was a massive monetary blood-letting. By 1933 the full-employment money supply would have been roughly 50 percent above actual levels, and our zeal for economic masochism had enabled us to accomplish the extraordinary feat of extinguishing 40 percent of our banks. (We had 25,000 banks in 1929, and we emerged in 1933 with about 15,000.)

Fiscal policy was also afflicted with its full share of gremlins in this unhappy period. The full-employment surplus moved from a deficit to a modest surplus in the critical 1932–33 period, a "wrong" swing of close to 2 percent of GNP. And the swing in the full-employment surplus from a deficit of roughly $2½ billion in 1936 to a surplus of less than $1 billion in 1937 (a perverse swing equal to about 4 percent of GNP) was certainly a major source of the downturn in 1937 that began before we had regained full employment—a downturn of great conceptual significance because it raised questions about the ability of our economy to sustain reasonably full employment.

The long-sustained period of abnormally high unemployment from late 1957 to mid-1965 is, of course, another illustration of an aberration in our economic performance whose sources can be traced to economic policy. The glacial pace of monetary expansion from 1956 through 1959 (excluding a brief interlude early in 1958) was certainly a major factor. The money supply (including time deposits) from the end of 1955 to the end of 1959 was allowed to increase at the rate of 3.1 percent per year, considerably short of that required for the economy to keep on a growth path consistent with reasonably full utilization of our productive resources.

Fiscal policy also was allowed to wander off course in a major way. In the recedence phase fiscal policy actually was working well. The full-employment surplus was declining rapidly to a $1–2 billion level by the end of 1958, and this contributed to the brevity of the decline and the strong subsequent upswing. At this point things began to develop less favorably. The full-employment surplus then rose from this $1–2 billion annual rate at the end of 1958 to the $14 billion zone two years later. Monetary policy also turned severely restrictive as the money supply, from mid-1958 to mid-1960 was permitted to increase at the rate of 2.4 percent per year—wholly inadequate for an economy whose basic capacity was rising then 3½–4 percent each year. Subjected to these fiscal and monetary drags, the economy faltered in 1960 before it achieved full employment. The administration's failure to provide leadership for a 1958 tax reduction cost the economy another recession (and its own party the White House in 1960). Here is a major lesson in the realities of political economy.

At the same time it must be remembered that this was an era of inflation-mindedness. The price level was rising at the rate of more than 3 percent per year. Of even greater significance was the surge of inflationary expectations, and decisions about things ranging from investments to the size of wage increases were being distorted accordingly. While fiscal and monetary policies did become too restrictive, a stern disinflationary policy was then in order, and it made a major (and underappreciated) contribution to the orderly subsequent expansion.

So much for a history that to some must seem ancient. Fortunately in recent years, some feel, the forces of darkness that produced these aberrant results have been dispersed. With the new economics we have ushered in an age of enlightenment. Since 1961, we have been told (about as often in lyric poetry as in prose) that the economic performance has been truly remarkable. Now it has been a better performance than we saw in the late 1950s. From 1960 to 1966 real output grew at the average annual rate of 4.8 percent per year—quite impressive for an economy whose long-run growth rate has been about 3½ percent. Moreover, there has been no recession since 1961 (though the expansion suffered a prolonged interruption in late 1962 and early 1963, and a recedence in the first half of 1967). And we had a major tax decrease in 1964 that clearly helped the economy to regain full employment somewhat over a year later.

Now it is not easy to gain perspective on the new economics. For one thing the precise substantive content of the phrase is astonishingly difficult to identify. There is certainly very little in its literature about objectives of economic policy that is new. . . .

Nor have there been major innovations in the instruments of

economic policy. The guidelines were a logical extension of increasing official attention before 1962 to the wage-price problem. There was a large tax reduction in 1964 that was needed and effective, equal in magnitude to 2.1 percent of the 1965 GNP (the year in which the full reduction became effective). We have had, however, other tax cuts of similar relative magnitude. A decade earlier the $7.4 billion tax reduction was equal to 2.0 percent of the 1954 GNP, and it was in the face of a substantial deficit in the budget. . . . Indeed, one of the best performances in tax reductions (or for fiscal policy generally) was in the mid-1920s when in three steps the revenue producing capability of the federal tax structure was reduced by $1.6 billion. . . . This was equal again to roughly 2 percent of GNP.

For a time the main basis for claiming that our capacity to execute policy has improved dramatically in recent years has been simply the improved performance of the economy. This better performance must mean that policies have also been different and better. Undoubtedly our policy capabilities have improved. Hopefully we learn a few things as we go along. What needs far more critical evaluation, however, is precisely this basic premise that our performance in recent years has been so superior that it is out of context with our historical experience. This is not so obvious as it may seem. The average annual rate of growth in the 1920s was equal to that since 1960—4¾ percent per year in both cases. And we did at least that well for a period that was twice as long from 1895 to 1907 (both cyclical "peak" years).

The real point here, however, is something more fundamental than a crude comparison of growth rates. That the growth capability of the economy was going to be unusually high in the 1960s was determined less by the new economics than by the birth statistics following the war that made a rapid subsequent rise in the labor force ineluctably certain. We are now in a period when the annual increments to the labor force are almost double their numbers in the 1950s, and there is some evidence that the rate of growth in productivity is also favorably affected by the higher rate of growth in output made possible by the more rapidly enlarging labor force. The test of policy is how the economy operated relative to this more rapidly rising potential.

And here the record since 1960 is simply not superior. In the low quarter of 1961, according to the Wharton index of capacity, the economy's operating rate was 80.5 percent. This was within a percentage point of the figure at the low point in 1949 and again in 1958, but it was below the 85.2 percent in the third quarter of 1954. The 1961 recession, in short, did not bring the economy's operating rate to a level unusually low by historical standards. In the year following the 1961 low point, the operating rate increased 6.2 percent. This is far less than the 13.4 percent improvement during the comparable period after the low point in 1958, or even the 9.4 percent after 1954. (There was a 15.8 percent gain after the 1949 low quarter, but this was influenced by the Korean Conflict.) Moreover, after the first year's improvement of the operating rate into early 1962, there was no further gain until the second quarter of 1964. Or, to put it somewhat differently, after the low point in 1961 the economy required sixteen quarters to accomplish a gain in its operating rate that required only four quarters in the post-1958 period—in both cases starting with about the same relative shortfall from par.

When we realize this, the absence of a recession in the 1960s also takes on a somewhat different meaning. It arose in part out of the unusually long, drawn-out path of the return to full employment, and when full employment was finally achieved in the final quarter of 1965, some of the old problems again became visible. And they have been exacerbated by an unusually erratic course of policy in 1966 and 1967. In 1965, as the economy was re-entering the zone of full employment fiscal and monetary policies should have become less expansive. Instead, they became more so. The rate of monetary expansion in 1965 accelerated from an 8.4 percent annual pace in the first half to a 10.6 percent rate in the second half. And the $8.6 billion full-employment surplus (at an annual rate) in the first half of 1965 shifted to a small deficit in the second half—a $9 billion swing in the wrong direction.

Then came the ill-fated January 1966 budget message, with its egregious underestimate of outlays for FY 1967, which immobilized fiscal policy and made it impossible to establish the case for a 1966 tax increase. Faced with an accelerating economy, the Federal Reserve panicked in 1966 and jammed hard on the brakes. There was an almost classic response. With the usual lag of two or three quarters, the economy in early 1967 faltered—with enough weaknesses to have produced a recession except for rapidly rising federal outlays (heavily for national security). During 1967, as if to cancel one error with another, the Federal Reserve has allowed the money supply to increase at a 12–14 percent rate—twice the economy's growth capability. And we now confront a budget for FY 1968 in a state of fundamental disequilibrium—with a prospective deficit that may be in the $20 billion range. These policies now expose us to a baleful combination of upward pressures on the price level, floundering credit markets, a major disequilibrium in our balance of payments and demands for direct controls. Some may be tempted to conclude that those now in charge of policy are simply less expert practitioners of economic policy than their predecessors in the early 1960s. Not necessarily. Those in the early 1960s had a far easier task than they readily admit. The disinflation of 1958–60 had established the basis for an orderly expansion. What then happened to be needed were expansive policies—which are also popular.

The real point is more fundamental. Departures from the full-employment growth path have had their origins primarily in the erratic management of economic policy, and this has its manifestations in the era of the new economics as well as earlier. The first great hope for a steadier course of economic expansion is, therefore, a steadier and more even-handed management of economic policy. . . .

Much of the discussion in recent years about strengthening the capability of policy to stabilize the economy has been in terms of introducing greater flexibility—e.g., giving the President limited power over tax rates. These proposals have merit. Most important ones would require approval of the Congress, however, and the Congress has seemed fully capable of restraining its enthusiasm about these suggestions. Moreover, the theory of strategy often implied here is that the primary task of policy is to dash about quelling uprisings whose origins are in the private economy. This is based on a faulty premise, and it is too crude and primitive a strategy for the modern economy.

Since a major source of departures from the path of vigorous and orderly growth and reasonably full employment has been the fitful and spasmodic behavior of fiscal and monetary policies, the most fundamental requirement for orderly movement along the full-employment growth path is that fiscal and monetary policies themselves pursue a more steadfast course. It is here that the greatest gains are to be had, and fortunately this does not involve colliding with any great constitutional issues such as the doctrine of the separation of powers. Moreover, it is worth repeating that this is not a recommendation for abdication to automaticity. It is a call for learning to operate these instruments of policy with more sophistication and exactitude, and within substantially narrower tolerances, than in the past.

If we can keep expenditures in reasonably close balance with revenues that the tax system will generate at full employment, and if the course of monetary expansion also moves more steadily along the full-employment growth path, we can reasonably expect that the economy will come even closer to a course broadly consistent with utilizing all of our "plans, functions, and resources . . . to promote maximum employment, production, and purchasing power." [1]

1. From section 2, Employment Act of 1946.

PART FIVE   The Perplexing Problems
of Cost-Push Inflation

The Strategy of Policy: Short Run
and Long Run

COUNCIL OF ECONOMIC ADVISERS

This selection was part of the 1970 Annual Report of the Council of Economic Advisers, which consisted of Paul W. McCracken, Chairman; Hendrik S. Houthakker; and Herbert Stein.

THE CURRENT INFLATION was generated by the mounting budget deficits and rapid monetary expansion that began in 1965 with the escalation of the Vietnam War and the massive increases in federal spending for domestic programs. These developments stimulated demand for output and labor at a pace which could not be met by growth in the labor force and other productive resources. The resulting pressures caused prices to rise rapidly. Any plan for arresting the inflation called fundamentally for arresting the forces which were causing it. In addition, it was clear that slowing down the inflation after it had gathered momentum would be more difficult than taking the steps necessary to avoid the inflation initially.

Steps to end rising budget deficits and to slow down monetary expansion had been taken in 1968. The Revenue and Expenditure Control Act of June 1968 had helped to shift the budget from a deficit of $25 billion in the fiscal year ended June 30, 1968, to a surplus estimated in January 1969 at $2.4 billion for the fiscal year 1969. Near the end of 1968, the Federal Reserve had turned to a policy of more restrained monetary expansion. Each of these moves, however, was only a beginning. Once they had

180

finally been taken, it was important that they remain in force long enough to do the job. Yet the shift in the budget position to surplus had been achieved with the help of a temporary tax surcharge which was scheduled to expire on June 30, 1969. With continuing strong pressure for increased expenditures in fiscal year 1970, the danger of sliding back into a budget deficit could not be ignored. Nor could it necessarily be assumed that the new and more restrained monetary policy would continue as long as needed. In 1966 monetary tightness had contributed to a dampening of the economy and of the inflation, but the economic slowdown led in turn to a shift back to highly expansive policies in 1967 and to a resurgence of inflation. It was commonly thought that this pattern might be repeated.

At the beginning of 1969, as earlier, there were disagreements among economists about the relative roles of rising budget deficits and rapid monetary expansion in causing the inflation of 1965–68. On one view the rising deficits were the driving force and they would have been enough to cause substantially the inflation that was experienced, even if there had been much less monetary expansion. On the other view the rapid monetary expansion was the primary factor; with it there would have been substantial inflation even with a stable budget policy, and without it there would have been little inflation even with rising deficits. These different views led to different emphases in policy prescriptions for 1969. Following the one theory the critical matter was at least to stabilize the budget in its current position of moderate surplus. According to the other theory a reduction of the rate of monetary growth was the decisive way to slow down the inflation.

The government could not prudently let the control of inflation depend on the choice of one of these strategies to the neglect of the other. Many uncertainties exist about the relative power of fiscal and monetary actions taken separately. There is much less doubt about the power of fiscal and monetary actions taken together. A reliable policy had to turn away from both the rising deficits and the rapid monetary expansion.

THE SHORT RUN: THE DIRECT INFLUENCE
ON WAGES AND PRICES

The Administration's plan of policy for 1969 did not include an attempt to revive wage-price guideposts, such as those existing in 1962–66. The results of our own experience and numerous trials of such policies in other countries over the preceding twenty years did not justify confidence that such efforts would help solve the inflation problem in 1969.

In their usual form these policies enunciate general standards of noninflationary price and wage behavior, coupled with appeals to labor and business for compliance. The degree to which representatives of labor and business have participated with government in defining standards and seeking compliance has varied from country to country. The sanctions invoked in support of the standards are usually informal and have varied in their severity and nature.

Experience with such policies in other countries has been remarkably consistent. In some cases success in holding down wage settlements or price increases has been achieved in particular industries. There is usually a period in which these programs may have some overall deterrent effect, though evidence here is less certain. After an interval, however, there is a point at which accumulating pressures make the programs ineffective.

American experience conformed to this pattern. In January 1962, the Council of Economic Advisers promulgated a set of guideposts intended to describe the course of wages and prices that would be consistent with general price stability and certain other objectives. The main element in the statement of these guideposts was that hourly wages should rise in line with the average long-term gain in output per man-hour. Prices should ordinarily be stable; but in a particular industry they could rise if productivity rose less than the average, and they should fall if productivity rose more than the average. A number of exceptions were specified—and indeed these were necessary—to meet requirements of equity and efficiency.

As originally put forth the guideposts were to serve a general educational function of encouraging voluntary patterns of behavior that would be non-inflationary. There was no suggestion that the government would apply them in particular cases or try to enforce them. But it was natural to question whether actions in particular cases conformed to the guideposts, and the government felt it necessary to comment on the justification for these actions. Once this threshold had been crossed, the government also became involved in attempting to insure compliance in particular cases where it was considered necessary. Usually the attempt consisted of discussions with the persons involved. Sometimes there were public exchanges of charges and counter-charges. In some cases the government relied upon its power as purchaser, regulator, and law-enforcer to encourage compliance.

With the upsurge of inflation and inflationary pressure after mid-1965, the difficulty of reconciling the guideposts with market forces became more intense. Labor and business were being asked to act as if prices were not rising, when in fact they were. As it became evident that steps necessary to keep prices from rising were not being taken, it also became more obviously unrealistic and inequitable to make these requests in specific cases. By the fall of 1966 the policy was widely recognized to be unworkable, and it was allowed to fade away. In subsequent years, there were only episodic actions with specific companies regarding prices.

Whether the policy changed the over-all behavior of the price level before it ran into intense inflation is uncertain. These were years of relative price stability. But they were also years of considerable slack in the economy, relatively high unemployment, and stable or declining farm prices. That is, they were years in which market conditions favored price stability. Econometric studies attempting to isolate a further contribution that guideposts might have made to price stability have produced uncertain results. The findings of some studies are consistent with the view that the guideposts may have had some effect in reducing the increase of the price level; other studies do not support this conclusion.

Whatever the uncertainties about this earlier period, the guidepost policy clearly did not work once the economy ran into strong and serious pressures of inflationary demand. By that time the question was not whether guideposts would have a measurable influence on the rate of inflation. It was whether they had any credibility and viability at all. The evidence is that they did not. The conspicuous cases in which guidepost policy could exercise some influence were too few and were overrun by the general tide of inflation in the economy as a whole.

The administration in 1969 recognized that the speed of the disinflationary process would depend in part upon how quickly business and labor became convinced that the economic climate was changing. If business and labor continued to expect demand and prices to rise rapidly, and if they pushed up wages and prices in anticipation, disinflation would come slowly and more painfully. This meant that the public's understanding of the determination to check inflation, of the policies being pursued, and of the progress being made would be important to success. There would be room and need for efforts to inform the public. But first there would have to be evidence that the new policies were actually working.

In the exercise of its ordinary functions the government has a considerable influence on conditions of demand and supply and consequently on prices in particular markets. It would be important for the government to make sure that its influence did not unnecessarily contribute to inflation in those markets, and beyond that to try to correct malfunctions in particular markets which might aggravate the consequences of the general inflation.

THE SHORT RUN: THE EXPECTED CHAIN
FROM POLICY TO RESULTS

As the process was viewed at the beginning of 1969, the fiscal and monetary restraint that was the core of anti-inflation policy would slow the rate of inflation through a series of steps which can be summarized as follows:

A Slowdown in the Growth of Total Spending · The growth in aggregate spending for goods and services as measured by gross national product, which was 9 percent from 1967 to 1968, would be reduced. The federal government's own purchases would not rise so fast, nor would its payments to state and local governments and to individuals—payments which these sectors ordinarily use to make their own purchases. By avoiding the tax reduction scheduled for midyear, the government would refrain from boosting private after-tax income and consequently from stimulating private spending.

Monetary restraint and the resulting scarcity and high cost of credit would slow down spending in various ways. Expenditures financed by borrowing—for new houses, for state and local construction projects, for business investment, and for consumers' durables—would be most directly affected. In addition, money balances would decline in relation to rising incomes and transactions, and the market value of other assets would be depressed because of higher interest rates. This would dampen the inclination of businesses and consumers to spend. These effects of monetary restraint on spending would not be immediate or follow a precise formula based on the amount of the restraint, but they would come if the restraint continued.

A Decline in the Rate of Growth of Production · The slowdown in the growth of purchases would mean a slowdown in the growth of sales; businesses cannot sell what others do not buy. Some businesses might respond to a decline in the growth of sales by allowing inventories to accumulate rather than by cutting their planned output, but this could only be a temporary reaction. Others might respond to a slowdown in the growth of sales by cutting prices in an attempt to keep volume up. But this was not likely to be the first response in 1969. Having already experienced several years of rapidly rising demand, costs, and prices, businesses would expect more of the same, and for the most part they would keep their own prices up and rising.

The most general and important response of business to a slowdown of sales would be a slowdown in the rate at which production was increasing. Initially this would involve a decline in the rate of growth and possibly some temporary decline in production itself. An absolute decline in output, however, would not be a necessary aspect of the disinflationary process. In a growing economy the labor force is increasing, new productive equipment is being added, new technology is being introduced, and the basic trend of labor productivity is rising; this means that the potential output of the economy also grows. Therefore, even though output is still rising absolutely, a slowdown in the rate of growth of output reduces actual production relative to its potential and is an anti-inflationary force. This is a part of the process that eventually builds up those back pressures which are essential to the development of a new stability in the level of costs and prices.

A Decline in Profits Per Unit • A deceleration in the rate of growth in real output would adversely affect productivity in the short run. The movement of fixed costs per unit of output would thus be less favorable for a time. After a sustained period of expansion and labor shortages, employers would tend to maintain work forces, and payrolls would tend to be fixed. The deterioration in productivity and increased costs per unit of output would reduce profits per unit. While even higher prices might consequently seem necessary, and while in many cases they might be posted, market conditions would make it difficult for such prices to hold, and the major effect would be heavier pressure on businesses to begin actions to reduce costs. The need to improve productivity and thereby pare unit labor costs would make labor "hoarding" more costly. Employment at overtime would diminish and layoffs would become more common.

A Slowdown in Wage Increases • As profits per unit weakened, employers would become more resistant to granting wage increases. At the same time, a softening labor market would lessen workers' insistence on large wage increases as a condition for employment, since they could not be so sure of finding another job quickly if they left a current one or rejected a new offer. Moreover, if business profits were less favorable, a major rationale for heavy wage demands would be removed. As a consequence, the average rate of wage increase would ultimately begin to diminish. However, in view of the momentum of past increases in wages and the cost of living, this could not be expected to happen quickly. Nor could it be expected to happen evenly in all sectors.

A Slowdown in Price Increases • While, as already indicated, the unfavorable developments in profits would create some incentive to mark up prices, more sluggish market conditions would encourage businesses to pursue temperate pricing policies, especially as this influence began to be reinforced by a slowdown in the rise of wage rates and unit labor costs. The reductions in wage and price increases would tend to reinforce each other. The longer price increases moderated, the weaker would become the expectation of further inflation. In turn, business and labor would be increasingly inclined to respond to the waning inflation by making appropriate price and wage adjustments, in preference to accepting a lower volume of production and less employment. With this change the economy would be on the road to regaining full employment without setting off another round of inflation. . . .

THE LONGER RUN: STABILIZING THE GROWTH OF GNP

The main lesson of stabilization in 1969 was the importance of avoiding in the future the kind of inflationary situation and pervasive inflation-mindedness that had built up by the end of 1968. Starting from that situation, a major change in the behavior of the economy and in expectations was required, a change that would run against the current of strong ongoing forces. No one could tell how fast that change could be successfully accomplished or the degree of monetary and fiscal restraint required to accomplish it.

The objective of stabilization policy in 1970 will be to move us toward a position where the main goal can be continuity. That position will have been reached when inflation has been brought down to a significantly slower rate, and real output is growing at about its potential rate. At that point growth of the GNP in current dollars at a steady and moderate rate, such as 6 percent per year, would serve to support steady growth of output at its potential rate with a far better performance of the price level than has been experienced in recent years.

The problem then will be threefold:

1. To stabilize the rate of growth of money GNP as far as feasible at a pace that will permit the economy to produce at its potential;

2. To adapt the economy so that it lives better with whatever remaining instability may develop and;

3. To press on with measures to reduce both inflation and un-employment further.

To stabilize the growth of GNP will require avoiding destabi-lizing moves in fiscal and monetary policies and instead using these policies to offset, or at least constrain, destabilizing forces arising in the private economy. One difficulty is that the attempt to use fiscal and monetary policies to counter fluctuations arising in the private economy may itself be destabilizing, if moves are not made in the right amounts and at the right times.

Stabilization by Fiscal Policy · Fiscal policy should avoid large destabilizing swings occurring at random or contrary to the clear requirements of the economy. The big upsurge of federal spend-ing (nondefense as well as defense spending) after mid-1965, which was unmatched by any general tax increase for three years, is a major example of such a destabilizing movement.

The likelihood of achieving economic stability would not be greatly affected by the size of the surplus or deficit, within a reasonable range, if that size were itself stable or changing only slowly, and if the effects on liquidity resulting from secular in-creases or decreases in the federal debt were offset by monetary policy. Therefore, it should be possible to decide on the desired full-employment surplus or deficit on grounds other than stability, and without sacrificing stability if the target itself is kept rea-sonably stable. If the budget position changes sharply in the short run in the absence of marked shifts in private demand, the adaptation of the private economy and the compensatory force of monetary policy may not come into play quickly enough to pre-vent large swings in overall economic activity. This is a major lesson for the 1970s.

If the surplus or deficit position of the budget that would be yielded by a steadily growing, full-employment GNP were kept stable, the actual figure would, of course, automatically respond to changes in the pace of the economy. If the economy were to grow unusually slowly in any year, receipts would rise slowly also, and the surplus would be below normal (or the deficit would be enlarged further). These variations in the size of the surplus or deficit would tend to stabilize the growth rate of the GNP. The question is in what circumstances and how to go beyond this and vary expenditure programs and tax rates to offset fluctuations in the private economy. There is now abundant experience with the obstacles to effective and flexible use of tax changes for this purpose. Moreover, recent experience and analysis suggest that the stabilizing power of temporary income tax changes may not be as great as had been hoped, and it might become less if they were used frequently, because people would tend to adjust their behavior to what they regard as the normal rate of taxation. Nevertheless, there will be situations in which tax rates must be changed in order to maintain the desired long-run deficit or surplus position and there may also be circumstances in which the effort should be made to use a temporary tax change to offset destabilizing shifts in private demand.

The possibility of varying the rate of increase of federal spending in the interest of stability is somewhat greater though still limited. Although tax and expenditure decisions are both politically sensitive, the fact that the President has some discretion to adjust the timing of expenditures within the limits of legislation avoids some of the complications that beset tax changes. Moreover, the effect of expenditure changes on economic activity can probably be more reliably foreseen than the effect of temporary tax changes. It is true that the part of the total expenditures that is open to deliberate variation is small, because of legal and implied commitments. Nevertheless, some variations can, in fact, be made, as they were in 1969, and it would be unwise to rule out the attempt to do more of this when the economic necessity is clear. . . .

Stabilization by Monetary Policy · Monetary policy can be devoted somewhat more singlemindedly to maintaining stability than can fiscal policy. Nevertheless, there are a number of difficulties in its use. Apparently the effects of changes in monetary policy are felt in the economy with widely varying and often long lags. Therefore, if policy that is intended to have a restrictive effect is continued until the effect is visible, the lagged consequences of what has been done may show up in excessive contraction. The attempt to counter this by a sharp reversal in policy to an expansive posture may, after a while, generate inflationary rates of expansion. In the present state of knowledge there is no ideal solution for this problem. Prudence, therefore, suggests the desirability of not allowing monetary policy to stray widely from the steady posture that is likely on the average to be consistent with long-term economic growth, even though forecasts at particular times may seem to call for a sharp variation in one direction or another.

The suggestion that monetary policy might well be steady, or at least steadier than it has been, raises the question of the terms in which this stability is to be measured. There is abundant evidence that the steadiness of monetary policy cannot be measured by the steadiness of interest rates. Interest rates will tend to rise when business is booming and inflation is present or expected; they will tend to decline in the opposite circumstances. Better results might be obtained by concentrating more on the steadiness of the main monetary aggregates, such as the supply of money, of money plus time deposits, and of total bank credit. This still leaves questions of policy to be resolved when these aggregates are tending to move in different directions, or at different rates of change, as they often do. There is no substitute for trying to understand in particular cases what the significance of the divergences is and what they indicate about the underlying behavior of the supply of liquidity.

Wage-Price and Other Structural Policies

COMMITTEE FOR ECONOMIC DEVELOPMENT

The Committee for Economic Development made these suggestions for dealing with the inflation problem on a structural basis in its November 1970 statement, Further Weapons Against Inflation.

THE EXTENT TO WHICH INCREASES in aggregate demand will generate cost and price advances at any given level of over-all capacity and employment is greatly affected by the *structure* and adaptability of *supply* and by the efficiency with which resources are being used. When resources—human, physical, and financial —can be promptly moved to the areas where they are in greatest demand and are most productively employed, upward pressures on prices tend to be minimized. These pressures, however, can become severe when the needed adjustments are impeded or blocked by artificial restrictions, institutional imperfections, or more basic supply imbalances. As the economy moves closer to high employment and capacity, moreover, bottleneck problems and other impediments to price stability tend to be sharply intensified.

INCREASING THE EFFICIENCY OF LABOR AND PRODUCT MARKETS

A very wide range of policies and measures is required to overcome structural impediments to price stability and to increase the productivity of our physical and human resources. Listed below are various types of policy actions that should, in our view, be given priority attention by the National Commission on Productivity and by government, business, and labor generally. If these actions are to produce results, there is a clear need to adapt our laws to a high employment economy. A comprehensive review of existing statutes and regulations should be undertaken to eliminate depression-born features that have an inherent inflationary bias, work counter to efficiency and resource mobility, and are inappropriate for a high employment economy.

Reassessing Labor Legislation · High on the agenda of such a review should be a reexamination of existing labor legislation. We believe a basic restructuring of our labor laws and regulations is needed to bring about a better balance in the relative powers of unions and management. This is particularly true for areas of the economy where union activities have led to undue restrictions on productivity, or on entry into particular trades. We also propose elimination of the existing eligibility of strikers for unemployment insurance benefits in the two states (New York and Rhode Island) that permit such payments after a strike has been in effect for a specified number of weeks.

Strengthening Manpower Policies · Improvement in labor legislation should only be one aspect of a broad program to enhance the mobility and productivity of our manpower resources. A key obstacle to reconciling price stability and high employment in recent years has been the slowness of the structure of labor supply to adapt itself to major changes in the structure of the demand for labor. Over the past decade, needs for occupations requiring substantial skills and training have risen very sharply while the demand for unskilled and semiskilled workers has increased only slowly. Thus, from 1959 to 1969 the average annual increase in white-collar jobs amounted to 2.9 percent, while professional and technical jobs rose by over 4 percent. During the same period the number of blue-collar jobs advanced by only 1.6 percent. As a result, serious shortages of white-collar personnel with professional and technical skills and of various types of skilled craftsmen and blue-collar workers emerged as the economy reached higher levels of demand, at the very time when unskilled and semiskilled workers remained in substantial excess supply.

Such disparities in part require active measures to break down artificial restrictions on entry into various professions and crafts. These restrictions include racial discrimination and other barriers to membership in certain unions and various unnecessarily burdensome professional licensing provisions. More broadly, they call for positive programs to expand training in skills that are in short supply; encouragement of more efficient use of personnel with lesser skills (expanded reliance on paramedical personnel in hospitals is an example); and upgrading the education and training of the large groups of persons who have few or no skills.

To help cope with existing or emerging manpower supply bottlenecks, we specifically recommend (a) expanded governmental and private assistance to apprenticeship-training programs in construction; (b) special governmental measures to assure that returning veterans of the Vietnam War will make adequate use of skills acquired in the service; and (c) increases in the very low current ceilings on earnings that now apply to persons eligible for social security and railroad retirement benefits.

As regards job placement, major further efforts should be directed not only at aiding disadvantaged groups but at much greater overall labor mobility and a more efficient functioning of the markets for all types of personnel. The current efforts of the U.S. Department of Labor to apply computer techniques in job placement are highly commendable. The use of such techniques needs to be greatly expanded, however, if there is to be a really efficient nationwide system of matching job vacancies and job seekers. Many other steps to improve labor mobility should be explored, notably provision of additional financial incentives for moving workers to areas where jobs are available; further tax changes that assist job search and relocation; improvements in counseling and transportation; and measures to increase the transferability of pension rights and other fringe benefits.

Raising the Efficiency of Product Markets · Measures needed to foster more vigorous competition and efficient functioning of product markets include steps to improve consumer information; active enforcement of antitrust statutes; and a reexamination of various laws and regulations that provide for minimum prices or call for excessively detailed regulation in areas where greater reliance on competitive forces would be preferable.

A much greater effort is required to curtail uneconomic subsidies and output restrictions that raise prices and interfere with efficient resource allocation. Some types of subsidies may, of course, be appropriate in particular instances—e.g., when they are used to strengthen productivity and skills, or if there is a need to protect particular groups of people from severe hardships caused by sudden or persistent declines in demand. As we have stressed many times in the past, however, the cushioning actions taken by government in these circumstances should be designed to facilitate rather than obstruct needed economic adjustments.

Agricultural price supports and acreage restrictions constitute one major example of governmental policies that contribute to inflation. They do this in three major ways: by holding consumer prices at levels well above those that would exist if market forces were allowed to have free play; by preventing the movement of resources toward more productive uses; and by adding unnecessarily to total budget outlays. We believe that a more appropriate approach would seek to cushion the adverse impact of lower farm prices on the incomes of individual farmers and to foster a constructive adaptation of farm personnel and other resources to changes in underlying market conditions. At the same time, there should be as little interference as possible with market influences on prices and supply.

Substantial further efforts are needed to reduce existing restrictions on the free flow of international trade, especially through the removal of nontariff barriers. Such action can often be achieved only through new international regulations, but there is also a need for immediate steps by the United States to carry out agreements that were made, contingent on congressional approval, in connection with the "Kennedy Round." While there should be adequate provisions for temporary relief to domestic industries in instances where sudden large increases in imports and discriminatory foreign practices threaten serious disruptions in the United States market, it is vitally important for over-all price stability and economic efficiency that this country continue to adhere to its basic commitment to liberal international trade policies. We also believe that the Tariff Commission should be required by statute to consider general price stability as an objective to be taken into account in its decisons.

Providing Positive Incentives for Productivity · An intensive exploration is required of the possibilities for new types of legislation or regulations that can make a positive contribution toward increasing productivity and fostering price stability. Measures to encourage productive long-term investment, such as the investment tax credit that this committee has long favored, are among outstanding examples. Tax policy generally should be designed to "develop a tax structure which stimulates or least deters effort and investment on the part of all segments of the private economy." More active governmental assistance needs to be given to pilot projects and research designed to raise productivity in many service activities and in construction. "Operation Breakthrough" in the housing field is one promising example. The availability, accuracy, and timeliness of statistics on productivity should be greatly improved, particularly in the case of the government and private service sectors.

THE ROLE OF VOLUNTARY WAGE-PRICE POLICIES

The structural measures discussed above should go a long way toward reducing the economy's inflationary potential at given levels of total demand. Applying such measures successfully, however, will in many cases be a prolonged and difficult task. Moreover, it does not seem likely that structural measures by themselves can deal with another important source of inflationary pressure that may be present even when the economy is operating significantly below full capacity—the "cost-push" that can be exerted by labor unions and business firms which possess a significant degree of discretion in setting wages and prices.

It is this element of discretion which creates a substantial risk at the present time, despite the marked dampening in over-all demand, that shortsighted policies by some unions and firms could lead to a self-defeating upward spiral in costs and prices. Already, more and more union wage demands tend to be based not only on the desire to make up for the rapid past increases in living costs but also to provide protection against expected future price advances. In the face of rising costs, many business firms for their part feel impelled despite lagging demands to try to raise prices in order to protect falling profit margins. The question thus arises whether—as a supplement to appropriate general demand policies and to measures for dealing with basic structural problems—more direct steps also should be taken to induce restraint in discretionary price and wage decisions.

One way to seek to accomplish this would be through the imposition of mandatory wage-price controls. However, this Committee is opposed to mandatory controls on wages and prices except in the event of a major war. Such comprehensive controls could require a huge and costly bureaucracy; would seriously impair the freedom and efficiency of the economy; and might well prove unenforceable under current conditions.

We have also given careful consideration to proposals that the President, as a drastic measure to break the existing inflationary psychology, call for a voluntary moratorium on all wage and price increases for a limited period of from six months to a year. We do not believe, however, that such a moratorium is likely to be enforceable under present circumstances and feel that it could actually be counterproductive by jeopardizing the development of more carefully worked-out—though still stringent—wage-price policies.

The adoption of voluntary wage-price or "incomes" policies in our view constitutes the most promising approach to the problem at this time. Such policies are directed only at firms and labor groups with some market discretion, and are particularly concerned with dealing with "cost-push" when there is no excess in total demand. They should not be confined to the manufacturing sector but can extend to other important areas where some leeway in wage or price setting exists, including industries which are not predominantly unionized. Under such policies, the government or a government-sponsored group defines the wage and price behavior that is conducive to or consistent with over-all price stability; seeks to enlist the voluntary cooperation of business and labor in exercising the needed restraint; and calls the public's attention to significant instances of excessively inflationary behavior.

Since the wage-price policies described here are based on voluntary cooperation, they involve far less extensive and detailed intervention in economic decision-making processes than direct controls. Those who favor such voluntary policies regard them as a means of avoiding eventual imposition of compulsory wage and price restraint, rather than as a step in this direction.

PAST EXPERIENCE WITH WAGE-PRICE POLICIES

A cautious early step toward a wage-price policy in the United States was taken at the beginning of 1958, when President Eisenhower's Economic Report stressed the importance of responsible price and wage decisions. The 1958 Report suggested that wage increases going beyond over-all productivity gains are inconsistent with stable prices and that price increases unwarranted by cost advances could, over time, be self-defeating.

These rather general admonitions were followed, in January 1962 by the promulgation by President Kennedy's Council of Economic Advisers of a more specific set of "guideposts" for noninflationary wage and price behavior. Essentially, these guideposts provided that if over-all price stability was to be maintained, wage increases should be geared to economy-wide productivity advances while prices in each industry should be geared to unit costs in that industry—i.e., most prices should ordinarily be stable, but there should be price declines in industries where productivity rises more than the average and increases where productivity advances less. Various exceptions were provided, notably to allow larger wage increases for workers in weak bargaining positions who had badly lagged behind; to facilitate premium payments needed to help shift labor and capital resources to areas of shortages; and to permit extra benefits for workers who were making special contributions to productivity.

Although the guideposts were initially conceived as largely educational and quite general, in subsequent years the wage guide was given more explicit numerical content in terms of productivity (formally for the first time in 1964). Moreover, there was an increasing tendency on the part of the administration to press publicly and privately for adherence to both the wage and price standard in particular instances. At the same time, the case for possible exceptions tended to be de-emphasized since it was feared that anything other than quite simple rules might weaken public support for the guideposts.

While prices and wages were unusually stable from 1962 to 1965, they began to rise markedly after the emergence of excessive over-all demand in 1966. From that time on, it became increasingly unrealistic to expect conformity with the guideposts. Labor, for one thing, could hardly be expected to accept wage increases geared to a 3.2 percent productivity standard when consumer prices were rising at an annual rate that was equal or higher. Although the Council continued to stress the basic productivity principle, it abandoned numerical guideposts by 1967. Thereafter, administration activities to induce moderation in price and wage behavior were confined to selective "moral suasion" or "jawboning" efforts—partly carried out publicly but more often through private conversations.

With the advent of the Nixon Administration, wage-price policies were at first formally abandoned, and the President himself made clear that the Administration would not seek to influence particular price and wage decisions. Then came the President's speech in June 1970, which included a general appeal for wage and price restraint and called for the spotlighting of outstanding cases of wage and price increases through periodic "Inflation Alerts" prepared by the Council of Economic Advisers and published by the new National Commission on Productivity. These initiatives have been widely regarded as a move toward a limited form of incomes policies, though they do not call for the development of "norms" of anti-inflationary behavior.

Did the wage-price policies of 1962–68 make any real difference in wage-price behavior? Considerable controversy still exists on this point. On balance, however, the available evidence seems to suggest that the guideposts did make a noticeable though modest contribution to stability in 1962–65, before excessive demand had emerged. Support for the view that the subsequent jawboning efforts also had some (though still smaller) moderating effect has recently been presented but this is much more difficult to evaluate.

Outside the United States, experiments with various types of wage-price or incomes policies have been carried out in many of the principal industrial countries, in some instances dating back to the 1940s. Experience has varied greatly. There appears to have been no case in which these policies have had continuous success and it generally appears to have been true that the policies did not work when total demand was excessive. Still, the record does suggest various particular instances or periods when incomes policies made a contribution to reconciling price stability and economic growth. It is interesting that despite various disappointments, most of the major European countries continue to make use of incomes policies in some form. This may well signify that if such policies are to remain effective, the specific techniques employed ought to be varied with some frequency.

SHOULD THE UNITED STATES EMPLOY WAGE-PRICE POLICIES?

Neither U.S. nor foreign experience with wage-price policies to date provides a clear-cut guide as to whether a new type of voluntary wage-price policy in the United States would make a substantial contribution toward containing inflation. If such policies are to be employed in this country at all, however, the present time seems to present an especially propitious opportunity for applying them. With aggregate demand no longer excessive, the types of cost-push influences at which such policies are directed are now in the forefront of the inflationary threat. On balance of considerations, we believe that the United States should include voluntary wage-price policies among its policy tools for reconciling price stability and high employment.

As already noted, properly conceived wage-price policies are not a substitute for appropriate fiscal-monetary policies or for actions to cope with basic structural problems. These measures must remain the first lines of defense against inflation. Rather, wage-price policies are designed to supplement and reinforce such measures by helping to reduce the economic and human costs of bringing inflation under control through general demand management.

Fundamentally, wage-price policies must work as an educational force that will cause economic decision-making units to take a broader view of their own long-run self-interest than they are likely to take in the absence of such policies. Their use is based on the presumption that management and labor can, at least in an important number of instances, be influenced to exercise greater restraint in wage demands and pricing decisions once they clearly understand that this will avoid a continuing wage-price spiral from which neither would gain. Just as many motorists will not automatically follow sensible ways of driving unless there are some traffic rules or signs, business firms and unions cannot be expected to exercise needed price and wage restraint without some indication that others will be asked to do the same in the context of some sort of ground rules that spell out the public interest. It is this sort of indication that wage-price policies can provide.

We believe it is desirable and appropriate that the basic educational role of these policies be reinforced by drawing the attention of public opinion to instances of excessively inflationary behavior. There should, however, be no governmental "arm-twisting" of individual firms and unions, based on actual or implied threats of actions other than presentation of relevant information to the public.

There is, of course, no full assurance that incomes policies will make a significant contribution to price stability. Even so, we believe there are enough favorable elements in the past record to make it worthwhile to give these policies a try. Our own observations suggest that major business firms would not be insensitive to official requests that they take the public interest in price stability into specific account when they make price and wage decisions. Since a wide range of considerations normally enters such decisions, a better definition of what the public interest requires in particular instances, especially when the decision is close, could well be the element that will tip the scale in the direction of greater price stability. Similarly, we believe that in connection with labor-management negotiations, there can be a beneficial effect if broad norms developed under wage-price policies serve as an explicit reminder of the public interest in price stability.

The use of wage-price policies is sometimes questioned on the grounds that they would have little influence on some of the areas of the economy where costs and prices have been rising most sharply—notably construction and various service activities —and that in areas where they can be effective, they would distort efficient resource allocation by interfering with the workings of free market mechanisms. Such arguments, however, tend to be based on a misinterpretation of what wage-price policies should be expected to accomplish. They cannot be a substitute for general demand policies or for the measures to deal with the structural problems of construction and of many service industries. They may, however, have an influence on containing inflation in these areas by helping to reduce the cost-push that may be transmitted from other sectors of the economy. Moreover, wage-price policies are intended to be applied only to segments of the economy where imperfections in the operations of free market mechanisms already interfere with optimum resource allocation.

In judging the potential success of the combined use of structural and wage-price policies, it should be noted that if they were to succeed in producing relative price stability with an unemployment rate of, say, 0.5 percentage points less than would otherwise be the case, the gains in terms of output would be very significant—quite apart from the reduction in human and social costs. Looking forward into the 1970s, a differential of 0.5 percentage points in the unemployment rate, and the effect on total man-hours and capacity utilization that go with it, would make a difference in the GNP of something on the order of $15 billion to $20 billion at an annual rate.

It can be objected, of course, that resort to wage-price policies carries the risk of producing various inequities. It is inherently difficult to develop norms of wage and price behavior that will in fact be fair to everybody, particularly if there is a premium on keeping the rules simple. Also, incomes policies frequently tend to impinge with special force on the larger firms and unions and on the particular wage and price decisions that are most clearly visible. Public attention is more likely to focus on the decisions of the bigger firms and unions even at times when the actions of smaller units, considered in the aggregate, have greater inflationary effects. A large price increase also stands a greater chance of being criticized than failure to reduce prices when productivity gains make this desirable.

Such objections lose much force, however, if support for the policy is actually widespread, based on a realization that cooperation with it is in fact in the common interest. From the viewpoint of the cooperating firms and unions—including those that are the most "visible"—the long-term gains in terms of preventing the development of a cumulative inflationary spiral may be much greater than the relative disadvantages they may suffer vis-à-vis those that are less affected by wage-price policies or refuse to cooperate. In this respect, voluntary compliance with these policies has much in common with the voluntary cooperation in various other fields that many of the larger corporations and labor groups already extend in connection with governmental appeals made in the public interest.

To the extent, moreover, that wage-price policies can be regarded as contributing to the simultaneous achievement of price stability and of high employment, the inequities that they may produce must be weighed against the fact that a failure to employ such policies may contribute to even greater inequities: the gross inequities connected with spiraling inflation or, alternatively, those stemming from the degree of increased unemployment or uneven impact of monetary policy that may be associated with attempts to defeat inflation through demand restraint alone.

WHAT KIND OF WAGE-PRICE POLICIES?

On the basis of the lessons of the past and of the emerging new economic challenges, we believe that an effective wage-price policy program will need to conform to the following requirements:

• The policies evolved should, to the maximum extent possible, be based on full and continuous consultation among government, business, and labor and should represent as wide a consensus among these groups as possible. The lack of a really active participation of business and labor leaders in wage-price policy formulation and application was a major shortcoming of earlier U.S. wage-price policies.

• To be meaningful, income policies should go beyond purely general appeals for wage and price restraint. They should include some ground rules or norms which define wage-price behavior that is consistent with the public interest in over-all price stability and that can be regarded as basically fair to all the groups involved.

• Such ground rules should be designed to assist rather than impede optimum resource allocation. Thus, any general rules should provide adequate exceptions for special price or wage adjustments that may in some instances be needed to correct critical imbalances between demand and supply.

· The program should be based on voluntary cooperation, depending for its effectiveness on keeping the public fully informed about significant instances of excessively inflationary behavior and the factors associated with them.

· The formulation as well as implementation of wage-price policies should be entrusted to an independent body within the government rather than be considered a direct function of the President or of his Council of Economic Advisers. Overly direct involvement of the presidency with particular wage and price decisions constituted a major drawback of earlier U.S. wage-price policies. The development of appropriate standards should be carried out, however, in close consultation with the Council of Economic Advisers and other relevant agencies in the administration, as well as with the Congress, representatives of state and local governments, and the private sector.

Several alternative institutional arrangements could satisfy these broad requirements. In our view, the creation of the National Commission on Productivity and the initiation of an "Inflation Alert" system constitute important steps toward the development of the kind of approach that we envisage. We recommend, however, that the announced new procedures be given added strength in a number of respects.

1. The fact-finding functions of the new "Inflation Alert" system should in appropriate cases be utilized to highlight important prospective wage and price developments rather than being solely directed at decisions that have already been taken. In particular, it would be helpful to alert public opinion to potential inflationary threats in advance of major scheduled labor-management wage negotiations. We do not imply, however, that advance notification of price changes should be required.

2. The National Commission on Productivity, or a new body, should be assigned the task of developing broad norms of appropriate noninflationary wage and price behavior that would give some guidance to business and labor groups which may be affected by Inflation Alerts.

3. There should be authorization for such a group to publish, after careful scrutiny of the facts, reports on instances of wage and price behavior by individual unions or companies, that de-

viate substantially from such broad norms as may have been established and that represent special threats to over-all price stability.

Over time, effective implementation of these functions may well prove to be a greater burden than should be imposed on the Council of Economic Advisers or on the new National Commission on Productivity. We recommend, therefore, that consideration be given to the creation of a three-man Board on Prices and Incomes, appointed by the President and subject to Senate confirmation, that would have principal responsibility for developing norms of noninflationary behavior covering private wage and price decisions that are subject to some discretion as well as changes in government wages and salaries. The Board also would be responsible for detailed examination of important instances of deviations from such norms. The Board should be composed of three distinguished citizens working on a full-time basis, who would represent the public at large. They should draw on the advice of the National Commission on Productivity and other appropriate bodies with key representation of management, labor, and government, while at the same time consulting closely with the Council of Economic Advisers. The Board should be assisted by a top-quality staff and have adequate access to needed information.

In the course of its experience with immediate policy issues, the Board can be expected to gain important insights into more basic factors contributing to inflationary wage and price pressures, and develop opinions regarding possible longer-range remedies. It should make reports to the Executive Branch and the Congress on its tentative conclusions in these areas and suggest which among the possible solutions deserve especially careful further exploration. Such remedies would presumably encompass steps to strengthen competitive forces in particular industries and labor markets, and in some exceptional instances might also include the possibility of compulsory arbitration. Every effort should be made to assure that suggestions developed through such a process be given very careful study and, if appropriate, be translated into early action.

Our support of voluntary wage-price policies is pragmatic. We do not know whether or not they will be needed on a permanent basis. But we do believe strongly that incomes policies should be tried now and be continued at least through the period of recovery. Indeed, it is during the period of renewed expansion that there is likely to be a particularly marked need for such policies.

What Price Guideposts?

MILTON FRIEDMAN

Professor Friedman expressed these doubts about the concept of cost-push inflation and these objections to guideposts in a conference held at the University of Chicago in 1966. This selection is a portion of his paper in Guidelines, Informal Controls, and the Market Place, *edited by George P. Schultz and Robert Z. Aliber.*

AN ANALOGY is often drawn between direct control of wages and prices as a reaction to inflation and the breaking of a thermometer as a reaction to, say, an overheated room. This analogy has an element of validity. Prices are partly like thermometers in that they register heat but do not produce it; in both cases, preventing a measuring instrument from recording what is occurring does not prevent the occurrence. But the analogy is also misleading. Breaking the thermometer need have no further effect on the phenomenon being recorded; it simply adds to our ignorance. Controlling prices, insofar as it is successful, has very important effects. Prices are not only measuring instruments, they also play a vital role in the economic process itself.

A much closer analogy is a steam-heating furnace running full blast. Controlling the heat in one room by closing the radiators in that room simply makes other rooms still more overheated. Closing all radiators lets the pressure build up in the boiler and increases the danger that it will explode. Closing or opening individual radiators is a good way to adjust the relative amount of heat in different rooms; it is not a good way to correct for overfueling the furnace. Similarly, changes in individual prices are a good way to adjust to changes in the supply or demand of individual products; preventing individual prices from rising is not a good way to correct for a general tendency of prices to rise.

Suppose that there is such a general tendency, and suppose that some specific price (or set of prices), say, the price of steel, is prevented from rising. Holding down the price of steel does not make more steel available; on the contrary, given that other prices and costs are rising, it reduces the amount that producers can afford to spend in producing steel and is therefore likely to reduce the amount available from current production. Holding down the price of steel does not discourage buyers; it encourages consumption. If the suppressed price is effectively enforced and not evaded by any of the many channels that are available to ingenious sellers and buyers, some potential buyers of steel must be frustrated—there is a rationing problem. Chance, favoritism, or bribery will have to decide which buyers succeed in getting the steel. Those who succeed pay less than they are willing to pay. They, instead of the steel producers, have the remainder to spend elsewhere. Those who fail will try to substitute other metals or products and so will divert their demand elsewhere; the excess pressure is shifted, not eliminated.

The situation is precisely the same on the labor market. If wages are tending to rise, suppressing a specific wage rise will mean that fewer workers are available for that type of employment and more are demanded. Again rationing is necessary. The workers employed have less income to spend, but this is just balanced by their employers having larger incomes. And the unsatisfied excess demand for labor is diverted to other workers.

But, it will be said, I have begged the question by *starting* with a general tendency for prices to rise. Can it not be that this general tendency is itself produced by rises in a limited number of prices and wages which in turn produce sympathetic rises in other prices and wages? In such a case, may not preventing the initial price and wage rises nip a wage-price or price-price spiral in the bud?

Despite its popularity, this cost-push theory of inflation has very limited applicability. Unless the cost-push produces a monetary expansion that would otherwise not have occurred, its effect will be limited to at most a temporary general price rise, accompanied by unemployment, and followed by a tendency toward declining prices elsewhere.

Suppose, for example, a strong (or stronger) cartel were formed in steel, and that it decided to raise the price well above the level that otherwise would have prevailed. The price rise would reduce the amount of steel people want to buy. Potential purchasers of steel would shift to substitute products, and no doubt the prices of such substitutes would tend to rise in sympathy. But there is now another effect. Steel producers would hire fewer workers and other resources. These would seek employment elsewhere, tending to drive down wages and prices in other industries. True, wages and prices might be sticky and decline only slowly, but that would only delay the downward adjustments and only at the expense of unemployment. . . .

The only example I know of in United States history when such a cost-push was important even temporarily for any substantial part of the economy was from 1933–1937, when the NIRA, AAA, Wagner Labor Act, and associated growth of union strength unquestionably led to *increasing* market power of both industry and labor and thereby produced upward pressure on a wide range of wages and prices. This cost-push did not account for the concomitant rapid growth in nominal income at the average rate of 14 percent a year from 1933–1937. That reflected rather a rise in the quantity of money at the rate of 11 percent a year. And the wage and cost-push had nothing to do with the rapid rise in the quantity of money. That reflected rather the flood of gold, initiated by the change in the United States price of gold in 1933 and 1934 and sustained by the reaction to Hitler's assumption of power in Germany.

The cost-push does explain why so large a part of the growth in nominal income was absorbed by prices. Despite unprecedented levels of unemployed resources, wholesale prices rose nearly 50 percent from 1933–1937, and the cost of living rose by 13 percent. Similarly, the wage cost-push helps to explain why unemployment was still so high in 1937, when monetary restriction was followed by another severe contraction.

The popularity of the cost-push theory of inflation, despite its limited applicability, stems, I believe, from two sources: first, the deceptiveness of appearances; second, the desire of governmental authorities to shift the blame for inflation.

One of the fascinating features of economic relations is the frequent contrast between what is true for the individual and what is true for the community. Time and again the one is precisely the opposite of the other. Each individual takes for granted the prices of the things he buys and regards himself as having no effect on them; yet, consumers as a whole greatly affect those prices by the combined effects of their separate actions. . . . Indeed, it is precisely this contrast between what is true for the individual and for the community that underlies many, perhaps most, common economic fallacies. They arise from invalid generalization from the individual to the community.

The widespread belief in the cost-push theory of inflation is a striking example. To each businessman separately, inflation tends to come in the form of increasing costs, and, typically, he correctly regards himself as having to raise the price at which he sells because his costs have risen. Yet, those cost rises may themselves reflect an increase in demand elsewhere and simply be part of the process whereby the demand increase is transmitted; and his ability to raise his price without a drastic decline in sales reflects the existence of excess demand. The monetary expansion and the associated increase in money demand take place through mysterious, widely dispersed, and largely invisible channels. The cost and price increases are their visible tracks.

In a recent elementary economics textbook, Alchian and Allen have given a vivid illustration of how a price rise produced by a demand increase can make itself felt to almost all the participants in the process as a cost-push:

Pretend that for some reason people's desire for meat increases. . . . Housewives reveal an increased demand by buying more meat than formerly at the current prices in the meat markets. . . . [T]he increased demand takes its toll of inventories. . . . [The] butcher will buy more meat than usual the next day in order to restore his inventory from its abnormally low level. . . . Just as butchers use inventories, so packers . . . also rely on inventories. . . . [A]ssume that the first day's change in demand was within that inventory limit and therefore was met without a price increase.

Packers restore inventories by instructing their cattle buyers . . . to buy more cattle than usual. But with all the packers restoring their inventories in this manner, the number of cattle available for sale each day are inadequate to meet the increased total demand *at the old price*. . . .

[T]he buyers will begin to raise their offers . . . until the price rises to the point where the packers will not want to buy more meat . . . than is available from the cattlemen. . . .

[T]he packers experience *a rise in costs* . . . [so] the packers must charge a higher price to butchers if they are to continue as profitable meat packers. . . . The butchers, in turn, post higher prices to the housewives. When housewives complain about the higher price, the butcher in all innocence, honesty, and correctness says that it isn't his fault. The cost of meat has gone up. . . . And the packers can honestly say the same thing.[1]

To almost all participants, therefore, a rise in price produced by excess demand appears to take the form of a rise in costs that enforces a higher price.

The interpretation of inflation as a reflection of cost-push is greatly fostered by governmental authorities. In modern times, the government has direct responsibility for the creation and destruction of money; it determines what happens to the quantity of money. Since inflation results from unduly rapid monetary expansion, the government is responsible for any inflation that occurs. Yet, governmental authorities, like the rest of us, while only too eager to take credit for the good things that occur, are most reluctant to take the blame for the bad things—and inflation generally is regarded as a bad thing. Their natural tendency is to blame others for the inflation that governmental policies produce—to castigate the rapacious businessman and power-hungry labor leader rather than point to the government printing press as the culprit.

The 1966 *Annual Report* of the Council of Economic Advisers is an amusing and distressing example. It has a 31-page chapter on "Prospects for Cost-Price Stability" that so far as I have been able to determine has only two passing references to "monetary policy" and does not even contain the word "money"—a treatment of money strictly comparable to the way a rigid Puritan writing a book about love might have handled "sex." . . .

Even granted that legally imposed and vigorously enforced wage and price ceilings covering a wide range of the economy would do enormous harm, some may argue that the enunciation of guideposts, their approval by businessmen and labor leaders, and voluntary compliance with them, or even lip service to them, is a palliative that can do no harm and can temporarily help

1. Armen A. Alchian and William R. Allen, *University Economics* (Belmont, Calif.: Wadsworth Publishing Co., 1964), pp. 105–7.

until more effective measures are taken. At the very least, it may be said, it will enable businessmen and labor leaders to display their sense of social responsibility.

This view seems to me mistaken. The guideposts do harm even when only lip service is paid to them, and the more extensive the compliance, the greater the harm.

In the first place, the guideposts confuse the issue and make correct policy less likely. If there is inflation or inflationary pressure, the governmental monetary (or, some would say, fiscal) authorities are responsible. It is they who must take corrective measures if the inflation is to be stopped. Naturally, the authorities want to shift the blame, so they castigate the rapacious businessman and the selfish labor leader. By approving guidelines, the businessman and the labor leader implicitly whitewash the government for its role and plead guilty to the charge. They thereby encourage the government to postpone taking the corrective measures that alone can succeed.

In the second place, whatever measure of actual compliance there is introduces just that much distortion into the allocation of resources and the distribution of output. To whatever extent the price system is displaced, some other system of organizing resources and rationing output must be adopted. As in the example of the controls on foreign loans by banks, one adverse effect is to foster private collusive arrangements, so that a measure undertaken to keep prices down leads to government support and encouragement of private monopolistic arrangements.

In the third place, "voluntary" controls invite the use of extralegal powers to produce compliance. And, in the modern world, such powers are ample. There is hardly a business concern that could not have great costs imposed on it by antitrust investigations, tax inquiries, government boycott, or rigid enforcement of any of the myriad of laws, or on the other side of the ledger, that can see no potential benefits from government orders, guarantees of loans, or similar measures. Which of us as an individual could not be, at the very least, seriously inconvenienced by investigation of his income tax returns, no matter how faithfully and carefully prepared, or by the enforcement to the letter of laws we may not even know about? This threat casts a shadow well beyond any particular instance. In a dissenting opinion in a recent court case involving a "stand-in" in a public library, Justice Black wrote, "It should be remembered that if one group can take over libraries for one cause, other groups will assert the right to do it for causes which, while wholly legal, may not be so appealing to this court." Precisely the same point applies here. If legal powers granted for other purposes can today be used for the "good" purpose of holding down prices, tomorrow they can be used for other purposes that will seem equally "good" to the men in power—such as simply keeping themselves in power. It is notable how sharp has been the decline in the number of businessmen willing to be quoted by name when they make adverse comments on government.

In the fourth place, compliance with voluntary controls imposes a severe conflict of responsibilities on businessmen and labor leaders. The corporate official is an agent of his stockholders; the labor leader, of the members of his union. He has a responsibility to promote their interests. He is now told that he must sacrifice their interests to some supposedly higher social responsibility. Even supposing that he can known what "social responsibility" demands—say by simply accepting on that question the gospel according to the Council of Economic Advisers —to what extent is it proper for him to do so? If he is to become a civil servant in fact, will he long remain an employee of the stockholders or an agent of the workers in name? Will they not discharge him? Or, alternatively, will not the government exert authority over him in name as in fact?

Inflation being always and everywhere a monetary phenomenon, the responsibility for controlling it is governmental. Legally enforced price and wage ceilings do not eliminate inflationary pressure. At most they suppress it. And suppressed inflation is vastly more harmful than open inflation.

Guideposts and pleas for voluntary compliance are a halfway house whose only merit is that they can more readily be abandoned than legally imposed controls. They are not an alternative to other effective measures to stem inflation, but at most a smoke-screen to conceal the lack of action. Even if not complied with they do harm, and the more faithfully they are complied with, the more harm they do.

Nonetheless, we should not exaggerate either the problem or the harm that will be done by false cures. Prices will almost surely rise in coming months. We shall probably continue to experience inflationary pressure on the average over the coming years. The price rise, however, will be moderate. A major war aside, I cannot conceive that the monetary authorities will permit the quantity of money to rise at a rate that would produce inflation of more than, say, 3 to 10 percent a year. Such inflation will be unfortunate, but if permitted to occur reasonably openly and freely, not disastrous. And, despite all the talk, prices and wages will be permitted to rise in one way or another. The guideposts will be more talked about than they will be voluntarily complied with or enforced by extralegal pressure. Hypocrisy will enable effective evasion to be combined with self-congratulation. Debasing the coin of public and private morality is unfortunate, but in moderate doses not disastrous. The greatest harm will continue to be done by the measures taken to peg exchange rates. It is well to keep in mind Adam Smith's famous comment, "There is much ruin in a nation," but only to avoid overstating a good case, not to condone bad policy.

Unreasonable Price Stability—
the Pyrrhic Victory Over Inflation

EDMUND S. PHELPS

The author, professor of economics at Columbia University, wrote this criticism of the Administration's anti-inflationary strategy in the spring of 1971 and revised it slightly to recognize the new economic policy begun the following August.

IN THE FIELD OF domestic policy, the Nixon administration will be longest remembered for its use of conventional monetary and fiscal·instruments to end a major inflation. The painful slump that has been the inevitable and predictable accompaniment of the classical exercise may be historic. The episode may mark, at least for a while, the last application (by the last economic liberal?) of what used to be called liberal economic policy in curbing the rate of inflation. The next contest with inflation—maybe in 1980—will probably witness, for better or worse, reliance on price and wage controls instead of the classical medicine. Of equal interest, the costs of the inflation fight may—and ought to—prompt a reappraisal of its worth.

Soon after taking office, the administration embarked on a plan to bring the inflation to a gradual halt by grimly tightening the reins on the money supply and on the federal budget. To have sought an abrupt halt of the inflation by such classical measures, it feared, might have risked an economic crash. On the other hand, to have acquiesced in a steady inflation, even at a moderate rate, would have strained the administration's conservative principles. To have resorted to a price and wage freeze would have offended its liberal principles. The course left was a slow winding down of the inflation rate over the presidential term. This was the Inflation Game Plan.

There is no denying that the operation was a technical success, much as originally foreseen. Quarter after quarter since the anti-inflation measures began to take hold, the annual inflation rate has fallen. It appears likely that the rate through 1971 will be about 4.5 percent. This compares with a 5.5 percent rise of the Consumer Price Index during 1970, and a 6.1 percent rise over 1969 when the first disinflationary steps were being taken. Certainly the economic theorist will always be grateful to the Nixon administration for this demonstration once again that money and taxes ultimately call the inflation tune. Yet academic theorists are among the very few with any real cause for gratitude. The shrinkage of inflation has been a Pyrrhic victory. The operation, while a technical success, has been too excruciating for the patient to endure.

The classical theory of inflation control is not difficult, although the administration has been reluctant to discuss it. Economists have long understood that the price level, being the money cost of buying consumer goods, tends ultimately to be governed by the relation of money to the producible quantity of goods. A reduction in the supply of money as a ratio to producible goods tends in the long run to lower the price level in about the same proportion. A cut in government expenditures or a rise in tax rates—hence a rise of the full-employment budget surplus—tends also to lower the price level in the long run. (They increase the demand for money as a ratio to producible goods.)

But, and this is crucial, there is no immaculate connection between money (or fiscal variables) and the price level. A slowdown of the money supply or a rise of the full-employment surplus causes a temporary business slump before it works its full effect on the path of prices. The reason is that the price and wage increases which a businessman or unionist sets are greatly influenced by his expectation of the rises that will take place in other prices and wages. Prices tend to rise at a rate equal to the inflation rate which people expect *plus* something more if business is abnormally good and *minus* something when business is abnormally bad. If a lower rate of inflation is to be achieved at the normal level of output and employment expectations of the inflation rate must be lowered. Unfortunately, these expectations of the inflation rate are sluggish, slow to respond up or down.

The classical method of reducing expectations of the inflation rate proceeds by disappointing those expectations as long as they are excessive. A slowdown of the money supply, or a cutback of government expenditures, causes fewer sales and soon less inflation than firms and workers were expecting. Expectations of the inflation rate are therefore revised downward in the light of bitter experience. With the expected inflation rate thus reduced, the way is paved for a return to prosperity at a lower inflation rate. But the exercise is effective only at an appalling social cost: The same disappointments that reduce expectations of the inflation rate act normally to depress production and employment. Unemployment and slack capacity increase until prosperity can finally be reclaimed at the lower rate of inflation.

This is harsh doctrine, and it is understandable that the Nixon administration has been reticent to discuss it. Yet there have been occasions on which candor broke through. In December 1970, speaking before New York manufacturers, President Nixon defended the Game Plan for what he termed "reasonable price stability." The workingman and businessman, having already paid a heavy cost in reduced employment and profits for the administration's desire to eliminate inflation, had now "earned the right," he said, to continue their sacrifices. In the same month, but somewhat less confident of our insistence on these sacrifices, Arthur F. Burns, Chairman of the Federal Reserve System, pleaded in Los Angeles for our continuing "fortitude to come to grips with inflation." More recently, in April of this year, the Director of the Office of Management and Budget, George P. Shultz, noting that "a portion of the battle against inflation is now over," told a group of Chicago businessmen: "Time, and the guts to take time, not additional medicine, are required for the sickness to disappear." Apparently the administration sees the inflation purge as a ritual test of our economic manliness.

Nevertheless, while the administration has liked to take credit for the ends being achieved, it often has failed to own up to the means being employed. The administration sometimes conveys the impression that keeping a tight rein on the money supply has a magical power over inflation without ever causing a lost job or an idle machine. The 6-percent unemployment rate that we are stuck at is blamed on fortuitous events, or unassailable policies, such as disengagement from Vietnam.[1] In attempting to protect the administration's policies from cries for monetary stimulus, Dr. Burns recently claimed that the economy is already "awash with liquidity." The remark was either disingenuous eye-wash or else a rare lapse for the usually astute Dr. Burns. The truth is that while there may be enough liquidity to float a slumping economic ship, there is hardly enough liquidity to buoy a prosperous one.

I have said that the present slump has been a matter of policy, the foreseeable outcome of the Game Plan, not an outcome of chance. In view of the confusion on this point, however, it may be worthwhile to examine briefly the mechanisms behind the present slump. Probably the primary cause of the prolonged sluggishness in the economy, and the factor primarily responsible for the recession to begin with, is the government's deliberate monetary policy: an unrelenting contraction of the money supply *relative* to the economy's capacity to produce and to the price level. What tends to mask the insufficiency of money for economic recovery is the never-ending confusion between rate of speed and distance covered. Some people assert that the present *rate of increase* of the money supply is adequate for the reattainment of prosperity. This is as unperceptive as saying that my horse runs fast enough when the other horse is ahead and runs just as fast. The proper task of the money managers in the Federal Reserve System is not simply to keep up with the real growth of the economy—plus whatever inflation rate is deemed "reasonable" over the long run. The need is to make up the arrears of the past.

Let me document the scarcity of money in this relative sense. The money supply in real terms, in terms of its purchasing power over goods, has been barely greater in the current year

1. Thus the *National Review* found reason to congratulate the President on the skillfulness of the Congressional campaign in this respect [December 1, 1970]: "And so, instead of being drawn into attempts to explain his economic policy, or the theory of fighting inflation, instead of being trapped into awkward statements about the 'acceptable level of unemployment,' Nixon seized the Social Issue. . . . The Democratic offensive on the economic issue came too little and too late for the smashing victory that might have been."

(1971) than it was three years before. Yet, over this period, the volume of production needed to provide the normal amount of jobholding has increased, with the real growth of the economy, by some 15 percent. As a result there is no longer enough money to finance full-employment production. As evidence, consider that in 1965—a "full-employment" year if we define full employment as 4.5 percent unemployed—the money supply was more than 24 percent of the corresponding GNP. In the second quarter of 1971, the money supply has been probably less than 20 percent of the level of GNP that at today's price and productivity levels would be needed for "full employment." And this is a time when, for a prompt return to full employment, the economy could use a monetary shove beyond the normal monetary prodding.

It is absurd therefore to worry, as some have done, that even a small improvement in the level of liquidity would risk "reigniting" the old rate of inflation. The present degree of liquidity, once related to the potential full-employment production level, is clearly inadequate even for maintaining the present inflation rate. "Full-employment liquidity"—the amount of liquidity (per unit of output) that would exist with the prevailing money supply if production were at the full-employment level—appears definitely to be deficient.

Much the same picture is presented by the fiscal side. Analogous to full-employment liquidity is the full-employment budget surplus. This is an estimate of what the budget surplus would be with the prevailing tax rates if production, and hence tax revenues, were at full-employment level. This full-employment surplus has swung from about $6 billion of hypothetical red ink in 1968 to a plus figure of $6 billion projected by the administration's Council of Economic Advisers in January 1971. If the Congress succeeds in adding expenditures and whittling away at taxes so as to decrease this figure by a few billion, it will not be because the Nixon administration wanted it that way. On the contrary, the administration has held up billions of dollars of Congressional appropriations for the purpose of producing a recessionary rise in the full-employment surplus.

This economic policy has been a costly mistake. I shall argue this on two grounds. First, "reasonable price stability"—if that means a flat price trend or one rising no more than 2 percent annually—is not the ideal state in our less-than-perfect economy. Second, even if it were ideal, price stability would not be worth the cost of the planned slump to achieve it. Yet such elementary objections to the goal of price stability are seldom, if ever, debated. Why? The reason, I believe, is that the public has been beguiled by a mystique that has somehow grown up around price stability.

Central to the mystique is the popular misunderstanding of the price level as the cost of "living." In fact it is nothing of the kind. The consumer price index is only the money cost of buying a given diet of goods—not the human cost in time, effort, or other sacrifice. Intellectually it is probably grasped that every rise in prices paid by buyers for a given assortment of goods is necessarily a rise in the prices received by the sellers of those goods. Yet people frequently talk as though they were only buyers and never sellers. They seem to forget that our real incomes depend upon the money prices of what we buy only as a ratio to the prices of the services we sell.

The question, "Would a rise in the price of turnips be good for me?" is, by itself, unanswerable. It needs a context. Similarly

TABLE 1. *Instruments of the Slump*

	1965	1968	1971
	(second quarter figures)		
1. Nominal Money Supply (billions of dollars)	162.5	188.4	219.2 [1]
2. Price Level (1958 = 1.00)	1.107	1.217	1.402 [2]
3. Real Money Supply = (1) ÷ (2) (billions of 1958 dollars)	147	155	156
4. Real "Full-Employment" GNP [3] (billions of 1958 dollars)	610	696	794
5. Full-Employment Liquidity = (3) ÷ (4) (in percent)	24.1%	22.3%	19.6%
6. Full-Employment Surplus [4] (billions of dollars)	1.0	−6.0	6.0

1. projected at 6% annual growth rate from the Jan. 1971 figure of 214.9
2. projected at 4% annual inflation rate from 1970 4th quarter level of 137.4
3. projected at 4.5% annual growth rate from actual 2nd quarter 1965 level
4. annual figures

with the effect of inflation. For an individual, as for society as a whole, whether real income will be enhanced or diminished by a rise in the inflation rate depends critically upon the nature of the forces causing the rise. Consider first an unanticipated rise in the inflation rate.

An unplanned, and hence at first unexpected, inflation is usually due to an unanticipated rise of aggregate demand for goods, as with the outbreak of a war. In that case output and employment are generally stimulated. For most of the population there will be the feeling of prosperity, and the fact of it as well if the production of consumer goods is also stimulated in the boom. The only people who tend to lose out are those whose incomes depend heavily upon private pensions and bond-holdings.

Yet the inflation, being unaccustomed, unwanted, and ultimately repulsed at heavy cost, comes to be held guilty of every misfortune experienced while it lasts. While crediting their every economic success to individual prowess, people tend to blame their every economic loss on the unaccustomed price rise, something beyond their individual control, never on the failure of their earning power to keep up. Cause is mistaken for effect when the surtaxes designed to moderate the inflation are blamed on it when in fact they would need to have been still larger to avert the inflation. Perhaps the crowning absurdity is that when the government punishes us with a recession in order to eliminate the inflation, the resulting bulge in unemployment and excess capacity is blamed on inflation rather than on the punishing hand. It is the purge of inflation, not the inflation itself, that is causing the city and state governments so much financial difficulty.

The guilt by association pinned on unexpected and unplanned inflation stands in the way of a fair hearing for the idea of planned inflation. For nearly all the associations, true and false, with unexpected inflation are irrelevant to planned and hence anticipated inflation. Suppose that the government were to adopt a positive inflation rate as the chosen target of its monetary policy. By its monetary and fiscal policies the inflation rate might be made to average around 4 percent rather than around the old norm of near zero. Such a 4 percent norm, being planned and customary, would be a quite different animal from the same inflation rate when it is unplanned and abnormal. The big difference would be that when some inflation rate has become the normal average over the business cycle and people have gained experience with it, they would learn to expect it and to count on it in the economic decisions they make.

The man in the street remains anxious. "What good does it do me to know that price rises are coming if I have no power to raise my income?" The economist replies: There is utterly no presumption or evidence that inflation, once it becomes the norm and is anticipated, will redistribute real income away from people with little or no market power. When producers are counting on higher prices all around, they tend to bid up the money wages of people without market power. People with market power have to see to their anticipatory wage increases themselves. Neither is there any good reason to expect that social security recipients, welfare recipients, small farmers, and other poor persons would lose ground on account of a rising price trend, once anticipated. The poor will suffer only if we make them suffer. In such an inflationary regime there would be as much shuffling of relative economic positions as in a zero inflation regime. But do not impute to inflation what the stars had held in store in any case.

Yet the mystique dies hard. There must be some powerful reasons, the layman will surmise, why wise men in authority have so long favored zero inflation as the norm of American monetary policy. Else why are the authorities now urging such heroic sacrifices to restore price stability?

There is, first, the theory that America must return to zero inflation in order to forestall a gold drain in our balance of payments, or some other mode of international monetary disaster. But the rest of the world is inflating faster than we are; and if we do not disinflate, it is unlikely the rest of the world will disinflate either. Moreover the international monetary system, for all its Byzantine complexities, could be adjusted and improved in such a way as to accommodate deliberate inflation.

There is, second, the theory that much of the financial community feels their bread to be buttered on the side of low inflation. Of course, their special interests, correctly perceived by them or not, should not be compelling; their losses from inflation might be other persons' gains.

We come at last to the heart of the mystique. Disinterested advocates of zero inflation candidly admit that their position is not science but religion. The weightiest and the most zealous proponent of zero inflation, Milton Friedman, makes not a single claim for the scientific merit of zero as against moderate anticipated inflation. Yet the myth of price stability is held to serve a useful social function. Humankind cannot stand much reality, Eliot wrote. Nor too much freedom either.

Without the functioning of the myth, it is contended, the monetary authorities might at first choose to sanction 4 percent inflation instead of zero. But there would then come a day, it is maintained, when there will be the same temptation to approve 8 percent inflation as there now exists to settle at 4. There would be no end to it, which of course would be intolerable. Q.E.D. But the logic is faulty. If one planned inflation rate were truly no worse than a lower one, as the argument assumes, then ever-rising inflation would be perfectly tolerable and even welcome. We could then have a perpetual controlled boom. But, of course, one inflation rate is not as good as any other.

Those who insist on the necessity of the price stability myth must therefore fall back on either or both of two positions. First, they can contend that the inflation rate, if left to free choice, will settle at too high a rate. We must ask why this should be blithely inferred. Other countries have managed moderate inflation rates (with the inevitable ups and downs). The other possible contention is that the economy will be less stable once the rock-like faith in the restoration of zero inflation is taken away. But it may be replied that an inherently desirable goal is more easily defended against tendencies to stray from it than a goal with no intrinsic attractiveness.

But the basic answer to the proponents of the role of myth is that we entrust graver national decisions to rational democratic process than the relatively mundane question of the most advantageous price trend. Why should we be barred, as if by some monetary constitution, from tinkering with the inflation rate in the way that we see fit? Of course the resulting policy may not be ideal. But it is quite possible that it would be distinctly better than the policy of ritual price stability.

Is there a scientific case for the establishment of some moderate inflation rate—say, between 4 and 5 percent per annum—as the norm for monetary and fiscal policy? Yes, and the arguments are not new in the economics profession. Saving the most telling for last, the arguments are these:

In a regime where a positive inflation rate is the norm, the expectation of that inflation rate serves as a kind of tax on holding money. Like every other kind of tax, it has its deleterious effects upon incentives. As the income tax discourages working for pay, the inflation tax discourages staying liquid. But like other taxes, the inflation tax does a job of holding down the claims of consumers upon resources so as to save some resources for use in capital formation. An optimal package of taxes would include some inflation so as not to place extra burdens on other kinds of taxes.

When the economy is geared to moderate inflation, it would be actually less prone to stubborn slumps and runaway increases of the inflation rate above the norm. Because liquidity would be less plentiful, there is less tinder around with which to spark a strong boom. And because, in recession, money markets would be less sloppy or elastic than otherwise, they would be more susceptible to central bank influence.

The speed-up of employment and job upgrading that would result from the policy shift to a higher inflation rate norm, though largely short-lived, would be of lasting and transforming benefit for many workers who would not otherwise have had such meaningful jobs and training opened to them so soon. In turn, a recession which lowers the inflation rate and which eliminates jobs even temporarily tends permanently to weaken the capacity for work of some of those disemployed. Their will to work, in Orwell's report of the thirties, atrophies like an unexercised muscle.

Finally, suppose that the reduction of production and employment resulting from the drive to reattain stable prices were wholly temporary. Even so, it would be improper to weigh dollar for dollar any future benefits from that price stability against those irretrievable losses of economic benefits in the present. The Congress and the Bureau of the Budget do not let public agencies have money for capital projects which can be justified only at a zero or negligible rate of interest. This investment in price stability demanded by the Federal Reserve, borne by us at the cost of substantial unemployment, should also be subject to a similar interest-rate test. We have to live in the present as well as the future.

The Basis for Lasting Prosperity

This selection is a shortened version of a lecture delivered by Arthur F. Burns, Chairman of the Board of Governors of the Federal Reserve System, at Pepperdine College on December 7, 1970.

NEARLY THREE YEARS AGO, I pointed out that once an economy becomes engulfed by inflation, economic policy-makers no longer have any good choices. To regain a lasting prosperity, a nation must have the good sense and fortitude to come to grips with inflation. There is, however, no painless way of getting rid of the injustices, inefficiency, and international complications that normally accompany an inflation.

Events of the past several years have lent poignancy to these simple truths. Recent experience has demonstrated once again that the transition from an overheated economy to an economy of stable markets is a difficult process. Elimination of excess demand was an essential first step to the restoration of stability, but this step has brought with it a period of sluggish economic activity, slow income growth, and rising unemployment. And while we have made some progress in moderating the rate of inflation, our people are still seeing the real value of their wages and savings eroded by rising prices.

The struggle to bring inflationary forces under control, and to return our labor and capital resources to reasonably full employment, is still going on. I am convinced, however, that corrective adjustments in the private sector over the past twelve to eighteen months are creating, in conjunction with governmental stabilization policies, the foundation on which a prolonged and stable prosperity can be constructed.

A cardinal fact about the current economic situation, and one that promises well for our nation's future, is that the imprudent policies and practices pursued by the business and financial community during the latter half of the 1960s are being replaced by more sober and realistic economic judgments. In my remarks to you today, I want first to review some of the key developments that lead me to this conclusion. Then I shall turn to the tasks that must still be faced in order to enhance the prospects for an early resumption of growth in production and employment in an environment of reasonably stable prices.

The current inflation got under way in 1964. Perhaps the best single barometer of the extent to which it served to distort economic decisions and undermine the stability of the economy is found in the behavior of financial markets during the late 1960s. In 1968, well over three billion shares of stock exchanged hands on the New York Stock Exchange—about 2½ times the volume of five years earlier. The prices of many stocks shot upward with little reference to actual or potential earnings. During the two years 1967 and 1968, the average price of a share of stock listed on the New York Exchange rose 40 percent, while earnings of the listed companies rose only 12 percent. On the American Exchange the average share price rose during the same two years more than 140 percent on an earnings base that increased just 7 percent.

A major source of the speculative ardor came from some parts of the mutual fund industry. Long-term investment in stocks of companies with proven earnings records became an outmoded concept for the new breed of "go-go" funds. The "smart money" was to go into issues of technologically oriented firms—no matter how they were meeting the test of profitability, or into the corporate conglomerates—no matter how eccentric their character.

This mood of speculative exuberance strongly reinforced the upsurge of corporate mergers which occurred during the middle years of the 1960s. No doubt many of these mergers could be justified on grounds of efficiency. But the financial history of mergers—including some of the great conglomerates—suggests that many businessmen became so preoccupied with acquiring new companies and promoting the conglomerate image that they lost sight of the primary business objective of seeking larger profits through improved technology, marketing, and management. When talented corporate executives devote their finest hours to arranging speculative maneuvers, the productivity of their businesses inevitably suffers and so too does the nation's productivity. These speculative excesses had to end, and it is fortunate that they ended before bringing disaster to our nation. . . .

Businessmen are reconsidering the wisdom of financial practices that distorted their balance sheets during the late 1960s. In the manufacturing sector, the ratio of debt to equity—which had been approximately stable during the previous decade—began rising in 1964 and was half again as large by 1970. Liquid asset holdings of corporate businesses were trimmed to the bone. On the average, the ratio of prime liquid assets to current liabilities fell by nearly half during those six years. In permitting such a drastic decline in liquidity, many of our corporations openly courted trouble.

Perhaps the most ominous source of instability produced by these financial practices was the huge expansion of the commercial paper market. The volume of commercial paper issued by nonfinancial businesses increased eightfold between the end of 1964 and mid-1970, as an increasing number of firms—some of them with questionable credit standings—began to tap this market. . . .

It took the developments of the summer of 1970, when the threat of financial crisis hung for a time over the commercial paper market, to remind the business community that time-honored principles of sound finance are still relevant.

As a result of that experience and the testing of financial markets generally during the past two years, corporate financial policies are now more constructive than in the recent past. This year, new stock issues have continued at a high level—even in the face of unreceptive markets—as corporations have sought to stem the rise in debt-equity ratios. Of late, borrowing by corporations has been concentrated in long-term debt issues, and their rate of accumulation of liquid assets has risen. Liquidity positions of industrial and commercial firms are thus improving, though it will take some time yet to rectify fully the mistakes of the past. . . .

By and large, our major financial institutions conducted themselves with prudence during the years when lax practices were spreading in financial markets. There were, however, some individual institutions that overextended loan commitments relative to their resources, others that reduced liquidity positions to unduly low levels, still others that permitted a gradual deterioration in the quality of loan portfolios, and even a few that used funds of depositors to speculate in long-term municipal securities. Fortunately, such institutions were distinctly in the minority. When the chips were down, our major financial institutions proved to be strong and resilient. And they are stronger today. As monetary policy has eased, the liquidity of commercial banks has been increasing. Even so, loan applications are being screened with greater care. The emphasis on investment quality has also increased at other financial institutions, as is evidenced by the recent wide spread between the yields of high and lower grade bonds.

These corrective adjustments in private financial practices have materially improved the prospects for maintaining order and stability in financial markets. But no less important to the establishment of a solid base for a stable and lasting prosperity have been the developments in 1970 in the management of the industrial and commercial aspects of business enterprise.

During the latter half of the 1960s, business profit margins came under severe pressure. The ratio of profits after taxes to income originating in corporations had experienced a prolonged rise during the period of price stability in the early 1960s. But this vital ratio declined rather steadily from the last quarter of 1965 and in 1970 reached its lowest point of the entire postwar period.

Until the autumn of 1969 or thereabouts, the decline in profit margins was widely ignored. This is one of the great perils of inflation. Underlying economic developments tend to be masked by rising prices and the state of euphoria that comes to pervade the business community. Though profit margins were falling and the cost of external funds was rising to astonishing levels, the upward surge of investment in business fixed capital continued. True, much of this investment in business was undertaken in the interest of economizing on labor costs. Simultaneously, however, serious efforts to bring operating costs under control became more and more rare, labor hoarding developed on a large scale, huge wage increases were granted with little resistance, and some business investments were undertaken in the expectation that inflationary developments would one way or another validate almost any business judgment. While the toll in economic effi-ciency taken by these loose managerial practices cannot be mea-sured with precision, some notion of its significance can be gained by observing changes in the growth rate of productivity.

From 1947 through 1966, the average rate of advance in output per man-hour in the private sector of the economy was about 3 percent per year. In 1967, the rate of advance slowed to under 2 percent, and gains in productivity ceased altogether from about the middle of 1968 through the first quarter of 1970. The loss of output and the erosion of savings that resulted from this slowdown in productivity growth are frightfully high.

The elimination of excess demand, which the government's anti-inflationary policies brought about, is now forcing business firms to mend their ways. Decisions with regard to production and investment are no longer being made on the assumption that price advances will rectify all but the most imprudent busi-ness judgments. In the present environment of intense competi-tion in product markets, business firms are weighing carefully the expected rate of return on capital outlays and the costs of financing. The rate of investment in plant and equipment has therefore flattened out.

Business attitudes toward cost controls have of late also changed dramatically. A cost-cutting process that is more wide-spread and more intense than at any time in the postwar period is now underway in the business world. Advertising expenditures are being curtailed, unprofitable lines of production discon-tinued, less efficient offices closed, and research and development expenditures critically reappraised. Layers of superfluous execu-tive and supervisory personnel that were built up over a long period of lax managerial practices are being eliminated. Reduc-tions in employment have occurred among all classes of workers —blue collar, white collar, and professional workers alike.

Because of these vigorous efforts to cut costs, the growth of productivity has resumed, after two years of stagnation. These productivity gains have served as a sharp brake on the rise in unit labor costs, despite continued rapid increases in wage rates.

In my judgment, these widespread changes in business and financial practices are evidence that genuine progress is being made in the long and arduous task of bringing inflationary forces under control. We may now look forward with some confidence to a future when decisions in the business and financial community will be made more rationally, when managerial talents will be concentrated more intensively on efficiency in processes of production, and when participants in financial markets will avoid the speculative excesses of the recent past.

Let me invite your attention next to the role that government policies have played this year in fostering these and related adjustments in private policies and practices.

The fundamental objective of monetary and fiscal policies in 1970 has been to maintain a climate in which inflationary pressures would continue to moderate, while providing sufficient stimulus to guard against cumulative weakness in economic activity. Inflationary expectations of businessmen and consumers had to be dampened; the American people had to be convinced that the government had no intention of letting inflation run rampant. But it was equally important to follow policies that would help to cushion declines in industrial production stemming from cutbacks in defense and reduced output of business equipment, and to set the economy on a course that would release the latent forces of expansion in our homebuilding industry and in state and local government construction. I believe we have found this middle course for both fiscal and monetary policy.

A substantial reduction in the degree of fiscal restraint has been accomplished in 1970 with the phasing out of the income tax surcharge and the increase in social security benefits. These sources of stimulus provided support for consumer disposable incomes and spending at a time when manufacturing employment was declining and the length of the work-week was being cut back.

I do not like, but I also am not deeply troubled by, the deficit in the federal budget during the 1971 fiscal year. If the deficit had originated in a new explosion of governmental spending, I would fear its inflationary consequences. This, however, is not the present case. The deficit in fiscal 1971—though it will prove appreciably larger than originally anticipated—reflects in very large part the shortfall of revenues that has accompanied the recent sluggishness of economic activity. The federal budget is thus cushioning the slowdown in the economy without releasing a new inflationary wave. The President's determination to keep spending under control is heartening, particularly his plea last July for a rigid legislative ceiling on expenditures that would apply to both the Executive and the Congress. However, pressures for much larger spending in fiscal 1972 are mounting and pose a threat to present fiscal policy.

Monetary policy this year has also demonstrated, I believe, that it could find a middle course between the policy of extreme restraint followed in 1969 and the policies of aggressive ease pursued in some earlier years. Interest rates have come down, and liquidity positions of banks, other financial institutions, and nonfinancial businesses have been rebuilt—though not by amounts that threaten a reemergence of excess aggregate demand. A more tranquil atmosphere now prevails in financial markets. Market participants have come to realize that temporary stresses and strains in financial markets could be alleviated without resort to excessive rates of monetary expansion. Growth of the money supply thus far this year—averaging about a 5½ percent annual rate—has been rather high by historical standards. This is not, however, an excessive rate for a period in which precautionary demands for liquidity have at times been quite strong.

The precautionary demands for liquidity that were in evidence earlier in 1970 reflected to a large degree the business and financial uncertainties on which I have already commented. It was the clear duty of the nation's central bank to accommodate such demands. Of particular importance were the actions of the Federal Reserve in connection with the commercial paper market in June 1970. This market, following the announcement on Sunday, June 21, of the Penn Central's petition for relief under the Bankruptcy Act, posed a serious threat to financial stability. The firm in question had large amounts of maturing commercial paper that could not be renewed, and it could not obtain credit elsewhere. The danger existed that a wave of fear would pass through the financial community, engulf other issuers of commercial paper, and cast doubt on a wide range of other securities.

By Monday, June 22—the first business day following announcement of the bankruptcy petition—the Federal Reserve had already taken the virtually unprecedented step of advising the larger banks across the country that the discount window would be available to help the banks meet unusual borrowing requirements of firms that could not roll over their maturing commercial paper. In addition, the Board of Governors reviewed its regulations governing ceiling rates of interest on certificates of deposit, and on June 23 announced a suspension of ceilings in the maturity range in which most large certificates of deposit are sold. This action gave banks the freedom to bid for funds in the market and make loans available to necessitous borrowers.

As a result of these prompt actions, a sigh of relief passed through the financial and business communities. The actions, in themselves, did not provide automatic solutions to the many problems that arose in the ensuing days and weeks. But the financial community was reassured that the Federal Reserve understood the seriousness of the situation, and that it would stand ready to use its intellectual and financial resources, as well as its instruments of monetary policy, to assist the financial markets through any period of stress. Confidence was thus bolstered, with the country's large banks playing their part by mobilizing available funds to meet the needs of sound borrowers caught temporarily in a liquidity squeeze.

The role that confidence plays as a cornerstone of the foundation for prosperity cannot, I think, be overstressed. Much has been done over recent months by private businesses and by the government to strengthen this foundation. If we ask what tasks still lie ahead, the answer I believe must be: full restoration of confidence among consumers and businessmen that inflationary pressures will continue to moderate, while the awaited recovery in production and employment becomes a reality.

The implications of this answer for the general course of monetary and fiscal policies over the near term seem to me clear. The thrust of monetary and fiscal policies must be sufficiently stimulative to assure a satisfactory recovery in production and employment. But we must be careful to avoid excessive monetary expansion or unduly stimulative fiscal policies. Past experience indicates that efforts to regain our full output potential overnight would almost surely be self-defeating. The improvements in productivity that we have struggled so hard to achieve would be lost if we found ourselves engulfed once again in the inflationary excesses that inevitably occur in an overheated economy.

As I look back on the latter years of the 1960s, and consider the havoc wrought by the inflation of that period, I am convinced that we as a people need to assign greater prominence to the goal of price stability in the hierarchy of stabilization objectives. I have recommended on earlier occasions that the Employment Act of 1946 be amended to include explicit reference to the objective of general price stability. Such a change in that law will not, of course, assure better economic policies. But it would call the nation's attention dramatically to the vital role of reasonable price stability in the maintenance of our national economic health.

At the present time, governmental efforts to achieve price stability continue to be thwarted by the continuance of wage increases substantially in excess of productivity gains. Unfortunately, the corrective adjustments in wage settlements that are needed to bring inflationary forces under control have yet to occur. The inflation that we are still experiencing is no longer due to excess demand. It rests rather on the upward push of costs—mainly, sharply rising wage rates.

Wage increases have not moderated. The average rate of increase of labor compensation per hour has been about 7 percent in 1970—roughly the same as 1969. Moreover, wage costs under new collective bargaining contracts have actually been accelerating despite the rise in unemployment. . . .

I fully understand the frustration of workers who have seen inflation erode the real value of past wage increases. But it is clearly in the interest of labor to recognize that economic recovery as well as the battle against inflation will be impeded by wage settlements that greatly exceed probable productivity gains.

In a society such as ours, which rightly values full employment, monetary and fiscal tools are inadequate for dealing with sources of price inflation such as are plaguing us now—that is, pressures on costs arising from excessive wage increases. As the experience of our neighbors to the north indicates, inflationary wage settlements may continue for extended periods even in the face of rising unemployment. In Canada, unemployment has been moving up since early 1966. New wage settlements in major industries, however, averaged in the 7 to 8 percent range until the spring of 1969, then rose still further. In 1970, with unemployment moving about 6½ percent, negotiated settlements have been in the 8 to 9 percent range.

Many of our citizens, including some respected labor leaders, are troubled by the failure of collective bargaining settlements in the United States to respond to the anti-inflationary measures adopted to date. They have come to the conclusion, as I have, that it would be desirable to supplement our monetary and fiscal policies with an incomes policy, in the hope of thus shortening the period between suppression of excess demand and the restoration of reasonable relations of wages, productivity, and prices.

To make significant progress in slowing the rise in wages and prices, we should consider the scope of an incomes policy quite broadly. The essence of incomes policies is that they are market-oriented; in other words, their aim is to change the structure and functioning of commodity and labor markets in ways that reduce upward pressures on costs and prices. . . .

I would hope that every citizen will support the President's stern warming to business and labor to exercise restraint in pricing and wage demands. A full measure of success in the effort to restore our nation's economic health is, I believe, within our grasp, once we as a people demonstrate a greater concern for the public interest in our private decisions.

If further steps should prove necessary to reduce upward pressures on costs and prices, numerous other measures might be taken to improve the functioning of our markets. For example, liberalization of import quotas on oil and other commodities would serve this purpose. So also would a more vigorous enforcement of the antitrust laws, or an expansion of federal training programs to increase the supply of skilled workers where wages are rising with exceptional rapidity, or the creation on a nationwide scale of local productivity councils to seek ways of increasing efficiency, or a more aggressive pace in establishing computerized job banks, or the liberalization of depreciation allowances to stimulate plant modernization, or suspension of the Davis-Bacon Act to help restore order in the construction trades, or modification of the minimum wage laws in the interest of improving job opportunities for teenagers, or the establishment of national building codes to break down barriers to the adoption of modern production techniques in the construction industry, or compulsory arbitration of labor disputes in industries that vitally involve the public interest, and so on. We might bring under an incomes policy, also, the establishment of a high-level Price and Wage Review Board which, while lacking enforcement power, would have broad authority to investigate, advise, and recommend on price and wage changes.

Such additional measures as may be required can, of course, be determined best by the President and the Congress. What I see clearly is the need for our nation to recognize that we are dealing, practically speaking, with a new problem—namely, persistent inflation in the face of substantial unemployment—and that the classical remedies may not work well enough or fast enough in this case. Monetary and fiscal policies can readily cope with inflation alone or with recession alone; but, within the limits of our national patience, they cannot by themselves now be counted on to restore full employment, without at the same time releasing a new wave of inflation. We therefore need to explore with an open mind what steps beyond monetary and fiscal policies may need to be taken by government to strengthen confidence of consumers and businessmen in the nation's future.

In the past two years we have come a long way, I believe, toward the creation of a foundation for a lasting and stable prosperity. Confidence has been restored in financial markets. Businesses have turned away from the imprudent practices of the past. Productivity gains have resumed. Our balance of trade has improved. The stage has been set for a recovery in production and employment—a recovery in which our needs for housing and public construction can be more fully met.

To make this foundation firm, however, we must find ways to bring an end to the pressures of costs on prices. There are no easy choices open to us to accomplish this objective. But that, as I indicated at the outset, is the tough legacy of inflation.

The Costs of Wage-Price Controls

WILLIAM POOLE

William Poole expressed these personal criticisms of controls, initially published in Brookings Papers on Economic Activity, *in September 1971 shortly after President Nixon froze wages and prices. Poole is a research economist with the Federal Reserve Board.*

. . . CONTROLS incur three different types of costs. The first is the loss of individual freedom resulting from central control over individual wage and price decisions. The second is the misallocation of resources resulting from controls. And the third is the administrative cost. All these costs are interrelated. For example, if administrative cost is kept low, enforcement of the controls will be weak and will have relatively little effect after a time. Also, it is obvious that the costs of controls are a function of their duration.

The resource allocation and administrative costs of controls are not likely to prove great if the controls last for at most several years, especially if they are selective or mild and really "buy" lower unemployment and greater price stability. In any event, a rich society can bear these costs. The important issue concerns the costs in individual freedom and the way in which they affect the nature of controls that are politically acceptable. The question is whether temporary mild controls will make any lasting contribution to the goals of full employment and price stability.

Considerable governmental power was applied when the wage-price freeze was put into effect. All contracts voluntarily reached by individuals and firms, with each other and with governmental units, have been suspended insofar as they provide for increases in wages and prices. . . .

Several examples may serve to amplify the references to "individual freedom." These examples should not be taken to concern "mere details," for one of the major arguments against controls is that there is no satisfactory way of handling these details. To consider the problems of enforcing wage controls, suppose that a firm wants to increase the pay of an employee to a level above the controlled level, perhaps because he is threatening to take a job with a competitor. An obvious technique is to promote him—indeed, so obvious that one of the first clarifications issued during the current freeze was that wages could be increased only in the event of a "bona fide" promotion.

What is a "bona fide" promotion? One approach is not to allow promotions into newly created positions. A firm is not permitted to create new vice presidents, or new foremen, or new senior accountants just to have more higher paying slots to put employees in. But clearly this approach to wage control cannot last very long since many firms have valid reasons for creating new positions.

What criteria can the controllers then use to distinguish between bona fide and control-avoidance promotions? Beyond the cases where the issues are clear-cut, many problems will arise, for example, in connection with corporate mergers and reorganizations. To offer another example, how does a government official know how many foremen are needed in a new plant producing a new product?

Comprehensive wage control is no easy matter. Many arbitrary decisions must be made. Wage control will be relatively easy and most complete over standardized types of jobs, including most blue collar and clerical jobs. Managerial and professional jobs, on the other hand, are more varied and more subject to change. The inequities will multiply, and so will the pressure for a more and more elaborate control machinery to limit the inequities by adjusting wages and salaries.

To obtain wage increases some individuals will be forced to change jobs because one firm, though willing, is not permitted to grant an increase in pay, while another obtains permission for a new position, or has a vacancy in an existing position. Excessive job changing is not only inefficient but also tends to break down wage control. To combat this tendency, controls may be imposed on job moves, or directly on the pay of individuals rather than of jobs.

Price control presents problems that are just as serious. How is the price on a new product to be determined? To set the price on the basis of the firm's cost requires the perhaps expensive attempt to understand its cost accounting methods. To set it equal to that of the closest competitive product is unsatisfactory if the new product costs more to produce but has superior characteristics that are not permitted to bring a higher price, or if it has roughly the same performance characteristics but costs less to produce. In the latter case the cost savings are not passed on to the purchasers of the new product.

Another problem arises when firms face cost increases, some of which in practice will prove unavoidable. Is a firm to be permitted to pass these increases on in the form of higher prices? If not, what happens if the firm simply stops production of an unprofitable item? Will a firm be forced to continue production of an item "vital to the national interest"? If cost increases on "vital" products, however defined, are considered a valid reason for price increases, how many officials will be required to administer the price controls?

Product specifications are constantly changing, sometimes reflecting improvement, sometimes deterioration. In comprehensive price control firms have an obvious incentive to reduce the quality of their goods and services. If the inflationary pressures to be suppressed by controls are powerful, control over product specifications will be required.

Although economists disagree as to the severity of these problems, they acknowledge their existence and believe that they will become more apparent with time. As problems appear, some economists will call for an escalation of controls, while others, like me, will argue that there is no natural end to the escalation of controls. How can these administrative problems be handled without a large bureaucracy? Only administrative guidelines that permit individuals, firms, and control administrators to know what changes in wages and prices, and in job and product specifications, are and are not permitted could make a small bureaucracy feasible. I do not believe such guidelines can be constructed, and, if these matters must be handled on a case-by-case basis, will not the sheer volume of cases overwhelm the control bureaucracy? Will the decisions by controllers be subject to legal appeal, and if so what is the case load likely to be?

Whether controls can work without a large bureaucracy is an

empirical question. In my view the issue involved is whether the inflation problem arises primarily from relatively few sources of market power, both on the labor side and the product side, that can be effectively controlled without an elaborate control machinery.

I believe that the economy is far more competitive than surface appearances would indicate. Suppose that mandatory controls were placed on the wages and prices of the 200 or the 500 largest corporations in the nation. Furthermore, suppose that prices were not permitted to increase at all, and wage increases were limited to the 3.2 percent productivity guideline. Assume, too, that the controls were really strict and all the problems of evasion were handled successfully. How would the experiment work out?

Those who favor this approach would predict that the rate of increase of prices and wages in the whole economy would be drastically slowed. Firms with controlled prices would take business away from those that raised prices and thereby effectively control all prices. Since the prices of uncontrolled firms would in fact be effectively controlled, they would be forced to limit their wage increases. Furthermore, wage demands made to the uncontrolled firms would moderate because the big, visible unions would not be obtaining big wage increases for others to emulate.

Those predicting failure for this approach expect, of course, that some evasion of the controls would take place. To the extent that it is stemmed, the controlled firms would lose their operating flexability. Their key employees would be bid away, and in some product lines they would find themselves unable to meet the market demand at the prices allowed. Customers, therefore, would turn to uncontrolled firms. Furthermore, the controls and the uncertainty of their application would limit the incentive for large firms to invest in expanded facilities, further eroding their positions.

Some find it hard to believe that in a situation of deficient aggregate demand such as now characterizes the U.S. economy there can be a significant number of cases in which controlled firms would be unable to meet market demand. This view underestimates the normal amount of dispersion in price changes, much of which is caused by differences in demand pressures in different industries. For example, from June 1970 to June 1971 the whole-sale price index rose by 3.6 percent. But of the ninety-eight detailed product categories in the index, nineteen had price increases of over 7 percent, and of these thirteen had increases of over 10 percent. Also, seventeen of the catgories had actual price declines, and of these six had declines of more than 3 percent. Of the thirty-six changes that were either increases greater than 7 percent or declines, twenty-four involved industrial commodities and twelve involved farm products and processed foods and feeds. There are, of course, many individual products within the ninety-eight categories and further disaggregation surely would show more variability.

I do not believe that the controllers will be able to rely on a few judicious exceptions to solve the problem of excess demand for some products and labor skills. To make many exceptions will risk pressures for still more. Furthermore, prices that would have declined without controls will tend to stay up because firms will fear difficulties in raising them in the future if conditions change. I expect that fewer price declines will occur under a system of controls than occurred in the period preceding the freeze.

I predict that in a relatively short space of time competitive forces would be operating so powerfully that the control experiment described above would be dropped or altered to meet the competitive situation. If the controls were altered, the uncontrolled sectors would determine the level of the wage and price controls in the controlled sectors, rather than the controls affecting the level of wages and prices.

These predictions are straightforward, but the experiment is unlikely to be undertaken. It simply is not politically possible to place strict controls on the largest firms. The reason lies beyond the political power they and unions hold and people's strongly held beliefs about equity. Rather, the reason is primarily the severity of the economic dislocations that would ensue from controls. To counter that it is "unrealistic" to set a 3.2 percent limit on wage increases when wages have been rising at two or three times that rate is not sufficient. If wage increases cannot be set at 3.2 percent, the economic realities control the controllers, rather than the other way round.

If mandatory controls on the largest firms and unions won't

work, there is, of course, little hope for a voluntary guidelines approach. Voluntary compliance is possible only when the guidelines are very close to what would have happened anyway.

THE RISKS OF CONTROLS

Some of those who favor temporary controls share my misgivings but nevertheless are eager to make the experiment. Even if the control effort collapses, something may have been gained and little will have been lost. Of course, if a thoroughgoing experiment works as poorly as I predict, it should at least end for some time the political pressures for controls. On the other hand, if the Phase II controls are not strict, failure of controls to work may only produce pressures for more stringent enforcement. Since the public has been promised more than mild controls can deliver, if they fail the danger is that semipermanent comprehensive controls will be invoked. Enforcement of controls of any variety is unlikely to be easy. Definition of "goods" and "services," and the large number of individual cases, will require many arbitrary decisions. The difficulties and dangers of bringing individual wage and price determinations into the political process on top of the many economic and other issues already there should not be ignored.

In my view, however, the major damage likely to result from controls is a postponement of the achievement of a stable full employment economy with a reasonably stable price level. I believe that there is no feasible method, including controls of the severity acceptable in our society, that would permit a quick return to both full employment and price stability. Controls may have the effect of hiding the genuine short-run conflict between full employment and price stability and lead to monetary and fiscal policies that are more expansionary than is consistent with progress toward the objective of sustainable economic stability.

AN ALTERNATIVE PROGRAM

. . . A strong case can be made for attacking some of the structural causes of high prices and excessive unemployment. It should be emphasized that the word used here is "high" and not "rising." Structural deficiences in the economy raise the level of un-employment consistent with stability in the rate of inflation, but do not by themselves cause the inflation. But while structural re-forms were being put into effect the result would be downward pressure on some wages and prices. This transitional effect would be most welcome, given the present public concern over infla-tion, and would help to generate support for the reforms.

Steps could have been taken—through executive action where possible and submission of new legislation where necessary—in at least the following areas: (1) modification or elimination of minimum wage laws; (2) modification of the tax laws to provide for the inclusion of all corporate profits rather than dividends alone in the definition of personal taxable income of common stock shareholders, in order to encourage increased dividend pay-outs and discourage corporate agglomerations; (3) antitrust action leading to dissolution of large firms in excessively con-centrated industries; (4) elimination of farm price supports to reduce the cost of food; (5) elimination of regulation of trans-portation fares and rates; (6) elimination of tariffs and quotas on imported goods and services; (7) strengthening of retraining pro-grams and employment services, perhaps including subsidies to encourage migration out of labor surplus areas. This list could no doubt be extended, but it is long enough to give the flavor of the reforms I would favor.

At the same time, to ease the burdens of unemployment, un-employment benefits should be extended and the welfare reform program enacted. In addition, temporary adjustment assistance should be provided to cushion the impact on individuals and firms unduly affected by the structural reforms proposed above.

The program outlined here has at least as good a chance of reducing inflationary expectations as does a temporary freeze fol-lowed by either mild controls or guidelines. The program is de-signed to go to the heart of the structural problems, providing extra stimulus now while minimizing the probability of over-shooting the full employment mark. If overshooting can be avoided, a real possibility exists of achieving a gradual decline in the rate of inflation at the same time that unemployment is falling. . . .

After the Freeze

GEORGE L. PERRY

George L. Perry offered these responses to Poole's criticisms of wage and price restraints in the preceding selection. Perry is a Senior Fellow at the Brookings Institution and co-editor of Brookings Papers on Economic Activity, *in which this selection initially appeared.*

WILLIAM POOLE has offered a model of incomes policy that is like balancing an egg. The policy can be far too oppressive—the egg falls left; or it can be totally ineffectual—the egg falls right. Finding a middle approach for policy that works is like trying to stand the egg on its head: It's clearly unstable and can't be done.

I don't think anyone in the administration is contemplating a permanent, comprehensive set of controls. And it is certainly not the program that I am prepared to defend or that most economists who favor an incomes policy of some sort have in mind. What is relevant is a middle-of-the-road program that can be adopted after the ninety-day freeze. Whether the middle road on incomes policy can work depends on the environment it has to work in. My view of the environment is different from Poole's. In the sand, the egg stands on its head very easily.

Recently I wrote about structural changes that have led to a deterioration of the tradeoff between inflation and unemployment. I developed measures of labor market tightness that took account of these changes and showed that labor markets had been extremely tight during the 1966–69 period. An inflation model based on these measures explained the rapid increases of wages and prices over this interval and through the first half of 1970. But even the structural changes identified there do not account for the rate of inflation the United States has been suffering in 1971. Labor markets are not tighter now than they were in 1965, even by my measures. Operating rates are not higher now than in the early 1960s. There is no way inflation in 1971 can be seen as a result of tight labor markets or excess demand in product markets; those conditions exist in only a few isolated sectors of the economy. Nor can inflation be explained by the weight in the wage index of long-term wage settlements that are still catching up for past inflation, although these headline makers may have important indirect, demonstration effects.

Although the concept lacks theoretical elegance, I am persuaded that inflation is now perpetuated to an important degree because of high "habitual" rates of wage and price increase. Although we conceal a lot of our ignorance about the inflation process when we employ past changes in wages or prices to help explain the present, we have to attribute a large impact to recent experience in order to explain today's situation. But the present rapid wage increases need not imply that shifts have occurred in some well-defined labor supply curve that would lead to a model of accelerating inflation. I see no evidence for this interpretation and choose the description "habitual" to emphasize this. If this habitual situation in wage setting is interrupted, there need be no consequences for real output and employment. I am offering a treadmill explanation of the present situation. A middle-road incomes policy is designed to get us off the treadmill, down to a lower habitual average rate of wage and price increase.

In this environment, I cannot share Poole's misgiving about a middle-road incomes policy. He fears that a policy that is enforceable only against large firms and unions would find controlled firms unable to meet the demands for some of its products. In this situation, he sees customers forced to switch their purchases to uncontrolled firms, and this development leading either to broader controls or to their complete abandonment. In today's economy, would this really be a problem? Not only are markets not tight enough, but controls need not be so rigid.

I am not dissuaded by Poole's finding that, for nineteen out of ninety-eight product categories, wholesale prices rose more than 7 percent during the past year while average wholesale prices rose only 3.6 percent. Some of the nineteen were agricultural products, raw materials whose prices are set in world markets, or products fabricated from them. Some may have been industrial products whose price increases resulted from increased labor costs. We do know that the first-year cost of many wage increases was more than 3.4 percent above the average rate of wage increase. And we know that long-run productivity experience varies substantially among individual industries, so that any given change in hourly wage costs is translated into widely differing changes in standard unit labor costs. Thus Poole's reported dispersion in price behavior makes a good case for flexible controls and intelligent price guidelines. But it does not persuade me that suppressed excess demand would be a problem. We could, of course, create that problem for ourselves—say, by trying to hold the price of lumber in the midst of the current housing boom. But that straw man should not be the subject of discussion.

If the nation can pursue a deescalation policy aimed at wages and prices broadly but, in practice, enforceable only in labor and product markets where market power is considerable, I would expect favorable results and only small costs. To opt for this kind of program is not to imply that oligopolistic industries and powerful unions are the main cause of the inflation. But they are a good place to concentrate an incomes policy for several reasons.

If we are to slow down the treadmill, highly visible price and wage situations are the one place in which the government can call attention to the new rules and show it means business. This kind of demonstration should help reduce the present "habitual" rate of price and wage increases in other sectors as well. I would expect weak markets over a long enough period to do it too. But that seems to be a long and costly process.

Furthermore, while these concentrated sectors did not give birth to the inflation, they have been an important factor in keeping it so healthy. Having been late to get started and having finally caught up, they are unlikely, of their own accord, to lead the way down toward price stability. That is not what union members pay their dues for. I find it somewhat contradictory that the same observers who doubt that such a limited incomes policy could work frequently stress structural changes to diminish market power among concentrated industries and unions as a longer-run inflation cure.

Finally, I want limited and flexible controls because I do not want more. A price-wage board can hope to exercise control in these visible sectors and do so in a fairly flexible way. They can consider ten appeals a month with some care. They cannot sensibly monitor prices and wages everywhere. I am against comprehensive controls just as Poole is and for the same reasons. The initial ninety-day freeze was short enough—and voluntary enough—to pose no serious problems of efficiency. It may have been the best way to start off. But I want to emerge from it with a limited and flexible system.

The circumstances behind the present inflation make this a particularly favorable time for such a limited program. With excess demands virtually absent, it is hard to visualize significant misallocations arising from a wage standard that deescalated average wage increases to, say, a 5 percent annual rate. Why should we expect to see the steel companies, who are under scrutiny, lose workers to small, competitive firms who are not? Firms have been granting large wage increases because they have become the general pattern. If the treadmill slows, so does the wage increase that an individual firm must grant to meet its labor requirements. To raise wages faster than this, firms would have to behave irrationally just because they are not under the scrutiny of controls.

Of course, there will be some reallocations through changing relative wages, but they do not require today's average inflation rate. Resources were reallocated in the early 1960s with no loss of efficiency and with a stable price level. Nor need the resource transfer be a flow governed by wage movements in the uncontrolled sector alone. A flexible control system would permit promotions, competition for particular skills in short supply, and similar departures from any general rule.

Under a new incomes policy, I expect prices generally to be governed by costs and so to present no special problem. For the areas where market power is great, a price-wage board would monitor price movements. While excessive price increases in oligopolistic sectors are not the main cause of the recent inflation, there are reasons to guard against them: First, it is important to demonstrate an evenhanded treatment of wages and prices under the incomes policy; second, we want to ensure a prompt passthrough of cost moderation into prices; third, we want to avoid the occasional instance in which administered pricing might contribute independently to inflation. The biggest problems would come from a few sectors in which classical market power is not the issue but in which prices have been rising inordinately for special reasons. If allowed to continue, these increases would make cooperation under the incomes policy in other sectors more difficult. For example, medical costs have been rising rapidly. Here the government could slow price increases by using its control over the medicare and medicaid programs.

A more difficult problem for incomes policies arises when the economy expands more and markets begin to tighten. Even here, an incomes policy should be helpful, just as I believe the guideposts were helpful in their day despite their almost totally voluntary nature. What we see as a fairly gradual tradeoff curve between inflation and aggregate market tightness arises, I believe, as an increasing fraction of only loosely connected individual markets grows tighter. Adjustments among the markets take place continuously through changing relative wages and prices. As the fraction of tight markets grows, the price changes average out to be more inflationary. On this highly simplified view, an incomes policy that modified the absolute price increases in the tighter sectors could still permit the needed adjustments, but with less net price increase than now occurs. An incomes policy need not break down until a substantial part of the economy experienced excess demand. . . .

Suggested Further Readings

Ackley, Gardner, *Stemming World Inflation* (The Atlantic Institute, 1971).

American Bankers Association, *Proceedings of a Symposium on Money, Interest Rates, and Economic Activity* (1967).

——, *Proceedings of a Symposium on The Federal Budget in a Dynamic Economy* (1968).

Ando, Albert, E. Cary Brown, Robert M. Solow, and John Kareken, "Lags in Fiscal and Monetary Policy," in the Commission on Money and Credit, *Stabilization Policies* (Prentice-Hall, 1963).

Brown, E. Cary, "Fiscal Policy in the Thirties: A Reappraisal," *American Economic Review*, LVI (1956).

Burns, Arthur F., *The Business Cycle in a Changing World* (National Bureau of Economic Research, 1969).

—— and Paul A. Samuelson, *Full-Employment, Guideposts, and Economic Stability* (American Enterprise Institute, 1967).

Chamberlain, Neil W., "The Art of Unbalancing the Budget," *Atlantic Monthly* (January, 1966).

Committee on Economic Development, *Taxes and the Budget* (1947).

Federal Reserve Bank of Boston, *Controlling Monetary Aggregates* (1969).

Friedman, Milton, *The Optimum Quantity of Money and Other Essays* (Chicago, 1969).

——, *Studies in the Quantity Theory of Money* (Chicago, 1960).

—— and Anna Jacobson Schwartz, *A Monetary History of the United States, 1867–1960* (Princeton, 1963).

Gordon, Robert Aaron, *Business Fluctuations*, 2d ed. (Harper, 1961).

——, *The Goal of Full Employment* (Wiley, 1967).

Hansen, Alvin H., *Economic Issues of the 1960's* (McGraw-Hill, 1960).

Harris, Seymour E., *Economics of the Kennedy Years* (Harper, 1964).

Hickman, Bert G., *Growth and Stability of the Postwar Economy* (Brookings, 1960).

Holmans, A. E., *United States Fiscal Policy, 1945–1959* (Oxford, 1961).

Holt, Charles C., C. Duncan MacRae, Stuart O. Schweitzer, and Ralph E. Smith, *The Unemployment-Inflation Dilemma* (Urban Institute, 1971).

Laidler, David E. W., *The Demand for Money: Theories and Evidence* (International Textbook Co., 1969).

Levy, Michael E., *Fiscal Policy, Cycles, and Growth* (National Industrial Conference Board, 1963).

Lewis, Wilfred, Jr., *Federal Fiscal Policy in the Postwar Recessions* (Brookings, 1962).

Maisel, Sherman J., "The Effects of Monetary Policy on Expenditures in Specific Sectors of the Economy," *Journal of Political Economy, vol. 76* (July/August, 1968).

Mayer, Thomas, *Monetary Policy in the United States* (Random House, 1968).

Okun, Arthur M. and Nancy H. Teeters, "The Full-Employment Surplus Revisited," in Arthur M. Okun and George L. Perry (ed.), *Brookings Papers on Economic Activity* (1:1970).

Organisation for Economic Co-operation and Development, *Inflation: The Present Problem* (December 1970).

Phelps, Edmund S., et al, *Microeconomic Foundations of Employment and Inflation Theory* (Norton, 1970).

President's Committee to Appraise Employment and Unemployment Statistics, *Measuring Employment and Unemployment* (Government Printing Office, 1962).

Ritter, Lawrence S., and William L. Silber, *Money* (Basic, 1970).

Sheahan, John, *The Wage-Price Guideposts* (Brookings, 1967).

Stein, Herbert, *The Fiscal Revolution in America* (Chicago, 1969).

Tobin, James, *National Economic Policy* (Yale, 1966).

U.S. Congress, Joint Economic Committee, *Staff Report on the Federal Budget, Inflation, and Full Employment* (1970); *The Wage-Price Issue: The Need for Guideposts* (1968); *Standards for Guiding Monetary Action* (1968); *Staff Report on Tax Changes for Short Run Stabilization* (1966); *Twentieth Anniversary of the Employment Act of 1946: An Economic Symposium* (1966); *Fiscal Policy Issues of the Coming Decade* (1965).